A COMMENTARY ON JEAN-PAUL SARTRE'S
"BEING AND NOTHINGNESS"

A COMMENTARY ON JEAN-PAUL SARTRE'S "BEING AND NOTHINGNESS"

JOSEPH S. CATALANO

The University of Chicago Press
Chicago and London

FOR MY STUDENTS

The University of Chicago Press, Chicago 60637
The University of Chicago Press, Ltd., London

© 1974, 1980 by Joseph S. Catalano
All rights reserved. Published 1974
Midway Reprint edition 1985
Printed in the United States of America

ISBN 0-226-09699-8

CONTENTS

PREFACE TO
THE PHOENIX EDITION

I think that anyone beginning to study *Being and Nothingness* would find it useful first to have read both Sartre's short monograph, *The Transcendence of the Ego,* and his semi-autobiographical novel, *Nausea.* Although the former lays the foundation for Sartre's view of consciousness, the latter is easier to read and is more interesting as an introduction to Sartre's ontology.

Nausea tells the story of Antoine Roquentin who, having traveled extensively, settles in the French town of Bouville to complete his historical research on the Marquis de Rollebon. There he is seized with the strange experience that he calls his "nausea." The nausea does not leave Roquentin, and he begins to realize that it never will: he is the nausea. His years of travel, his research into the past, and his general immersion in the world had obscured his awareness of himself. But now the nausea reveals to him the true character of his freedom and his responsibility.

The nausea reveals to Roquentin that human consciousness is the true source of the meaning in the world, or, to be more exact, that consciousness is the origin of the meaningful reality itself that we call "the world." Indeed, each human being as a unique center of freedom is responsible for adding meaning to the world. Thus a man cannot look to the world for the meaning and justification of his life; rather he must be the one who brings meaning and justification to the world. The nausea is therefore the dizzy realization that man's own freedom is the source of the world's meaning.

Roquentin does not become aware of the significance of his

nausea all at once. Cultural sediments, levels of meanings, habitual ways of living have to be loosened up before he can become aware of the interplay between consciousness and the world. What is significant is that this awakening does not occur as the result of philosophic reflections but by the strange way things affect Roquentin's body and the new way his body responds to things. Indeed, the visceral import of the term "nausea" draws immediate attention to the importance and centrality of the body in Sartre's thought.

Further, *Nausea* illustrates the reciprocity between consciousness and the world; it shows in a vivid way that we are first and foremost immediately aware of something other than consciousness itself. We note that Roquentin is not portrayed as stopping his daily routine in order to reflect on his "nausea"; instead he is shown trying to understand what is happening to him by starting a diary. In *The Transcendence of the Ego* Sartre had already shown that reflection ordinarily cannot be relied on as a tool for understanding ourselves; when we stop to reflect, the "self" doing the reflecting is not exactly the same as the "self" being reflected upon. Although in *Being and Nothingness*, Sartre describes a state of "pure reflection" in which consciousness does attain fleeting glimpses of itself, even this reflective self-awareness is an aspect of the intentionality of consciousness by which it spontaneously goes out to its object.

Nausea is a vivid expression of that revealing intuition of being that is mentioned in the Introduction to *Being and Nothingness* and is developed throughout the work. But whereas *Nausea* proceeds by a "logic of discovery," and shows how Roquentin gradually becomes aware of the experience of nausea itself, *Being and Nothingness* proceeds with a "logic of exposition," and describes an ontology that both gives meaning to the experience of nausea and shows how it is possible. Of course, Sartre's ontology does not develop from a single experience: other experiences, such as the awareness of absence, are also bases for his descriptive ontology.

The concrete, literary mode of discourse used in *Nausea* is an interesting counterweight to the philosophic mode used in *Being and Nothingness*. This philosophic mode proceeds from the abstract to the concrete, and Sartre constantly reminds his readers that each subsequent chapter brings him a step closer to his goal, which is an understanding of the concrete situation of man's existence. In itself, his method should not lead to any special difficulties; nevertheless, I suspect that it is the occasion for the frequent misinterpretations of his view of consciousness.

When, as often happens, the chapters of *Being and Nothingness* are consulted as if they were a series of independent tracts on different subjects, then Sartre's method can lead to misconceptions; for *Being and Nothingness* is an integral work, with a deliberate logic of exposition. Of course, since *Being and Nothingness* is a phenomenological study, Sartre is commited to a descriptive method and not to a deductive exposition of being. Still, his systematic way of developing his thesis from the abstract to the concrete gives a clear order, or logic, to his descriptive studies, a logic that makes it dangerous to extract the individual chapters from their context.

For example, that the chapters "The Origin Of Negation" and "Bad Faith" are merely the first two chapters of Part One is often overlooked. The long first chapter, "The Origin of Negation," may give the illusion of completeness because it proceeds from an abstract notion of nothingness to an understanding of concrete nothingness, but this first description of concrete nothingness is itself abstract in relation to what follows. Similarly, the second chapter, "Bad Faith," is also generally misunderstood because it is read as if it were an independent study on the nature of self-deception, and not as merely a preliminary description of freedom, which is filled out later in the book, especially in the last two chapters.

Frequently the descriptions of Sartre's view of consciousness read as if the writer had jumped from the chapter "Bad Faith" in Part One to the chapter "Concrete Relations with Others" at the end of Part Three. This leap escapes the difficult chapter "Transcendence" in Part Two and misses the crucial chapter "The Body" in the middle of Part Three. Further, given Sartre's method of proceeding from the abstract to the concrete, the mere fact that *Being and Nothingness* ends with the two chapters "Being and Doing" and "Doing and Having" should itself make it clear that Sartre does not regard his own descriptions of consciousness and freedom to be concrete until he has sketched the way we act and behave. But even this statement must be qualified. Sartre considers his entire ontological description to be, in a wider context, abstract, since it does not consider the ethical dimension of human existence. In *Being and Nothingness* Sartre maintains that an ontology describes the "is" and not the "ought" of human actions.

I have kept these few remarks within the original scope of the commentary, and I have neither attempted to give an overall judgment on *Being and Nothingness* nor considered any subsequent philosophical development of Sartre's thought. I think the latter issue would only be distracting to one first approaching the study of *Being and Nothingness*; I believe, too, that the subsequent phases of Sartre's thought, specifically his unique Marxism as given in the *Critique of Dialectical Reason*, can only be understood after first comprehending his ontology.

Nevertheless, something should be said about the overall program in which he first presents his ontology. It is interesting that neither Sartre nor Heidegger was able to complete his philosophic program as initially planned. Heidegger's *Being and Time* was first presented as only part of a phenomenological study on the question of being, and Sartre's *Being and Nothingness* was supposed to be completed with a study on ethics. Their failure to continue with their outlines is, I believe, a testimony to the honesty of their phenomenological approach; at the end of their early studies they "saw" the world differently and learned enough from their own descriptions that they were unable to continue with their previously designed formal approach.

Regarding the absence in the commentary of any judgments about the "truth" of what is contained in *Being and Nothingness*, I have indeed frequently given internal criticisms where I thought these appropriate, but I have refrained from any general evaluations of Sartre's ontology. I think that such evaluations make it difficult for a reader to come to his own judgment about a philosophic work: philosophy is not apologetics. More importantly, a judgment about a philosophic work is itself a philosophic enterprise in which the task is not simply to affirm or deny certain conclusions that apparently summarize a philosophic position, but rather to engage in a dialogue that presupposes a thorough knowledge of the text itself.

The understanding of Sartre's thought has suffered from quick judgments and short summaries. If *Being and Nothingness* is approached as an integral work, then Sartre's phenomenological ontology is seen to be rich, profound, and unique: rich in its delineation of the situational aspects of our free acts; profound in the way it centers the human body, which defines and is defined by the world; and unique, I believe, in the history of philosophy, in its attempt to stretch the finite to provide a complete ontology of being. But perhaps the most important aspect of Sartre's thought for our generation is its ability to unveil our self-deceptions and to oblige us to accept the free molding of our selfhood and our environment. If our own thinking on the human condition takes Sartre's philosophy into account, we will never lose sight of our responsibility to turn our earth into a planet in which the freedom of each human being is reflected in his environment. Robert Denoon Cumming, in his excellent introduction to his anthology, *The Philosophy of Jean-Paul Sartre,* maintains the plausibility of the verdict that Sartre is "the only philosopher of our time." Cumming's remark may be extravagant, but it is an extravagance neither ill-timed nor wholly without reason.

I see that I have been indulging somewhat in the apologetics that, until now, I have tried to avoid; but although an apologetical approach is never philosophical, it is not always unjustified. The weight of much of the secondary literature regarding *Being and Nothingness* demands some counterbalance, for too often this literature stresses, out of context, I believe, the one sentence at the end of Part Four, "man is a useless passion," but ignores the important place that the book, as a whole, gives to human existence. In general, this literature also overlooks Sartre's remarkable thesis that each human life is not only an attempt to give meaning to its own existence, but is also an outline of a solution to the universal problem of being. Sartre's formulation of his thesis, given in the first chapter of Part Four, is a useful guide for the study of his long tract on ontology: "My ultimate and initial project —for these are but one—is, as we shall see, always the outline of a solution of the problem of being. . . . It is the very way in which I entrust myself to the inanimate, in which I abandon myself to my body . . . which cause the appearance of both my body and the inanimate world with their respective value."

PREFACE

Anyone who attempts to read *Being and Nothingness* is aware of its difficulty. Unlike Sartre's literary works and popular expositions of existentialism, *Being and Nothingness* is addressed to a specific philosophic community, and consequently, with no knowledge of phenomenology, even the student of philosophy finds this work somewhat mystifying. Furthermore, Sartre's style presents a problem. Sartre is in love with language (his autobiography is entitled *Words*). The result of this affair with language is a work of strange proportion and mixed clarity—rich and clear in illuminating examples, often brief in the elaboration of historical reference, and overly concise in philosophic explanation and expression. Then, too, at times the styles overlap, the literary invading the philosophic, as when Sartre describes man as that being who is what he is not and is not what he is.

The difficulty of reading *Being and Nothingness* has given rise to a number of excellent works that summarize, paraphrase, and evaluate this cornerstone of Sartre's philosophy but that do not pretend to help one to read the book itself. This commentary is solely on *Being and Nothingness* and does not consider either works that postdate *Being and Nothingness* or the question of any subsequent evolution in Sartre's thought. It is written primarily as an aid to acquiring that firsthand knowledge that can be obtained only by studying the text itself. Ideally, therefore, it should be read in conjunction with *Being and Nothingness*. Nevertheless, every effort has been made to make the commentary readable independent of Sartre's work.

Since Sartre's philosophy is of interest to people with varied backgrounds, we will assume that the reader does not have any specific knowledge of philosophy. Enough immediate background and outline of Sartre's thought is provided in the first chapter to make an intelligent start in reading *Being and Nothingness*.

In a work as massive as *Being and Nothingness*, no commentary of this length can elaborate on every sentence that the reader thinks is obscure. In general, more commentary is offered on Sartre's Introduction and early chapters, where the thought itself is most difficult and where the reader, perhaps, has less background. Throughout the commentary a clear exposition of the most obscure and difficult passages is attempted. At times, this will necessitate an interpretation, and the reader will be informed that such is the case. Finally, since we are not concerned with comparing Sartre's thought with that of the various philosophers and psychologists he mentions, we will accept his presentations and evaluations at face value.

ACKNOWLEDGMENTS

I owe a great deal to my colleagues and students for their encouragement and assistance in writing this commentary. My colleagues helped to provide a milieu in which writing and teaching, if not easy, were at least possible. My students, particularly at the New School, used versions of this manuscript as notes; I expanded or modified many sections because of their comments.

My primary expression of gratitude, however, is to Charles Sherover for proposing the writing of this commentary and for editing the manuscript.

NOTE TO THE PHOENIX EDITION

Since the first appearance of this book, Martin Heidegger has died (May 26, 1976), and the complete *Critique of Dialectical Reason* has been published (tr. Alan Sheridan-Smith, New York: Philosophical Library, 1976).

J. S. C.

BACKGROUND

This background chapter and Sartre's own Introduction attempt to introduce the reader to a complete philosophic milieu. This task leads to a circularity that cannot be avoided: the Background and Introduction serve to place the rest of the book in its proper context, and reciprocally, the rest of the book clarifies these early sections. It is therefore advisable to read these sections carefully, but it is not necessary to understand every reference or line of argument before proceeding with the rest of the book.

DESCARTES AND SARTRE

As a Frenchman, Sartre was almost required by his philosophical community to give serious attention to the most important of French philosophers, the seventeenth-century philosopher-mathematician René Descartes (1596–1650). Descartes brought to philosophy the same spirit of detachment, the same confidence and expectation, that he had as a mathematician. It was his intention to establish a philosophy that would be accepted as universally as mathematics itself.

If philosophy is to have the certitude of mathematics, Descartes reasoned, philosophy must develop like geometry, clearly and distinctly, from universally accepted first truths. Descartes believed that he had found a crucial first truth with which to begin constructing a philosophy in the very activity of thinking. He claimed that if we begin philosophic thinking as we should, by trying to doubt everything, we find the one thing we cannot doubt is that *we* are thinking or doubting. "... I am, I exist, is necessarily true every time that I pronounce it or perceive it in my mind," he writes in his *Meditations*. This certitude of our existence as the necessary subject of our thoughts, including our doubts, is often referred to simply, as the "cogito" (*cogito ergo sum:* I think, therefore I am).

From the cogito, Descartes concluded that the I, or self, is essentially a pure mind or thinking substance and is more easily and directly known than one's body and the world. In succeeding meditations, Descartes tried systematically to rebuild all that he had previously doubted. Since he had doubted everything, including the validity of the senses and, consequently, the existence of his body and the world, he had only his mind and its ideas with which to begin his quest for an absolutely certain philosophy. Closed within his own mind, his next step was clear: to direct all his critical reflections immediately to the content of his mind, his ideas, to determine which are true representations of reality and which only appear to represent realities outside the mind but are merely modifications of the mind itself.[1] For example, Descartes reasoned that the idea of three dimensions represents external bodies, since whenever we think of the idea of a body we must think of it as three-dimensional. The idea of color, however, does not represent color in external bodies, since whenever we think of the idea of a body we do not have to think of it as colored.[2]

The conception of knowledge—first, a direct awareness of ideas as the immediate object of knowledge, and then a reasoning process to determine which ideas are copies of realities and which are merely modifications of the mind itself—is Descartes's most significant break from his Scholastic heritage, a heritage that con-

---

1. This simplification of Descartes's argument is sufficient for our purposes. Descartes, however, makes it clear that he needs the existence of God to guarantee that ideas, which are themselves clearly and distinctly related, de facto correspond to extramental realities.

2. Since Descartes had doubted the existence of his body, with its senses, and consequently the external world, all his sensations (for example, the sensation of color) as well as conceptions become for him direct objects of consciousness to be critically examined to see whether they correspond to realities outside his consciousness.

sidered ideas means by which we know things directly. It is also a crucial step in the development of philosophy from Descartes to Immanuel Kant (1724–1804).

It is Descartes's initial philosophic project and goal, rather than the actual development of his philosophy, that strongly influence philosophers. The initial doubting of the existence of the world, the consequent certitude of the self as a thinking substance immediately aware of its own ideas as possible copies of reality, and the dualism of mind and matter—these aspects of Descartes's system (Cartesianism) haunt philosophy and provide the context for much of Sartre's thinking.

Sartre, and indeed all the existentialists, agree with Descartes that the first object of philosophic reflection is man himself. In Sartre's first novel, *Nausea*, he clearly shows his debt to Descartes as well as the distinctiveness of his own approach to philosophy.

> I jump up: it would be much better if I could only stop thinking. Thoughts are the dullest things. . . . and they leave a funny taste in the mouth. Then there are words, inside the thoughts, unfinished words, a sketchy sentence which constantly returns: "I have to fi. . . I ex. . . Dead . . . M. de Roll is dead . . . I am not . . . I ex. . ." It goes, it goes . . . and there's no end to it. It's worse than the rest because *I feel responsible and have complicity in it.* For example, this sort of painful rumination: *I exist,* I am the one who keeps it up. I. . . .
>
> My thought is *me*: that's why I can't stop. I exist because I think . . . and I can't stop myself from thinking.[3]

The Cartesian influence is here evident. It is also clear that, unlike Descartes, Sartre finds that relations with matter, emotions, and responsibility for one's free interpretative involvement in the world are simultaneous with the awareness of oneself as existing.

In *Nausea*, it is things and not logic that awaken the main character, Roquentin, to his true self as a completely free agent in the world. Sartre does not begin philosophy by a logical analysis of ideas, as Descartes suggests, but by an awakening to reality as simply being there without any necesary reason for its existence and by an awareness of himself as absolutely free. The nausea is a kind of dizziness in

3. *Nausea*, trans. Lloyd Alexander (New York: New Directions, 1949), p. 135 (italics mine). All references are to this edition.

the face of one's freedom and responsibility for giving a meaning to reality; it is visceral cogito.

Although generally influenced by Descartes's philosophy, Sartre's view of knowledge and consciousness is radically different. This break from the Cartesian tradition develops for Sartre mainly through the influence of a German philosopher, Edmund Husserl (1859–1938).

HUSSERL AND SARTRE

To understand Husserl's approach to philosophy and his relation to Sartre, it will help to recall Descartes's attempt to build a philosophy on the firm foundation of his own existence, and his subsequent task of proving the existence of a world external to his consciousness. It is important, however, at this point, to be very clear about the precise nature of Descartes's doubt concerning the existence of the world.

The "world," for Descartes, certainly appeared to be there, and his own most critical doubts could not make the world cease to appear to exist independently of his consciousness of it. Thus, for example, it certainly *seemed* that the desk he was writing on existed outside his consciousness. But Descartes's question was whether what certainly and clearly appeared to exist actually existed independently of his awareness of it. This distinction is not as strange as it seems. Science has accustomed us to believe in a similar paradox, namely, that the way things appear to our senses are not always the way they appear to our scientific reason. Our scientific knowledge, however, does not change the way things appear to our senses. For example, we still continue to see the sun rise and set even though we "know" that this is not the case.

It is not clear that Descartes explicitly viewed his doubting of the world in this way, but it is implicit in his philosophy and it is this precise point that leads us to Husserl's relation to Sartre. Husserl was familiar with the difficulty that Descartes and subsequent philosophers had in attempting to prove the existence of the external world. But he was also struck by the simple fact that regardless of our doubts concerning the existence of the world, it continues to *appear* to exist. For example, the apple that appears to be existing in front of me, and which I seem to perceive as "out there," continues to appear as existing "out there" regardless of my speculations about its actual external existence. In fact, I can continue to make a distinction between an apple that I am now remembering and the apple that appears to exist outside my mind, regardless of whether the latter actually exists. For the apple that I *seem* to be perceiving as resting on the table continues to *appear* different from the apple that I am now remembering having seen on a tree last spring. It is not simply that the "apples" are different, but that, according to Husserl, apples *appear* in the process of "remembering" different from the way they *appear* in the activity of "perceiving." It may be difficult to describe accurately these differences between the remembered apple and the perceived apple, but when we have done so, we will have "essentially" distinguished the difference between the apples *regardless of whether the one actually exists outside our mind.*

Husserl therefore claims that if we put aside, or "bracket," the question of the existence of things, they will still appear to be essentially the same. He is thus led to redefine "objectivity." To say that something is "objective" does not mean that it exists outside our minds, but that it can be accurately described to be the way it appears and that this description can be communicated to others. For example, the fundamental difference between remembering an apple and perceiving it can be "isolated" from our individuality and subjectivity, and further, this "essential" difference can be shared with others.

Consequently, while Husserl agrees with Descartes that true philosophical reasoning must be scientific and more rigorous than any of the physical sciences, he insists that its method should be descriptive rather than deductive.[4] According to Husserl, this descriptive technique, or phenomenological method, carefully examines each object of consciousness, for example, the perceived-apple or recollected-apple, in relation to its specific activity or consciousness, perception or recollection.

In this respect, we may have earlier misled the reader when we distinguished between the way things appear to ordinary perception

---

4. The reader who wishes to broaden his knowledge of phenomenology is recommended to read Husserl's own small and very readable work, *The Idea of Phenomenology* (The Hague: Martinus Nijhoff, 1964).

and the way they appear to scientific perception. Husserl certainly would not claim that things appear to scientific perception in a way that is more real than the way in which they appear to ordinary perception. Rather, he would no doubt maintain that the scientist describes the objects of ordinary perception as these objects are modified by the scientist's instruments. Thus, light appears to the scientist as a wave or photon, because he is examining not merely the light reflected from an apple, but the light that is analyzed by instruments, interpreted through mathematics, and conceptualized in models. The point is that "what appears" (or phenomena), for example, the light or photon, must always be "seen" in relation to a precise activity of consciousness, for example, ordinary or scientific perception; and reciprocally, the activities of consciousness, ordinary or scientific, are themselves specified by their distinctive objects. In relation to a precise activity of consciousness, "what appears" can always be described *objectively*, in the sense that it can be isolated from the individuality of the observer and communicated to others; that is, it can be described as it essentially would appear to any consciousness engaged in this same activity of consciousness. Husserl thus claims that though the mind is active, it is not so active as to hide permanently the basic structure or makeup of what is given to it.

Nevertheless, Husserl is aware that our habits and acquired view of things hide from us consciousness' original grasp of evidence and "essence." *We often confuse and overlap scientific and ordinary perception of reality*—for example, the earth truly "appears" to circle the sun to one elsewhere in the solar system, but to one situated on the earth, the "sun" (that is, a pattern of color) really appears to rise and set, and further, this appearance is objective in the sense that the phenomenon appears this way relative to all consciousnesses situated on the earth. Also, to use an image of Sartre's, the roots of a tree may appear as a complicated pump to one "viewing" them through the images of science; but the roots are certainly not a pump in any literal sense and it is difficult, but not impossible, for us to obtain a view of a root as it originally appears to our consciousness uninfluenced by the knowledge of how we are supposed to perceive it.

Phenomenology has been described as a return to objects as they originally present themselves to our consciousness. Husserl's phenomenology includes a process ("reduction") by which we continually reexamine both the object and consciousness until we clearly "see" exactly how the object originally presents itself to consciousness and how consciousness appropriates the object to itself. Again, if as phenomenologists we turn our attention to the perception red of an apple, what we finally grasp is the characteristic of a perceived-apple-red as distinct from a remembered-apple-red (perhaps, that the perceived-red is more vividly intermingled with the "texture" of the apple). Consequently, for Husserl the world loses nothing of its distinctiveness or richness if we bracket the question of its existence and concentrate on what is given to our consciousness. In fact, for this very reason phenomenology has been described as a newfound wonder in the face of the world.

According to Husserl, the phenomenological method reveals the objective structure, or makeup, of being rather than merely the structure of the mind, because consciousness is, by its very nature, consciousness *of* an object. Consciousness is not, as for Descartes, the self-awareness of an independent and self-sufficient mind examining its own ideas to prove which of them truly represent reality. Rather, consciousness automatically refers to or "tends to" its object; it is *intentional*. Habits of thinking can hide from us, but not destroy, consciousness' original intention of objects.

Intentionality, for Husserl, gives us a new way of looking at the Cartesian cogito (that is, the certitude and nature of our consciousness). The task is no longer to discover which of our ideas represent extramental reality; rather, it is to describe our original intentions and their related objects. This description will reveal the "objectivity" of the object, regardless of whether or not the object, as it manifests itself to consciousness, also exists independently of consciousness.

The objects of consciousness, the givens, are termed by Husserl "phenomena." The term was first used extensively by Kant. For Kant, phenomena are things as known by the mind and as distinguished from things as they might be in themselves—the "noumena." For example, the perception of red of an apple is, for Kant, a phenomenon that hides rather than reveals the apple; it is how the apple appears to us rather than the way it exists in itself. Kant would maintain that the "apple" (that is, some unknowable thing) exists independently of our knowledge of it, but he would deny that we could know its true nature because of the mind's active role in knowledge.

Husserl would agree with Kant that phenomena are things as they are known by our consciousness, but he denies that the phenomena hide the true nature of the thing. According to Husserl, the true phenomena, the objects as seen after the proper use of the phenomenological method, are objective ways of *being;* they are necessary ways of existing, if a thing is to exist. Thus the perceived-red of an apple, as distinct from a recollected-red, is the necessary way an apple must *exist* as red if it *is* to exist as red.

For Husserl, phenomena usually present themselves to us as aspects of a more unified object. An apple, for example, presents itself to me differently, depending on where I stand to view it. Nevertheless, *all these aspects manifest themselves as aspects of the apple: they all somehow fall into place and unite themselves into a unity—"apple."* Husserl maintains that the unification of these aspects requires a unifying structure within consciousness itself. This unifying structure he calls a "transcendental ego." It is "transcendental" because it cuts across, or transcends, the individual act of consciousness while remaining basic to each act; it is an "ego" because it is the same *I* that is conscious of all the aspects and unites them into a unity. Husserl's notion of a transcendental ego is important for our purposes because Sartre will take issue with it.

Sartre, in general, follows both Husserl's understanding of phenomenology as a descriptive science and his notion of consciousness as always consciousness *of* something. He rejects Husserl's phenomenological reduction, with its consequent intuition of essence, and Husserl's transcendental ego. Sartre maintains that existence, and not essence, is directly given to consciousness. This intuition, or immediate grasp of existence, is the core of Sartre's philosophy of existence and the foundation of *Being and Nothingness.* A full understanding of the significance of this intuition will be had only after studying *Being and Nothingness.* A brief look, however, at Sartre's existentialism will be useful as a general orientation to this major work.[5]

Jean-Paul Sartre has characterized his philosophy as "existential-

5. The relation between Hegel (Georg Wilhelm Friedrich Hegel, 1770–1831) and Sartre has not been discussed in this Background because Sartre, in his Introduction, does not explicitly acknowledge his debt to Hegel and does not

ism"—notably in his essay "Existentialism Is a Humanism." Although the term "existentialism" is ambiguous and applies differently to different philosophers, the term draws attention to Sartre's fundamental intuition of existence, and the consequent priority that existence has in his whole philosophy.

The distinction between essence and existence comes to contemporary philosophy mainly through the influence of the medieval scholastics, who considered essence and existence distinct aspects of all reality. Essence was viewed as the answer to the question of *what* a thing is; it was considered to be the basic nature, or "structure," of a thing. Thus, for many of the scholastics, man is essentially a rational animal. Existence, on the other hand, answered the question *whether* a thing is; it was, for them, that fundamental act that causes a thing to be, independent of our thinking of it. Thus a whale, unlike a mermaid, exists independently of anyone thinking about it.

Sartre considers much of philosophy to be "essentialistic" because it emphasizes the priority of essence over existence. For Sartre, Husserl is essentialistic because he insists that the fundamental purpose of philosophy is to arrive at a knowledge of what things are. Furthermore, and for Sartre this is the heart of the issue, Husserl's suspending, or bracketing, of existence does indeed rob the world of its richness. Sartre would no doubt maintain that Husserl could bracket existence because the latter considered existence as such as adding nothing to the richness of a phenomenon. For Husserl, red "is" fundamentally red, man "is" man, a perceived tree "is" a perceived tree, regardless of whether these essences exist. Sartre described his reaction to this view of existence in *Nausea*:

> It left me breathless. Never, until these last few days, had I understood the meaning of "existence." I was like the others, like the ones walking along the seashore, all dressed in their spring finery. I said,

---

indicate that Hegel's dialectic is the immediate context of his work. While it is clear that Sartre's terminology and much of the content of specific sections owe a great deal to Hegel, I believe the scope of this relation to be one of interpretation. Therefore, Hegel's position is discussed only where Sartre explicitly mentions it. The following two works consider the relation of Sartre to Hegel in some detail: Hartman, Klaus, *Sartre's Ontology: A Study of "Being and Nothingness" in the Light of Hegel's Logic* (Evanston: Northwestern University Press, 1966); and Bernstein, Richard J., *Praxis and Action* (Philadelphia: University of Pennsylvania Press, 1971), particularly Pts. I and II.

like them, "The ocean *is* green; that white speck up there *is* a seagull". . . . When I believed I was thinking about it, I must believe that I was thinking nothing, my head was empty, or there was just one word in my head, the word "to be." Or else I was thinking . . . how can I explain it? I was thinking of belonging, I was telling myself that the sea belonged to the class of green objects, or that the green was a part of the quality of the sea. . . . If anyone had asked me what existence was, I would have answered, in good faith, that it was nothing, simply an empty form which was added to external things without changing anything in their nature. And then all of a sudden, there it was, clear as day; existence had suddenly unveiled itself. It had lost the harmless look of an abstract category: it was the very paste of things, this root was kneaded into existence [p. 171]. . . .

Existence has, for Sartre, a priority over essence because existence is "the very paste of things." But if existence is prior to essence, existence is prior to meaning, since essence designates the fundamental meaning in things. Sartre accepts this logic. Existence precedes all possible meanings, both in man and in nature. (In *Nausea*, Sartre says that existence is *absurd*, not with a relative absurdity that takes on meaning in a higher context, but with an absolute absurdity.)

For Sartre, the priority of existence over essence applies in a very special way to man. All that is distinctive in man results from man's actions and does not precede those actions. Sartre will admit that conditions common to men, such as having a body and being born, do, in fact, precede man's actions. But these conditions do not make man distinctively human. What makes man distinctively man is his free interpretations of, and reactions to, these common conditions. For Sartre, man can be said to "create" his essence by his actions. Man's essence follows his actions; he is this kind of man because he acts in this kind of way. If man had an essence that preceded his actions, this essence would determine man's actions, making it impossible for him to be truly free.

The priority of existence over essence is also evident in Sartre's notion of the self. In an early published article, "The Transcendence of the Ego," Sartre criticizes Husserl's transcendental ego, that is, the *I* that unifies our individual acts of consciousness. Sartre claims that a transcendental ego would *preexist* all of man's actions, since it is meant to unify these actions. Also, a transcendental ego would be essentially the same in each man, since its unifying action is essentially the same in each man: the various perspectives of an apple are essentially unified, by each individual, into the same entity, "apple." Consequently, Sartre maintains that a transcendental ego would be a sort of essence preceding man's actions. Furthermore, a transcendental ego would "inhabit" every act of consciousness, blocking consciousness and making it impossible for consciousness to be intentional, that is, totally and perfectly *of* an object. Sartre, on the contrary, insists that consciousness should be perfectly "clear," or translucent, so that it can reveal the object as it is, and also that consciousness, or the "self," cannot be conceived as an essence preceding man's actions. Let us examine more closely Sartre's view of consciousness and the self, although we will return to a more detailed discussion in Chapter Two.

In opposition to Husserl's understanding of the ego as transcendental, Sartre proposes his own notion of the ego as *transcendent,* that is, as being *outside* the internal "structure" of consciousness and existing as an *object* for consciousness. Sartre claims that Husserl was not consistent with his own notion of consciousness as always *of* an object. According to Sartre, the intentional character of consciousness must be absolute: it must be *all* and *only* "of," and not an ego conscious of objects. An ego that would preexist *in* consciousness and be transcendental would bring an opaqueness to consciousness precisely because it would make consciousness into a kind of "thing." Therefore, Sartre claims, *the ego cannot preexist in consciousness but must be an object of consciousness.*

Sartre elaborates his notion of the transcendence of the ego by claiming that in a sense there are two selves. There is the personal *I* (the ego), which we become aware of in our reflections and attempts to discover ourselves. It is the *I* that we conceive of as preceding our intentions and actions, the *idea* we and others have of ourselves. It is the *I* endowed with all its psychological, hereditary, and cultural traits. *This personal* I, *however, is a thoroughly reflective and derivative knowledge of the self resulting from our intentions and behavior.*[6]

---

6. Sartre is aware that this "produced" ego is not Husserl's transcendental ego. Nevertheless, the transcendental ego, to the extent that it is that which unifies our actions, is still regarded by Sartre as a "what" and consequently a derived notion of the self.

On the other hand, the true self is, for Sartre, prepersonal and indistinguishable from the self-knowing-this-object.[7] Sartre will say that when we are absorbed in an action we are directly conscious of *what* we are doing and not of a self performing the action. He admits, nevertheless, that if someone asks us *who* is doing the action, we would respond, "I." Sartre concludes from this that we are always *indirectly* conscious of a "self" in the direct consciousness of an object. All consciousness of an object, precisely because it is an *awareness* of an object, is indirectly a *self*-consciousness-of-an-object, but directly a self-consciousness-of-an-*object*. For example, when we are absorbed in viewing a movie, we are immediately and directly aware of the movie and indirectly aware of ourselves.

For Sartre, Descartes's cogito and, to a lesser extent, even Husserl's transcendental ego are ultimately derived and produced objects, resulting from our reflections on our total human condition. It is the self that we present to ourselves and the world as an object to be examined. The more fundamental self, however, is the prepersonal awareness that is present every time we are conscious of an object.

Sartre's existentialism is double-edged. Existence precedes essence both in man and in things. Matter simply is; it lacks all necessary reason for being. One can find no justification for matter's existence either in things, since they lack an essence, or outside things, since, for Sartre, there is no God. Man, also, is just thrown, without any prior meaning, into the world. But there is an important qualification. With the existence and advent of man reality, or being, becomes meaningful and a "world" comes-to-be.[8]

In his study of the priority of existence, Sartre has a precursor, Martin Heidegger (1889–   ). Heidegger was a student of Husserl's for many years before he developed his own existential approach to phenomenology in his *Being and Time*. Sartre's *Being and Nothingness* is, in a sense, a reply to Heidegger's work. For Heidegger, time is the most important aspect of reality, and time comes to

---

7. I believe that the term "prepersonal" is more accurate than the term "impersonal," which is sometimes used to describe the pre-reflective cogito. It is clear that Sartre is objecting to a derived knowledge of ourselves being accepted as our true "self." But, it is also clear that he admits that the pre-reflective cogito is an awareness and as such is not blind; in fact, Sartre explicitly refers to the pre-reflective cogito as "personal." See p. 109.

8. For a discussion of the term "being," see p. 14 and p. 26, n. 5.

reality through man's existence. Heidegger is very concerned with the historical evolution of philosophy and the influence of history on the human consciousness. In *Being and Nothingness*, Sartre is not as concerned with history; rather he focuses his attention on man's ability to interpret freely his heritage as well as his environment.

For Sartre, it is not time but nothingness that is the core of human existence, and that man brings to all reality. One of the main tasks in this commentary will be to try to appreciate Sartre's notion of nothingness. For the present, we may recall Sartre's insistence that *consciousness must be perfectly translucent, perfectly clear, so that it can reveal the object as it is.* Sartre further reasons that consciousness cannot be a reality, for if it were, this reality would have its own identity and thus would hinder consciousness from revealing perfectly its object. Only *nothingness*, for Sartre, can be perfectly clear and can perfectly reveal reality. Only nothingness, as we will see, lacks identity with itself and is totally *of* another. Being, for Sartre, cannot reveal something other than itself, for its own reality would get in the way. Only nothingness is not itself. As will be made clearer further along, Sartre is referring to a concrete nothingness, such as is often experienced in the perception of someone's absence (missing a fourth at bridge or perceiving that a friend is not at an accustomed meeting place), and not to an abstract concept of nothingness, such as the concept of a void or a square circle.

To understand further Sartre's insistence on the importance of nothingness, it may help to consider that while Sartre does not believe in the existence of any spiritual realities, he also rejects materialism as an oversimplification of the human condition. The only existent, for Sartre, is matter. It is *nothingness* that distinguishes man from the purely material. For Sartre, there is no God and no spirit. There is only matter and nothingness—existence and nothingness—being and nothingness. From these two, man and the world arise.

THE TITLE:
BEING AND NOTHINGNESS

The term "being" usually has at least two related meanings in any philosophy. It can mean whatever *is*, that is, whatever has any reality, whether it is an idea or an existing tree. The term "being" can also mean what is most basic to any reality, that is, the quality that primarily distinguishes any kind of reality from complete non-existence. Although Sartre frequently uses the term "being" in both senses, his most frequent use of the term is in the sense of that which is most basic to any reality; for example, he frequently uses such phrases as the "being of consciousness" and the "being of phenomenon." *It is important to become familiar with this use of the term "being."*

Clearly, the two senses of "being" (as whatever is in any way whatsoever and as what is as the fundamental aspect of a reality) are closely related. In the final analysis, "being" as the most basic aspect of a reality is viewed also as the source of all other reality. Thus, for Sartre, being as existence is that which primarily distinguishes reality from nothingness and which is also the foundation of all other aspects of being, including essence.

As already mentioned, the term "nothingness" in the title is used by Sartre to call attention to the fact that "concrete" nothingness somehow functions in a most fundamental way within being. The terms "being," "essence," and "existence" refer to the heart of Sartre's philosophy, and further qualifications will have to await the study of *Being and Nothingness*.

THE SUBTITLE:
AN ESSAY ON PHENOMENOLOGICAL ONTOLOGY

The subtitle, "An Essay on Phenomenological Ontology," clearly shows Sartre's indebtedness to both Husserl and Heidegger. The term "phenomenological" refers to Husserl's phenomenological method of descriptions, which Sartre will radically modify. The term "ontology," used by Heidegger in *Being and Time*, signifies, generally speaking, a basic descriptive study of being itself as distinguished from those disciplines that examine—in a restricted sense—only certain beings. Thus ontology studies existence itself as it manifests itself in all reality, while a science like biology examines only the life characteristics of living things.

The term "ontology" is inherited from Christian Wolf (1679–1754), who used it to signify a deductive science of being, whereas it is used by Heidegger and Sartre to mean a descriptive study. Traditionally, the term "metaphysics" also signifies a study of being itself. Sartre, however, distinguishes ontology from metaphysics. Metaphysics, for Sartre, is concerned with the question of *why* there is anything rather than nothing. Sartre claims that he is interested only in the fundamental descriptions of being, and not in speculations about its origins—although, as we will see, he occasionally indulges in such speculations.

THE INTRODUCTION:
THE PURSUIT
OF BEING

Sartre's Introduction is the most difficult part of his book. It is important, however, to understand this Introduction if we are to understand *Being and Nothingness* as an ontology, that is, as a fundamental description of being itself. Sartre writes for the informed reader—one already acquainted with Husserl and Heidegger—and his style is here particularly terse, his argument compact. But generally, the Introduction is not obscure and the time and effort spent in understanding it is a worthwhile investment that will result in an easier and more critical reading of subsequent chapters. Indeed, one should not be discouraged at the need for several readings, since even professional philosophers not trained in phenomenology find the Introduction, as well as other sections of Sartre's work, very difficult.

Nevertheless, the entire book will clarify this Introduction, and the reader is urged to attempt to understand the work as a whole before reexamining some of the more difficult details contained in the Introduction.

The general problem considered in Sartre's Introduction is the relation of thought to reality, or as Sartre would prefer to put it, the relation of consciousness to being. Sartre reexamines the entire question whether consciousness can apprehend reality and whether the reality thus apprehended is the essential nature of things or rather their brute existence.

We recall from the Background that (1) phenomenology is a descriptive study of what appears to consciousness, and that Sartre, as a phenomenologist, accepts that the proper way to begin philosophy is to reflect on phenomena; (2) phenomenological descriptions do not merely describe the workings of the mind, but reveal reality itself; and (3) reality, for Husserl, is essence.

Sartre's main task in the Introduction is to reveal, through the proper use of the phenomenological method, that consciousness is in immediate contact with the existence of things. Sartre therefore simultaneously praises Husserl for showing, contrary to Kant, that the proper study of phenomena reveals rather than hides reality and chides him for bracketing existence and viewing reality as essence.

Sartre's general argument is that phenomena reveal the existence of both consciousness and things. There are thus two main "movements" in the six sections of the Introduction. After a preliminary but important analysis of phenomena to show that, in general, existence is not reducible to phenomena, or meaning, (sections I and II), he shows, in particular, that the *existence*, or *being*, of consciousness is not identical with phenomenon (section III). For example, when we perceive red, the *being* of our consciousness is not reducible to, or exhausted in, the perception of red. This conclusion is painstakingly arrived at, because logically all that Sartre has, to begin his reflection, are phenomena, e.g., the perceived-red. Nevertheless, this is the easier and less critical of the two conclusions of the Introduction, and neither Kant nor Husserl would dispute that consciousness has a reality that is not totally reducible to its perceptions. The second movement is the more critical. In it, Sartre shows that the very fact of phenomena, the awareness of any object, reveals the existence of things (sections IV–VI). Here Sartre parts company with both Kant and Husserl, since, contrary to Kant, Sartre insists that phenomena reveal reality, and contrary to Husserl, he claims that the reality that the phenomena reveal are not the essences of things but their brute existences.

Although there are two "movements" in the Introduction, the basic sweep of the argument is to show that consciousness is in immediate grasp of the existence (*l'être*) of things, the *being* of things, and that this being of things is not reducible to our awareness of things as a meaning.

The entire Introduction is also an examination of the intentionality of consciousness, that is, the thesis that we are immediately aware of an object and not of consciousness itself. Sartre interprets this to mean that we are directly aware of existence itself.

I. THE PHENOMENON

The main difficulty in reading the first section of the original text is that Sartre is preparing us for a radical reinterpretation of phenomenology. We recall, from the Background, that Husserl brackets existence in order to focus on what is for Husserl the heart of reality, essence. Sartre attacks Husserl's phenomenology from two points (we must keep in mind that we are concerned only with Sartre's view of Husserl, which is mainly of the early Husserl). First, he begins to show that Husserl's phenomenology replaces the reality of the thing by its objectivity and thereby loses the unity of the existing thing. Second, he indicates that even on the level of essences, Husserl faces the serious problem of an infinite series of appearances to guarantee the objectivity of the object.

The first sentence of this section is thus both a praise of Husserl and a foreshadowing of a break with Husserl's phenomenology. Sartre writes: "Modern thought has made considerable progress by reducing the existent to a series of its appearances."[1]

It is as if Sartre were already warning us that if Husserl can reduce things to their appearances, seen as objective aspects and grasped as "meanings," then the existent thing vanishes in its uniqueness as existing. But we are anticipating Sartre's argument, which begins by an examination of *phenomenon.*

By the term "phenomenon" Sartre means the appearance, in the sense of the manifestation, of any object to consciousness. He notes that the term is ambiguous. "Phenomenon" can mean either an appearance that hides the true reality of an existent or an appearance that reveals reality to consciousness. In the first sense, "phenomenon" can mean an illusion, as a stick in water appears to be bent; or the term can signify the exterior aspect of a thing as opposed to its interior nature. More technically, "phenomenon" in the first sense is the Kantian phenomenon—an appearance hiding the true reality or noumena. Sartre, however, following Husserl, uses the term "phenomenon" in the second sense, as signifying reality's own manifestation or appearance to consciousness. Thus what appears to the mind trained by the phenomenological method is the manifestation of being itself. Being does not hide itself.

Sartre proceeds by noting that Husserl's understanding of phenomenon has helped to eliminate from philosophy many embarrassing dualisms—views that reality is composed basically of two kinds

1. *Being and Nothingness,* trans. Hazel Barnes (New York: Philosophical Library, 1956), p. xiv, hereafter referred to as BN; *L'être et le néant* (Paris: Gallimard, 1943), p. 11, hereafter referred to as EN.

of being. In the Background, we have seen that Cartesianism views the mind as a spiritual substance and matter as pure extension in space. This view of reality led the Cartesians into the difficult, if not unsolvable, problem of the relation of two fundamentally independent substances, particularly in considering man, who has obviously both a mind and a body and is affected by each. All dualisms are therefore "embarrassing" insofar as they must explain how the two realities are related to each other and why they are each considered "reality" or "being."

The embarrassing dualisms that Sartre considers are interior and exterior, being and appearance, potency and act, appearance and essence. He agrees that the phenomenologies of Husserl and Heidegger have made progress in eliminating dualism but questions whether they have been completely successful.

First, from the Background it is clear that the dualisms of interior and exterior and of being and appearance are eliminated by Husserl's view of phenomenon as reality's appearance to consciousness. Unlike the Kantian phenomenon, which is relative both to the mind knowing it and to the thing-in-itself hiding "beneath" it, Husserl's phenomenon is relative only to the consciousness knowing it. For example, Kant would maintain that the perception of an apple-red is relative both to the position of the perceiver and to the intrinsic hidden nature of the quality of the apple. Husserl, on the other hand, claims that the perception of the red of an apple is relative to the perceiver but views the redness thus manifested as an aspect of the apple's reality. There is thus, according to Husserl, no real distinction between the appearance of red and its being or between the interior of red and its exterior—that is, after the proper use of the phenomenological method.

According to Sartre, Aristotle's dualism of potency and act also falls under Husserl's phenomenology. Aristotle considered that activities such as seeing or thinking presuppose the capacity, or potency, to see or think. Thus Aristotle reasoned that what distinguishes a blind person from a healthy person with his eyes closed is the latter's "capacity," or potency, to see. But for Sartre, capacity, precisely as capacity, is hidden; consequently, it could not be true being.

Finally, phenomenology eliminates the dualism of appearance and essence. In the succeeding paragraphs, Sartre will indicate a problem in Husserl's attempt to unify appearance and essence. For the present, he notes that the essence is that which gives unity to all the various appearances of a thing and that the essence is itself an appearance and not something hidden beneath the appearances. Therefore, Sartre reasons, the essence is more than a mere name that we give for convenience to a haphazard series of an object's manifestations—a position that is often termed "nominalism." For example, the term "apple" is more than a mere label for a series of manifestations that have no unity among them. Although an apple has many perspectives, we somehow recognize, in the perception of any one of these perspectives, that all the aspects belong to a true totality, "apple."

There is admittedly some obscurity in the above explanation. What precisely is the phenomenon as essence uniting the series of manifestations of the object? We recall, from the Background, that Husserl realized that any object, such as an apple, manifests at any given time only one aspect (*Abschattung*) of itself to consciousness. Nevertheless, Husserl claimed that the transcendental ego unifies all preceding and succeeding aspects into a true unity of the object, for example, "apple." Furthermore, the phenomenological method (reduction) can reveal the essential reason for this unity, since this unity is itself an appearance, or phenomenon. Finally, since the essence is itself a manifestation of the object, it is possible to "see," or intuit, the essence. This immediate intellectual seeing, or intuition, of an essence *in* the aspects of an object and the simultaneous revealing of the essence by the object in its aspects (the essence or totality "apple" revealed in the perception of this side of the apple) is one of the most difficult points to understand in Husserl's philosophy.[2] Sartre seizes upon this point as an obscurity and weakness that, as he will now show, leads Husserl back to dualisms.

For Sartre, Husserl's notion of phenomenology requires that the existent known have the capacity for an *infinite* number of (possible) appearances, and thus the dualism of finite and infinite enters philosophy. Sartre maintains that if the object could be reduced to a finite number of appearances, it would lose the very objectivity Husserl

2. The issue is further obscured because Husserl seems to claim both that the transcendental ego itself brings about or "constitutes" the essential unity of the object from its aspects and that the "law" uniting the aspects somehow comes from the object itself.

claimed for it. For example, the objectivity of this apple before me demands that the upright apple that I now perceive is the same as the upside down apple that I could perceive. If I were conscious only of the apple as upright, I would not be aware of that precise objective unity "apple" but merely of one of its aspects. Does it follow, however, that the object "apple" must have the capacity for an infinite number of manifestations?

Though objects manifest themselves to me through only one aspect at a time, I transcend, or go beyond, that one aspect, uniting the present aspect perceived with the total series of which it is only a part—the totality of past and future perceivable aspects.[3] Sartre claims that Husserl's own principles demand that this series of manifestations be infinite.

An example may help in understanding Sartre's critique of Husserl. If, for example, the apple before me can manifest itself to me in a finite series of appearances—its color, shape, weight, or position—then there would be a point when I *totally* grasp the object within my consciousness. But does not the very objectivity of the object demand that I be conscious that the apple can always reappear differently to me and to other minds and still be an "apple"? If I decide to turn the apple upside down or to look at it through sunglasses, does not the "apple" now transcend its former series of appearances and include within it these new manifestations? It is still an "apple," upside down, still an "apple" seen through sunglasses. The objectivity of the apple thus demands that it be capable of an infinite number of manifestations and still retain its unity as an "apple."

Sartre observes that we seem to have only one dualism, finite and infinite, which is after all an advantage.[4] For the present, he leaves this problem and concludes by recalling that at least the phenomenon does not hide an unknowable thing-in-itself, the noumenon. This

3. Indeed, if consciousness stopped completely at a single aspect, I would be conscious only of that aspect; I and the aspect perceived would be one—it would fill me and I it. In Sartre's terms, there would be only an intuitive and subjective plenitude.

4. Sartre also hints that we seem to be back to the dualism of being and appearance. For the true being of the apple would seem to be the infinite series of its possible appearances, which can never manifest itself as infinite, while the apple always appears to be finite.

conclusion leads Sartre to examine the more immediate problem of what kind of reality Husserl's phenomenon really has.

The essence of phenomenon is "to appear," and this means that phenomenon must appear to someone. But are we to conclude that the reality of the object is identical with the reality of consciousness? Indeed, is the being of the object (the being of the apple) identical with its phenomena, that is, with its appearances to consciousness. Granting that Husserl has shown that the *objectivity* of the object is identical with its phenomenon, or appearance—and even here Sartre has noted Husserl's problem of the object's infinite possible manifestations—the question then arises whether the *being* of the object is identical with its objectivity. Sartre will devote the following sections to showing that, in general, being is not reducible to phenomenon (section II); that, in particular, the being of consciousness is not identical with the object perceived (section III); and, finally, that the being of the thing perceived is not identical with its objectivity or manifestations (sections IV–VI). Thus, starting with phenomenon (for example, the perception of an apple), Sartre will show that both the being of consciousness and the being of the apple perceived are not totally reducible to the consciousness of the apple.

Sartre will thus reveal two "transphenomena" to every phenomenon, that is, two regions of being that arise from phenomena but are not reducible to phenomena—consciousness and brute existence. In this way, he attempts to avoid every form of idealism, a philosophy that, to a greater or lesser extent, emphasizes a priority of knowledge over existence.

II. THE PHENOMENON OF BEING AND THE BEING OF THE PHENOMENON

We have seen, from the Background, that phenomenology implies that being does not hide permanently behind our knowledge of it but rather manifests itself to consciousness. Also, we have noted that the term "being" can mean either whatever is in any way whatsoever or what is as the basic reality of a thing. In the first sense, we say a tree is a being, a phenomenon is a being. In the second sense, we ask what is the *being* of a tree, what is the *being* of a phenomenon. The problem we now consider involves the relation of these meanings of being.[5] It concerns the basic kind of reality a phenomenon is, namely, whether it is fundamentally an essence or an existence. An analogy may help to bring out the significance of this question concerning the being of phenomenon.

A person dreams of a magic lamp that manifests itself in its various aspects—shape, the appearance of a genie, and so forth. There is then a phenomenon of the lamp. But what is the being of this phenomenon? Of course, we are concerned with being in the sense of the basic kind of reality of a thing. But this can be either essence or existence. Thus the being of the phenomenon magic lamp can be either the essence of the lamp—that aspect that is the principle of all its magic qualities—or the kind of existence the phenomenon has, namely, a dreamed existence.

In an analogous way, Sartre notes that there must be some kind of phenomenon of being in its most general sense, since we can speak of being and clearly have some comprehension of it; for example, we can examine the difference between actual being and possible being or between mental being and extramental being. Thus, in some way, being is manifested to us through its concrete appearances, such as the phenomenon of *this* apple. But we are then left with the question

5. Strictly speaking, Sartre is not concerned merely with comparing the various usages of the term "being." As a phenomenologist, he considers many of our expressions concerning being as not mere matters of linguistic convenience but as referring to a comprehension of being that itself is ultimately based on some manifestation of being. Nevertheless, some confusion may arise in reading this section because Sartre does not explicitly distinguish the related meanings of the term "being." In fact, the two senses of being referred to are implicitly related by him to a third sense, as when we speak of concrete being, *this* tree. Both the general and the more specific senses of being must refer to concrete being if we are not to be considering the empty concept of being. Thus I can question what red has in common with other beings (in some way it *is*) or I can consider the *being* of red (whether it is basically an essence or a certain kind of existence). Sartre's point is that the examination of concrete being reveals the nature of *all* being, i.e., that through the manifestations of particular beings there is some kind of manifestation of Being ("being" in general). He no doubt considers his argument as basically unaffected by the various ways of looking at being. Indeed, this seems to be the case. For no matter what sense of being we are using, it would seem to be always true, for Sartre, that the phenomenon of being is not on the same level as the being of phenomenon. The phenomenon is always on the level of knowledge or some content of consciousness, while being is, as we will see, existence.

whether the being of the existing thing, for example, this apple, is the same as the being of its manifestation to consciousness—that is, *is the kind of being an apple has of the same "quality" or "nature" as the kind of being its manifestations have?* We can see what Sartre is aiming at if we return to Husserl. According to Husserl, the being, or reality, of an apple manifests itself to consciousness with a certain evidence or "essence." And when the mind knows the essence of an apple, it also knows the true being of an apple.

In general, for Husserl, reality manifests itself to consciousness as a "what," an "essence," or a "phenomenon." Thus reality and phenomenon are basically on the same level: the *phenomenon* of being is fundamentally on the same level as the *being* of phenomenon. This is true, according to Husserl, even if we are comparing the *phenomenon* of an existing apple with the *being* of the apple. For, as we saw in the Background, Husserl claims that if we bracket, or suspend judgment about, the de facto existence of the apple, it still appears to be what it is, namely, an existing apple, and it appears as distinct, for example, from a recollected apple. Thus existence enters into the object as one of its aspects.

Sartre, of course, would agree with Husserl that we can contemplate the difference between an existing and a recollected apple. But his point here is that existence-as-an-aspect-of-an-object is radically different from *existence*. Our access to brute existence is of a fundamentally different order from our understanding of brute existence because brute existence is fundamentally different from its objectification by consciousness.[6] Consequently, for Sartre, the phenomenon of being is not the being of phenomenon—the *manifestation* of existence is not the *existence* of existence-as-an-aspect-of-an-object.

It may further help to understand Sartre's objection to Husserl if we return to our analogy. The dreamer, a phenomenologist, of course, reflects when he awakes on the dreamed-lamp. He recognizes that his description of the dreamed-lamp is not the experience of

6. Although boredom and nausea are not a conceptual knowledge of existence, they are an access to existence that is an awareness of existence. This access to existence is through the being of the pre-reflective cogito, a being that *is* a "knowing," in the sense of an immediate revelation of existence (see pp. 132–135 and pp. 146–147).

dreaming the lamp, but he maintains that the experience would add nothing to the "richness" or description of the dreamed-lamp. Indeed, even if there should be no such experience as dreaming, the object dreamed-lamp is *perfectly* distinguished from the object perceived-lamp. Thus the actual experience of dreaming is homogeneously, or uniformly, related to the object dreamed. Analogously, this phenomenologist would claim that there is no heterogeneity between the perfect description of an existing apple and our direct consciousness of it.

According to Sartre, both Husserl and Heidegger err in that they conceive the passage from the phenomenon to its being as a passage from the homogeneous to the homogeneous, that is, a passage from the concrete meaning of the existing thing to its essential meaning. Thus, while they do not absolutely identify phenomenon and being, they keep the two on the same level, the level of meaning.[7]

It is clear that, for Sartre, the being of phenomenon is not itself a phenomenon, a meaning, or something hidden beneath phenomenon.[8] Rather, being is simply the condition of all disclosure or revelation. It is the foundation of the revealing quality of things, it is that which gives things the quality that reveals, rather than hides, the essences of things, somewhat as the dreamer's mind is the *condition* for the lamp appearing to the dreamer.

It is in this second section of the Introduction that Sartre sees his phenomenology as radically departing from Husserl's and Heidegger's understanding of reality. *That reality is existence and that existence is revealed to consciousness through such pre-reflective*

7. Sartre refers to Husserl's eidetic reduction: the step in the phenomenological method in which the concrete phenomenon is seen to be an essence. For example, a perceived-red is seen to be a distinct "structure" (whatness) from a remembered- or imagined-red. Sartre, in this respect, also refers to Heidegger's ontic-ontological characterization of the human reality: that concrete being (ontic) that questions the fundamental reality of his own being as well as the nature of being in general (ontological). Sartre interprets this to mean that the *phenomenon* of the human reality reveals the *being* of the human reality, since man is seen to be fundamentally a questioning being and his being, or existence, is finally identified with his nature as questioning.

8. He also claims that being is not the presence of the thing to consciousness, since absence also reveals being. Sartre here hints at a notion of nothingness that is central to his ontology. As we will see in Part One, Chapter One, it is a concrete nothingness, such as missing a fourth at bridge.

awareness as nausea or boredom are the pivotal point of this entire Introduction and the beginning of Sartre's reinterpretation of the phenomenological method. As noted, Sartre points out that we can, of course, examine being like any other object. We can, for example, inquire into the nature of dreamed-being, although we are then no longer in immediate contact with the being of dreams, but rather with the meaning of dreamed-being. *And similarly, when we examine being, we obtain a knowledge of being rather than an immediate access to being itself.*

From the above, it is clear that, for Sartre, any access we have to being must be nonconceptual. Indeed, according to Sartre, we do have a revealing intuition of existence, that is, an immediate access to being. It is through boredom or nausea that we become aware of being as brute existence. Being is thus revealed to us not in a concept but in immediate confrontation with reality. If being were revealed to us in "knowledge," Sartre would claim that we would still be faced with the problem of the being, or existence, of that knowledge. This point will be examined in more detail in the next section.

There is some difficulty in relating the opening paragraphs of this section to the concluding paragraphs. Sartre speaks of a revealing intuition of the phenomenon of being. This can mean either that nausea, for example, can be experienced through a particular phenomenon—the perception of a song—or that there is a unique phenomenon of nausea or boredom. The ambiguity arises because Sartre is beginning to change the meaning of the term "phenomenon." For if phenomenon means the revelation of reality to consciousness, then phenomenon must reveal existence. However, Sartre agrees with Husserl that being also manifests itself as an essence, or structure, to consciousness, and Sartre will usually agree to call being's manifestation as an essence "phenomenon." Thus Sartre usually opposes "being," in the sense of existence, to "phenomenon."

Furthermore, Sartre's use of the term "the existent" (*l'existant*) can be misleading to one not familiar with phenomenology. The existent for Sartre does not mean a thing existing independently of consciousness that is known only by some representation within the mind. The existent is the thing as known; the existent is a phenomenon and truly reveals itself.

But Sartre's point is that the being of the existent does not consist in being revealed. Although being is coextensive with phenomenon and not hidden beneath phenomenon, it is not subject to the phenomenal condition, which is to exist only as an object for consciousness. *Being is that which reveals (the existent), although being is not itself simply that which is revealed.*

Nevertheless, when the context is clear, we will sometimes refer to the being of the existent as the *"brute* existent," hoping that this term will not imply something hidden beneath the existent. We will return to this discussion of terminology in the last section of the Introduction.

Sartre will devote the next section to proving that the being of consciousness is not identified with the object known (phenomenon), and the remaining sections of the Introduction to proving that the being of the existent known is neither the being of our consciousness nor the objectivity of the existent known. For example, the being of a tree is neither our consciousness of the tree nor the "meaning" of a tree—even if this meaning were comprehensive and included "existing" as one of its aspects. The being of a tree is not exhausted by even the most comprehensive understanding of a tree.

For Sartre, as we have said, there is a transphenomenality of phenomenon; that is, the being of phenomenon is a condition for phenomenon but not reducible to phenomenon. There are, as we noted, two transphenomena—consciousness and existence.

III. THE PRE-REFLECTIVE COGITO AND THE BEING OF THE *Percipere*

Sartre has concluded that the being of phenomenon is not itself a phenomenon; being does not have the phenomenal character of an essence but, rather, is transphenomenal in nature. Now he shows that, from one viewpoint, this transphenomenality of being is the pre-reflective cogito; for example, our awareness when we are absorbed in watching a movie.

He fixes the context for his study between the extremes of a certain realism and idealism: a realism that attempts to relate ideas as representations to the things represented and consequently leads to the already rejected dualism of appearance versus reality; and idealism, which claims that the existence of things consists in the knowledge we have of them—as Berkeley (Bishop George Berkeley, 1685–1753) puts it, "to be is to be perceived" (*esse est percipi*).

Cartesian realism views consciousness as directed immediately toward its ideas as representations of reality or as modifications of consciousness itself. For the Cartesian, the task of philosophy is to reflect on our ideas and to reason which of them truly reflect reality. This view of consciousness and its objects is entirely incompatible with the phenomenologist's view of consciousness as directly *of* an object, as a manifestation of reality. Sartre, therefore, concentrates on the more difficult problem of distinguishing his view of consciousness from Berkeley's and Husserl's. In this context, he considers Husserl's phenomenology as close to the idealism of Berkeley, since Husserl brackets existence and considers objects as essentially unrelated to existence. Sartre's basic objection to idealism is that a philosophy of knowledge must be based on a philosophy of being; that is, the question of *how* we know reality presupposes an answer to the question of the "nature" of reality. Sartre thus wishes to separate himself from a long tradition—beginning with Descartes and Kant—that claims, in general, that we should first investigate the workings of the mind before examining to what extent the mind knows reality.[9] He considers this "critical" tradition to be erroneous because knowledge presupposes existence, at least the existence of the knower. Thus there cannot be knowledge of knowledge *ad infinitum*, and eventually we must recognize that knowledge must be an aspect of being itself.

Again, our analogy with the dreamer may be useful. Suppose we wish to investigate how our mind works while it is dreaming. It is clear that our study would presuppose that our dreams are a modification of our being and that they depend on our being—for otherwise, we may be dreaming that we are studying dreams and dreaming that we are dreaming that we are dreaming . . . Thus if knowledge is not based on a being that is itself not knowledge, then the entire series knowledge of knowledge of knowledge . . . evaporates into nothing.

Sartre is therefore back to his earlier conclusion that the *being* of

9. At most, this statement indicates a logical priority. Kant would maintain that phenomena reciprocally reveal both the limits of knowledge and the limited way reality appears to us.

phenomenon is not reducible to phenomenon, or knowledge, but is, from one viewpoint, the transphenomenal being of the subject. Knowledge refers to the being of the knower. The being of the knower, however, is the very consciousness experienced in the act of knowledge.

We have progressed from phenomenon to the transphenomenal being of the subject—consciousness. Much of what Sartre now says concerning consciousness has already been discussed in the Background.

We have seen that consciousness is intentional, that is, that it is directly and immediately related to something—its object—other than consciousness. Thus consciousness, by its very nature, is relational: it is *of* an object-other-than-consciousness. Since consciousness is directed outward and not toward itself, there is a true connection between consciousness and the world.

Although consciousness is directed outward, it is still an *awareness*, and therefore there is, in a sense, consciousness of consciousness. We must be careful, however, not to understand this immediate consciousness of consciousness, or self-consciousness, as split into a consciousness-knowing and a consciousness-being-known. We can, of course, reflect on our consciousness and be aware of it as an object to be studied. But for Sartre, this deliberate act of reflection is a secondary act, a turning of our consciousness on itself. In this act of reflection, we must be aware of ourselves reflecting on ourselves. Thus whatever knowledge we obtain of ourselves must simultaneously be an awareness as well as a knowledge; for example, if I reflect that I am tired, I am also aware that I am reflecting. I can, indeed, now make that awareness, namely, that I am aware that I am tired, into a new object and become aware that I am aware . . . There is only one way to avoid an infinite regress, and that is to recognize that while awareness, or consciousness, can be made into an object, it is immediately not an object or knowledge of the self, but the (transphenomenal) being of the knower. Consequently, consciousness, by its very being as an awareness, is *pre-reflectively* a (self-) consciousness. (Sartre states that in speaking of consciousness of the self [*de soi*], the *of* [*de*] is to be put in parentheses as denoting a grammatical necessity. Hazel Barnes notes that in English we can simply use the term "self-consciousness." But to emphasize that this "self" is not an object, we will often put the term "self" in parentheses.)

Thus when Descartes thought that he had discovered the certainty of his own existence in his reflections on himself, he must have already been *aware* of his certainty: he must have been pre-reflectively aware of himself reflecting.[10] Consequently, for Sartre, the true self is pre-reflectively a self-consciousness. To be more precise, consciousness is *directly* an awareness of something other than itself and simultaneously and indirectly an awareness of itself, as when we are absorbed in a book, we are directly aware of reading and indirectly aware of *ourselves* as reading.

Sartre thus insists that the intentional character of consciousness does not imply a split between the object and the (self-) consciousness of the object. The intentional character of consciousness requires that the object not be considered as a *thing* residing *in* consciousness. For example, we often think of ourselves as "hearing" sounds and "seeing" colors while not being aware of them—perhaps we conceive of ourselves as accustomed to them. But if we accept this picture of perception literally, it means that we are conceiving the objects of perception and our perceiving consciousness as having independent existences: the objects exist in us and we may or may not be conscious of them. According to Sartre, however, hearing and the consciousness of hearing cannot be distinguished even logically. Nevertheless, this does not mean that the being of the object perceived is absorbed in consciousness, for this would make consciousness into an independent existence. Sartre wishes to keep a delicate balance—insisting that consciousness is intentional and therefore necessarily related to an object other than itself, and yet insisting that the being of consciousness and the being of the thing known are not reducible to the consciousness-of-the-object. For example, when we perceive the red of an apple, our consciousness has no other direct object than the perceived-red, and still the being of our consciousness and the being of the red are not reducible to our perception of red.

The being of consciousness and the being of things are related and

---

10. Of course, consciousness must be able to *immediately* reflect on itself, otherwise Sartre's entire phenomenology, as a reflection on consciousness, would be invalid. Sartre will thus later distinguish a "pure" reflection from an "impure" reflection (cf. pp. 125–131).

yet very different from each other. Sartre will devote the entire book to elaborating this relation and difference. For the present, he merely sketches some of the characteristics of the being of consciousness, just as in the last section of his Introduction, he will sketch some of the characteristics of the being of things.

Consciousness, we repeat, by its nature is a revelation of a reality other than consciousness. *If we are to recognize that consciousness reveals and does not hide reality, then we must be prepared to see consciousness as a pure translucency (translucidité).* Consciousness can have no opaqueness, for this would "color" its object. Sartre will show, in Part One, Chapter One, that the translucency of consciousness requires that consciousness be a "concrete nothingness." There can be no "laws" or "nature" of consciousness, since these would require that consciousness reveal its object in accordance with those laws or nature. The thing would then be hidden by the mind's knowledge, and we would be back to the Kantian distinction between the thing-as-known and the thing-in-itself.

Since consciousness has no nature or laws, Sartre concludes that it must be pure activity and self-determination.[11] Of course, from the aspect of the thing known, consciousness is determined by knowing a certain *what*—my perception is determined by the redness of the apple before me. Nevertheless, the being of consciousness is not determined by its object, since the object comes into existence as an object-known only because consciousness determines itself to be the awareness of this aspect of reality rather than another.

Thus, for consciousness, existence precedes essence; that is, what is known comes-to-be as a known only because consciousness activates itself as the awareness of a particular aspect of reality.[12]

---

11. Although Sartre will later elaborate the proposition that consciousness is a concrete nothingness *in* being, he warns us here that this does not mean that consciousness arises from nothing. "Nothingness," as an explanation of consciousness, is consequent upon that concrete nothingness *in* being that is consciousness.

12. Consciousness, for Sartre, cannot proceed from a potency or cause, since phenomenology eliminates the dualism of potency and act. Furthermore, if we conceive of a cause of consciousness, we are still faced with the problem of the origin of consciousness: either we must face the problem again in a cause, which is conscious; or we must explain how consciousness can originate from an unconscious cause.

Sartre concludes that consciousness is a nonsubstantial absolute. It is absolute because, as the *being* of the knower rather than the knowledge of the knower, consciousness is not relative to the object known; for example, it is the pure awareness of the apple-red (as perceived from here). For the same reason, namely, that it is being, consciousness is also nonsubstantial, since a substance would have a self-identity that would prevent the perfect clarity needed by consciousness to be the pure revelation *of* a being.

In the title of this section, Sartre uses the term *"percipere,"* an infinitive meaning "to perceive." He therefore questions whether the pre-reflective cogito is the *being* of the act of perception.[13] It is clear that the pre-reflective cogito (or consciousness) is the transphenomenal being of our act of perception. Thus knowledge is ultimately based on being and not on further knowledge.

To summarize: from the viewpoint of what-is-known, consciousness is identified with its "object," since consciousness has no "nature" of its own; from the viewpoint of its being, however, consciousness is not an object, a "what," or a phenomenon, but rather the pure relational being that is an *awareness-of*.

IV. THE BEING OF THE *Percipi*

It may be useful to pause and reflect on Sartre's general procedure in the Introduction. As a phenomenologist, he begins with a study of phenomenon—that very appearance that does not hide reality but reveals it. He sees a twofold transphenomenality within phenomenon: every phenomenon is (1) an awareness of (2) something, for example, the *perception* of a *cup*. From the viewpoint of awareness, he arrived, in the previous section, at consciousness as the transphenomenal being of the perceiver; that is, the existence (*l'être*) of

13. The phrase "being of *percipere"* is technically ambiguous, since it can mean the being of the object perceived precisely as a perceived or known being, namely, that knowledge is, in a general sense, a kind of being; or it can mean being as opposed to knowledge, that is, that knowledge, even as a kind of being, is ultimately based on a being other than knowledge. Sartre uses the term in both senses and shows that whatever "being" knowledge has, this "being" is ultimately based on a being other than being-known. This line of argument is particularly evident in the subsequent sections of the Introduction.

consciousness (awareness) is not reducible to the object perceived (the cup). From the viewpoint of the thing known, he will now show that the existence (*l'être*) of the thing known is not reducible to its objectivity.

At first, this appears to be a return to the Cartesian dualism of mind and matter. But Sartre intends to keep the twofold transphenomenality of phenomenon without falling into such a dualism. He has already taken pains to distinguish his pre-reflective consciousness from the Cartesian cogito and to insist that consciousness is not the substantive Cartesian mind. His task is now to show that the being of the thing perceived (the cup) is not the being of consciousness—although it will later be revealed to be the foundation of consciousness—and also that it is not, as Descartes's matter, a created being.

Sartre makes it clear that he considers his procedure also to avoid the idealism of both Berkeley and Kant. Idealism, he notes, begins by examining the known as known; its aim is to establish those conditions of thought that validate the sciences—for example, the law of causality as a necessary way of unifying phenomena. Thus far, however, we already have attained a being, consciousness, that is the foundation of thought itself and is that unique mode of being that is simultaneously a mode of apprehension. Further, as an immediate nonconceptual apprehension of itself, consciousness is not subject to the dualism and relativity of the subject-object relation of knowledge.

In order to avoid idealism completely, however, Sartre must now show that the being of the thing perceived is independent from the being of consciousness. He does this in two steps. First, he shows that the perceived object (e.g., cup), precisely as it is an object perceived, cannot be identified with the act of perceiving it; that is, the perceived object, regardless of whether it exists independently of being known, still has a unity that is not explicable by the act of perceiving it. Second, he shows that this unity leads us to recognizing the independent existence of the thing perceived.

In the first step, Sartre notes that even if we limit our consideration to the thing perceived precisely as perceived, it still has a being that is not perfectly identified with our perception of it. As we have seen, the thing perceived—the cup—is the synthetic unity of its infinite possible manifestations, including future possible ones. Indeed, we perceive the totality "cup" in and through the perception of a single aspect or perspective of the cup. Thus the cup is perceived as having an objectivity that is not identified with our perception of it, although it is not, at this point, clear that the cup has an existence independent of our perceiving it.

Of course, we might object that the thing perceived is relative to our perception of it, but Sartre shows that this does not imply that the being of the thing perceived is relative to our perception. Clearly, the characteristic mode of the *percipi*—the act-of-being-perceived—is passive; for example, the cup is that-which-is-perceived. Consequently, if the being of phenomenon consists in being-perceived, this being would then be passive. But passive being, Sartre says, elaborating on a distinctive characteristic of his philosophy, is the result of activity; for example, we actively assume the attitude of being-offended.

Furthermore, by an inversion of the principle of action and reaction, passivity must be found equally on the side of the agent acting as on the side of the one receiving the action. Sartre's point may be seen by considering an isometric exercise in which the right hand pushes the left hand. The right hand can push the left only because the right offers resistance, and thereby allows itself to be pushed by the left hand. Analogously, red can *be* perceived only if perception is that-which-can-be-affected by the perceived-red.

In the previous section, we have seen that the being of the perceiver, as consciousness, is pure spontaneity—nothing can act on it and it cannot act on anything. Also, if the being, or *esse*, of the thing perceived consists in our perception of it, Sartre hints that we would be faced with the same contradiction that he finds in creation: the creature receiving its being from the creator and simultaneously remaining distinct from the creator.

Similarly, if the being of the thing perceived consists in our perception of it, this being would be a received being and not a being of its own. At the same time, however, this received being would transcend our consciousness, since in its infinite possible manifestations, it transcends our finite knowledge of it. Thus the perceived cup would be totally a received being, produced by our consciousness (assuming consciousness could produce anything), and yet the cup, in its total objectivity, would be more than our knowledge of it.

But we might, with Husserl, still attempt to identify the *being* of the thing perceived with its *objectivity*. Sartre therefore continues with an involved discussion of Husserl's attempt to give due independence to the being of the thing perceived.

For Husserl, the synthetic unity of the object comes not only from the activity of the transcendental ego but also from the essence or content of the object itself. The various aspects of a cup unite themselves into the unity of the cup not only because of the activity of the ego, but also because there are certain "principles" or "laws" within the content of the object cup that necessitate that the various aspects fall, as it were, into place. These "laws" provide a certain given, a certain *hyle* (from the Greek, meaning "matter"), to perception. This hyle, for Husserl, is not the matter of existents, since, for him, phenomenology brackets the question of actual existence. Nor is it the being of consciousness, but rather the matter on which consciousness acts. For Sartre, this hyle is a hybrid being, neither consciousness nor part of the world, and it cannot be the being of the thing perceived.

Sartre therefore concludes that Husserl cannot adequately account for the objectivity of the object. The objectivity of a cup, for example, does not come from the activity of consciousness, nor can it be explained as that which is passively received by consciousness (since consciousness receives only this or that particular aspect of a cup and not its totality). Further, Sartre concludes that if the being of the thing perceived were passive, it would also be relative to the agent responsible for the passivity. The thing perceived would always have its being only in relation to the agent and not within itself, and thus the cup would not be recognized as a "cup" by others. Passivity and relativity, therefore, cannot consist in the act of being perceived. But again, neither is the being of the thing perceived the transphenomenal being of consciousness, since *the thing known, in its unity, always transcends our knowledge of it.*

Nevertheless, we are still only on the first step of the argument and have not clearly proved that the *being* of the existent is not reducible to its being known; e.g., we have not proved that the being of an apple is not reducible to its objectivity.

We are thus led to the last two sections of the Introduction, which are concerned with the true being of the thing perceived—the transphenomenal being of the "content" of phenomenon, the *being* of the existent.

V. THE ONTOLOGICAL PROOF

The examination of intentionality—the thesis that consciousness is directly a revelation of a being other than consciousness—is for Sartre an "ontological" proof. Traditionally, the ontological proof, or argument, refers to Anselm's and Descartes's argument for the existence of God—an attempt to reason from the meaning or concept of "God" to the fact of his existence.

Anselm reasons that, by definition, "God" is that being greater than which cannot be conceived. Even an atheist, Anselm states, must agree to this nominal definition of the term "God," otherwise the atheist is not denying what the believer affirms. But then, as the greatest being conceivable, God must exist, since a nonexisting God is nothing, and the mind can clearly conceive of many things more perfect than nothing—for example, an existing ant. That is, even the *concept* of an existing ant is more perfect than the *concept* of a nonexisting God, contradicting the original nominal definition of God. Descartes's argument (particularly in the fifth meditation of his *Meditations*) is more technical but essentially the same.

Sartre's ontological argument is different from Anselm's and Descartes's in one very important respect. Sartre's argument is based on the relation of a *being* (consciousness) to another *being* (being-in-itself) rather than on an analysis of concepts. This is why Sartre regards that the demand of consciousness for a being-other-than-consciousness must be met, while denying the validity of the ontological argument for the existence of God.

Sartre notes that the description of consciousness can be taken in two senses: one, closing the subject within itself; the other, by an ontological argument, leading outward to the being of phenomenon (for example, the being of an apple).

In the first sense, consciousness, as consciousness *of* something, is taken to mean that consciousness "constitutes" or brings about its object—that the "something" is produced by consciousness itself. Sartre, however, recalls the conclusions of the preceding section, particularly the analysis of passivity, to rule out this possibility. Furthermore, as noted in the preceding sections, the object, in its total objectivity, is the synthetic totality of all its possible manifestations and thus is more than any concrete perception of it. Consequently, Sartre concludes that consciousness cannot produce the objectivity of the object, and certainly not its being, the source of its objectivity.

Sartre gives another reason why consciousness cannot produce the being of the thing-known. *He claims that objectivity results from "absence" and "nothingness" rather than from the presence and fullness of the perspective perceived.* For example, when we perceive a cup, the intentionality of consciousness is not to the aspect or side of the cup present to our consciousness but to the totality cup. This totality is the synthetic unity of all the possible aspects, present and future, of the cup. Clearly, however, this infinite series of possible manifestations transcends what is present to our consciousness, that is, it transcends our knowledge of the cup. Consequently, the objectivity and being of the cup transcend the presence of the cup and our consciousness of the cup. Thus the objectivity of the thing perceived and its being—for being is the foundation of objectivity—come to consciousness as something outside consciousness' productivity. Consciousness is therefore an awareness of something other than consciousness, in the sense of an awareness of a *being* that is other than the being-of-consciousness.

We see now the significance of the earlier analysis of self-consciousness. If consciousness were first turned on itself, it would be self-contained and we would have to reason to the existence of external things. Rather, the being of consciousness is first and directly a revelation of a being-other-than-the-being-of-consciousness.

Therefore, there is a twofold transphenomenality of phenomenon: one leading to the being of the subject, the other to the being of things. But the being of the subject and the being of things are related differently to phenomenon. The being of consciousness is the awareness aspect of phenomenon, the perception of the cup. The being of things is that existence that is the condition of things manifesting themselves to consciousness, the being of the cup that enables it to appear to consciousness precisely as a cup. Sartre's entire book is an elaboration of these two modes of being and their relation within "phenomenon." The last section of the Introduction, however, will be devoted to a preliminary sketch of the being of existents, being-in-itself, and its relation to the being-of-consciousness.

VI. BEING-IN-ITSELF

The study of phenomenon has led us to the transphenomenal being of consciousness, or *awareness,* and this in turn has led us to the transphenomenal being of phenomenon, or *being-in-itself.*[14] It is, however, of the nature of being-in-itself, or brute existence, not to be revealed completely to consciousness. This does not mean that existence hides its true nature; rather, it manifests itself in the series of its appearances—for example, an apple reveals its true being in the various ways it appears to consciousness.

Consciousness, however, is not limited to revealing certain existents, but naturally tends to understand *any* existent. In this way, consciousness naturally tends to understand all being. Sartre will elaborate on this point, particularly in Part Two, Chapter Three, "Transcendence," but here he merely notes that consciousness tends to reveal all being-in-itself as the foundation of meaning; i.e., the ontological argument of the preceding section is valid for the whole realm of consciousness and being. Consequently, man has a vague (preontological) awareness of existence as such.

The average person is certainly not explicitly aware that this vague knowledge is indeed a knowledge of existence as such, for this explicit awareness requires a training in ontology. Nevertheless, in agreement with Heidegger, Sartre claims that man has a natural questioning of being, although he may never use philosophic techniques to explicate this awareness. Such explication will be the task of his book. But even granting an explication of being, we must remember that *being is not a meaning.*

---

14. The term "being of phenomenon" has admittedly been used ambiguously. In the early part of the Introduction, it has meant the twofold transphenomenality of phenomenon (section II)—consciousness and being-in-itself. But since, as we will see, being-in-itself is the foundation of the being-of-consciousness, Sartre, from this point, will mean by the "being of phenomenon" the being of "things," being-in-itself.

Sartre agrees that meaning has its own kind of being, but he insists that the being of meaning is not the being of existents. For example, the meaning of an apple is a kind of being, although it is not the being-in-itself of the apple. The being of meaning, of course, has a relation to the being of existents, a relation that is most specifically considered in the chapter on Transcendence.

Although there are indeed two transphenomenal regions of being, the being of the existent and the being of consciousness, the "being" that is referred to in this section is the being of the thing perceived, being-in-itself. Thus Sartre notes that:

1. The present description of being is concerned only with (*a*) the being of phenomenon, or being-in-itself (*l'être-en-soi*), and this description is radically different from that of (*b*) the being of consciousness, or being-for-itself (*l'être-pour-soi*).[15]

2. There are thus two related realms of being: (*a*) the being of phenomenon and (*b*) the being of consciousness.

Although we must treat each separately, the true nature of each will be understood only when its relation to the other is brought to light. Nevertheless, we have already ruled out both the realistic and idealistic solutions to this relationship. First of all, a realistic interpretation, which claims that existents act upon and cause ideas in consciousness, has been eliminated by the analysis of the purely spontaneous character of consciousness. Second, the idealist position, which claims, to a greater or lesser extent, that a critique of knowledge precedes a study of being, has been ruled out by showing that being is not a meaning (in particular, the idealisms of Berkeley and Husserl have been shown to be false by exhibiting the absent element in the objectivity of the phenomenon). Further, an examination of the intentionality of consciousness has revealed the untenability of both the realist's and idealist's positions.

15. The terms "being-in-itself" and "being-for-itself" refer to stages in the Hegelian dialectic. In Hegel's logic, being-in-itself, as the positive aspect of quality, is the determinate state of being precisely as it is identified with its positive aspect. (But, for Hegel, this is not concrete existent.) Being-for-itself, as the true infinite, is being as it has synthesized within itself all otherness. For Hegel, being-in-itself and being-for-itself are stages in the dialectic; for Sartre, however, they represent irreducible but related givens. For a brief discussion of Hegel's dialectic, see pp. 58–60.

Sartre will continually return to an examination of realism and idealism in his approach to particular problems, and he will constantly try to show that his solutions avoid the extremes of Cartesian realism and all forms of idealism.

Sartre has several important reasons for using the terms "being-in-itself" and "being-for-itself" rather than the more familiar terms "things" or "man." In referring to things as *in*-themselves, Sartre wishes to draw our attention to the absolute unity that matter has with itself. An apple is an apple; it does not have the task of becoming what it should be. The being of an apple is not in question for itself. The being of an apple is *in-itself* and thus has no relation with itself.

Man, however, is said to be a *for-itself* because he is not perfectly one with himself. This lack of identity with himself allows man to reach out beyond himself and relate all things to himself and for his own purposes. Consciousness is thus a being for itself because it has a natural tendency to relate all being to its own purposes.

Sartre also avoids using such terms as "things" and "man," or "mind" and "matter," because of the dualism that these terms imply. In *Being and Nothingness*, Sartre attempts to describe the human reality and material existents as forming a relation, being-in-the-world. The terms "in-itself" and "for-itself" are used to stress the intimate relation of consciousness to matter as well as to keep evident the differences of these two realms of being.

Further, the terms "being-in-itself" and "being-for-itself" remind us of the phenomenological origins of our investigations. For the examination of phenomenon reveals the existent and yet also reveals that the being of phenomenon is not reducible to its objectivity. This point is extremely important. As awkward as the phrases "being of consciousness" and "being of phenomena" are, these phrases remind us that our investigation is phenomenological. We are not referring to things and minds existing independently of each other and related merely externally to each other as one complete entity to another complete entity—as, for example, a chair is merely externally related to a table.

There is still another reason why Sartre avoids using such terms as "man" and "things." In the history of philosophy and in common interpretation, these terms often imply a hierarchy of natures—

minerals, plants, animals, and man—a hierarchy in which man as the rational animal is the noblest substance, or thing, among many existing things. But as we have seen, the human reality is nonsubstantive; its being is to be totally consciousness-of. Whatever the relation of the for-itself to the in-itself, it is not the relation of one substance, or "thing," to another substance, or "thing."

Nevertheless, despite these warnings and in order to help make the terms "for-itself" and "in-itself" more familiar, the terms "things" and "man" will frequently be used throughout this book. (Also, in such phrases as "the for-itself's relation to itself and the in-itself," the terms "man" and "things" can help eliminate the necessity of using the pronoun "itself.")

One final word here about terminology. Generally, the terms "human reality," "human being," "for-itself," and "consciousness" have the same meaning in Sartre's philosophy; and they will, for the most part, be used interchangeably throughout this commentary. But there is perhaps a slight difference that should be indicated here. The terms "human reality" and "human being" are the most general, and with the reservations mentioned above, are used wherever the term "man" would normally suffice. The term "for-itself" is often used to stress the unique relation of man to things and to himself. The term "consciousness" refers specifically to the *being* of man, to that which first manifests itself as the unique and distinguishing characteristic of the for-itself. In the chapter on the for-itself (Part Two, Chapter One), Sartre will reveal that lack, possibility, and value also are "aspects" of man's being. But in our phenomenological description of phenomenon, consciousness as awareness (and from here on the terms "consciousness" and "awareness" will be used interchangeably) is that which first manifests itself as the being of man. (From the earlier brief discussion of the title of Sartre's book, it will be recalled that when we use a phrase such as "the *being* of man," the term "being" is used in the sense of what is most basic or fundamental in reality, and to repeat, for Sartre, this is existence—existence that is not reducible to phenomena.)

This last section of the Introduction, however, is not concerned with the being of man, but with a brief description of the being of things, to which we will now return.

Although the entire book will be a description of being-in-itself (or, simply, the in-itself) and its relation to being-for-itself (or, simply, the for-itself), Sartre here gives three general descriptions of the in-itself that follow immediately from our discussion thus far:

1. Being is in itself (*l'être est en soi*).
2. Being is what it is (*l'être est ce qu'il est*).
3. Being is (*l'être est*).

Two things should be noted about these three descriptions. First, although Sartre has dropped the phrase "of phenomenon" and refers merely to *being* (*l'être*), it is still clear from the entire context that he is describing a *region* of being—the in-itself. It is true that in anticipation of his distinction between being and nothingness, he already refers to this region as "being." Nevertheless, the entire purpose of the Introduction, as well as Sartre's own explicit remarks, makes it clear that consciousness, in some way, is being.

Second, Sartre is not attempting to *define* being. As a phenomenologist, he is merely *describing* some of the characteristics of being-in-itself. A definition, as distinct from a description, classifies an object both by naming the general class to which the object belongs and by naming that which distinguishes the object from other members in its class. Thus, traditionally, man was considered both as belonging to the general class "animal" and as distinct from other animals by "rationality." Clearly, "being" cannot be defined, since there is nothing more general than being and since everything that would distinguish one object from another object is itself being. A description, however, does not attempt to classify an object but merely attempts to make the object more known. Thus, for example, Aristotle often described potency and act, although he never attempted to define or classify these aspects of being. In a similar way, Sartre is attempting to reveal being-in-itself by describing it from three viewpoints.

1. To describe being as *in-itself* is to draw our attention to the absolute unity that things have with themselves (for example, an apple is an apple). Things do not have their reality constituted by a relation. They are *in-themselves* and neither potency nor becoming describes their being. A tree, for example, "becomes" only in relation to consciousness, and without consciousness, each stage of the tree's growth is perfectly at one with itself. The

continuity of the stages of a tree's growth, as well as its every movement, requires a consciousness to gather these stages into the totality "tree." In *Nausea*, Sartre describes his view of the in-itself as lacking all motion and potentiality:

> Of course a movement was something different from a tree. But it was still an absolute. A thing. My eyes only encountered completion. The tips of the branches rustled with existence which unceasingly renewed itself and which was never born. The existing wind rested on the tree like a great bluebottle, and the tree shuddered. But the shudder was not a nascent quality, a passing from power to action; it was a thing; a shudder-thing flowed into the tree, took possession of it, shook it and suddenly abandoned it, going further on to spin about itself. All was fullness and all was active, there was no weakness in time, all, even the least perceptible stirring, was made of existence [p. 178].

Sartre also notes that the view of the creation of the world has obscured our notion of being-in-itself. We have been in the habit of trying to conceive a creature as a being that simultaneously exists as an independent being and depends on God. But, according to Sartre, the simple fact is that if the being of a creature is not to be absorbed in the being of God, then the creature must exist in and by itself as uncreated. We are not to conclude from this, however, that it is proper to describe being as uncreated and uncaused. These are human labels. Causality, passivity, and movement are all human designations that, as we will see, relate being-in-itself to our conduct and behavior. Being-in-itself simply *is*. It is totally identified with itself and is beyond affirmation and negation. *The difficulty with trying to make this clear is that technically a "thing," such as a "tree," already presupposes a relation of the in-itself to consciousness.* A tree, an apple, and a cup are *meaningful* entities and thus are not true examples of being-in-itself. The in-itself is rather the "brute" being of things, that is, that which reveals things as objective, as phenomena, but which is not itself their objectivity.[16] Nevertheless, where the

---

16. Sartre, however, does not appear to be perfectly consistent in his use of the term "in-itself"; sometimes he uses the term to refer to the "brute" existent, and sometimes to existence as already altered by the advent of consciousness (see p. 141, n. 6 and p. 132, n. 1).

context is not misleading, we will often use *"things,"* such as an apple or a tree, as if they were examples of the *in-itself.* Otherwise, we will speak of the *being* of things, the *being* of apples and trees.

2. To describe beings as *"that which is what it is"* is to stress that things are not truly *selves.* This is an attempt to eliminate a possible misunderstanding in the description of being as in-it*self.* A self is a consciousness of its own selfhood and thus is not perfectly one with its selfhood. The brute existent, however, does not *have* unity; rather, it *is* its unity. Thus, strictly speaking, an apple is what it is and it is not one with it*self.* Nevertheless, the term "itself" will still be used in describing being-in-itself, and the force of the "in" must be understood as eliminating any selfhood implied by the term "itself." Sartre further states that when we state that being is what-it-is, this is not merely tautological. It is not an "analytic" principle in which the predicate simply explicates what is already in the subject—for example, a square is a four-sided plane figure. Rather, the statement "Being is what-it-is" is not analytical, since it does not describe all of being, which would include the being of consciousness, but only being-in-itself. The being of consciousness, we will see, is described as that which *is* what-it-is-not and *is not* what-it-is. Therefore, the "is," in the statement "Being is what-it-is," must be taken in a restricted sense; it refers to the being of phenomenon and indicates that being-in-itself is perfectly identified with itself. The perfect identity of being-in-itself, however, does not mean that all being is one, but only that each existent is perfectly identified with itself.

3. To describe being-in-itself as that which *is,* is to draw our attention to the fact that things exist without reason or justification. Being-in-itself does not have a necessary reality as its foundation, nor can being-in-itself be deduced from the possibility of being. For to say that something is necessary is to claim to *reason* to a necessary connection between it and some other reality. Necessity is thus a relation involving *meanings* and not existents. Existence simply *is.* Also, being-in-itself cannot be derived from possibility, since, as Sartre will make clear in the chapter on the for-itself, possibility is an aspect of the human

reality. Possibility enters into being-in-itself through man's concrete projections in the future; for example, the possibility of landing on the moon arose when the state of man's technology was such that he could realistically intend this goal. To claim that being-in-itself *is*, is to stress that the existent is simply there, that it is "contingent." Sartre states that we can express the contingency of the existent by stating that the existent is superfluous (*de trop*). Things have no meaning, no connections among themselves, no justification for their being. There is neither God nor necessary laws of nature to justify the fact that there are existents.

Sartre concludes his Introduction by reminding us that we are now faced with the monumental task of describing the two realms of being, the in-itself and the for-itself, as well as the task of describing the relation of each realm to the other and of showing how they both are, in some way, being.

PART ONE
THE PROBLEM OF
NOTHINGNESS

Part One of Sartre's book is important and controversial. Here Sartre introduces us to his description of concrete nonbeing. Briefly, Sartre shows that negative judgments such as "John is not here" have a foundation in a nonbeing that is within being and, further, that this nonbeing comes to being through the particular nonbeing that is the human consciousness, or the for-itself.

It may serve as a useful introduction to anticipate Sartre's general approach to the problem of nothingness. As a phenomenologist, Sartre is concerned with taking a new look at experience and with revealing the ontological, or fundamental, source of experience. Phenomenology is opposed to constructing theories that explain away such original experiences as absence or dread. For both Sartre and Heidegger, these experiences are not abnormal, nor do they result from peculiar dispositions of certain individuals. In brief, these experiences are not merely subjective. Consequently, Sartre's and Heidegger's ontological descriptions attempt to show such experiences as arising from the very being of the human reality.

To understand Sartre's approach to nothingness, therefore, one must constantly keep in mind the experiences of nothingness with which he begins his ontology. What are these preontological experiences of nothingness? Before calling attention to a few of them, it is necessary to stress that they are to be approached pre-reflectively, before all interpretation, no matter how deep-rooted the interpretations may be. The most familiar experience is absence—the immediate and pre-reflective awareness of someone as missing. For example, while walking with someone in a crowd, I suddenly turn and *perceive* that the person is not there. The use of the term "perception" is crucial. For besides the joyful or sad emotional response at realizing that the person is missing, the experience of absence is primarily a perception of absence. (Strictly, Sartre would not wish to distinguish completely between emotion and perception in the experience of absence.) Again, consider that I was planning to place a bet on a certain horse and then changed my mind. The horse wins the race. I immediately experience regret, based on the awareness that I could have placed the bet.

It is doubtful if anyone has not had experiences of absence or regret. They are given to us pre-reflectively and uncritically as an immediate awareness of someone not-being there or as an awareness of not-doing something that we could have done. The usual explanations of these phenomena are that they are "merely psychological" and that they are not really what they first appear to be. In a sense, we are told that we are in an abnormal state when we have such experiences, that we are overly excited, emotional, and simply not thinking. Sartre, on the contrary, insists that we must accept them for what they are—pre-reflective awareness of "nothings" (*négatités*)— and that it is not the role of the philosopher to attempt to explain away these immediate perceptions.

Besides the more obvious experiences of absence and regret, Sartre draws our attention to the phenomenon of questioning as involving nothingness. He reveals that questioning arises from a concrete nothingness within man and that this nothingness within man is the origin of those concrete *nothings* such as absence that are within the world. Although this nothing within man is the more fundamental nothing, it is also the least apparent. Sartre will thus describe it last in Part One, Chapter Two, where he will reveal that "bad faith," or our ability to lie successfully to ourselves, is based upon a nothingness within ourselves.

Sartre is well aware of the great difficulty in attempting to describe this concrete nothingness. But he insists that this task must be approached if the pre-reflective awareness of such phenomena as absence is not to be explained away. In sections I and II of Chapter One, Sartre approaches this task by calling attention to the fact that negative judgments are based upon a concrete nothing within the world and within man. Then, in sections III and IV, he shows that all previous approaches to nothingness treat it as an empty concept or mere void and thus explain away the concreteness of nothingness. Finally, in section V, he lays the foundation for his own description of nothingness.

1
The Origin of Negation

I. THE QUESTION

The Introduction, Sartre notes, was marred by a too abstract consideration of phenomenon and consciousness. The characteristic of abstraction is to consider realities as distinct, although they cannot exist separately.

Some examples may help us in understanding Sartre's view of abstraction. The shape of a clay statue can be considered separate from the clay, though neither can exist apart from the other. The total reality is rather a gestalt, or whole; and if in our analysis we forget this original synthetic totality, we will later never comprehend the true nature of the totality as a unity. Also, if we analyze the *Mona Lisa* into its colors and intensities, as recorded by a very sensitive apparatus, the resulting analysis may list every color on the canvas in its proper intensity, but it will leave out that synthetic unity that is the *Mona Lisa*. Only if we start with the painting as a totality and constantly keep in mind that we are studying it as this one whole will the resolution of its colors meaningfully contribute to a further understanding of the painting as more than the sum of its parts.

In a similar way, we must keep in mind that phenomenon and consciousness form, with the object known, a "synthetic" unity (one that is more than the sum total of its parts). Also, the being of phenomenon and the being of consciousness constitute a totality, which Heidegger calls "being-in-the-world." This totality has a real priority over its conceptually distinct parts (or moments) "man" and "world," which, like the shape and clay of a statue, can be considered separately, although they cannot exist apart from each other.

According to Sartre, this synthetic unity of consciousness-in-a-world is at least the de facto situation, regardless of what might be. In fact, we will see that while Sartre declares a certain priority of being-in-itself over consciousness, he still insists on the synthetic relation of being-in-the-world. Therefore, he examines in this chapter: (1) the precise synthetic relation that is being-in-the-world, and (2) the natures "man" and "world" that constitute this synthetic unity.

In examining these questions, Sartre's method is to study human conduct. He insists that human conduct is not a mere psychological state walled within the subject; rather, like consciousness, it is of, and toward, the world.

The immediate problem is thus to recognize the specific human conduct that will particularly reveal the relation being-in-the-world and that will serve as a guide to future study. For Sartre, this key human conduct is the *attitude of questioning, or inquiry itself.*

Any inquiry, even the question "Is there a conduct that reveals man's relation with the world?" is an attitude toward the world. This inquiry is clearly more than a mere combination of words, and as Sartre will show, it is also more than a psychological state. When we question, we inquire not merely about our ideas but also about the external world. We expect a "reply" from reality, a yes or no, a revelation of something or nothing, as when we inquire whether John is home. There is little difficulty in understanding that John's presence at home is, in a sense, reality's reply to our inquiry. But Sartre emphasizes the position that the absence of John at home is also reality's "reply" to our inquiry—that is, that both presence and absence are external to (transcend) consciousness and yet are essentially related to consciousness, forming a synthetic unity with it.

The most obvious objection to considering concrete *nothings* (*négatités*) as transcendent (that is, outside our consciousness) is to insist that such negations as "absence" refer merely to statements or negative judgments existing only in our mind. Sartre will elaborate his answer to this objection in the next two sections, but here he notes that if nothings were not transcendent, then all negations would be equated with fictional negations, such as a mermaid does not exist, a square circle does not exist. But according to Sartre, many negations reveal a truth that could only be justified by recognizing nonbeing as an element of the real.

For the present, Sartre calls attention to two nonbeings (*deux non-êtres*) in every attitude of questioning. There is the expectation of the questioner, which, as we will see, presupposes a certain nothing within the nature of knowledge; and the possibility of a "real" nonbeing within being. The question bridges the gap between these two nothings by declaring the subject's expectation of a reply from nonbeing or being.

II. NEGATIONS

Sartre begins considering the objections to accepting nonbeing as a constituent of the real. The answer to each objection follows a pattern that will be repeated throughout this work: (1) *to affirm that nonbeing does indeed come to reality only through man;* (2) *to deny that nonbeing is thereby an abstraction, merely subjective, or merely psychological.*

First, he notes that his own claim, in the Introduction, that being-in-itself is beyond affirmation or negation would seem to rule out the possibility that nonbeing can exist in being. But we already noted that this early consideration of being is too abstract. The more important objection, however, is that nonbeing would seem to be merely the abstraction or concept we form by comparing the results of various negative judgments: John is not here; I do not have a thousand dollars; mermaids do not exist. From these judgments, I would then form the concept of nonbeing as the class possessing all these "nonexistents." Each negative judgment, precisely as a mental process, would seem, therefore, to be a full psychic activity with the same completeness as any affirmative judgment. Then the only distinctive reality a negation would have would be a mental reality produced by the mind reflecting on its judgments, a pure mental construct, or in Sartre's terms, a "noema-correlate."[1]

The problem we now face is whether negative judgments are the foundation of our awareness of "nothingness," or whether the concrete nothings within being provide the foundation of both negative judgments and the consequent general concept of nothingness.

Sartre admits that nonbeing does indeed arise out of human expectation, but he denies that nonbeing is thereby a mere concept or reflective activity of consciousness. We should now recall that our study of the relation being-in-the-world led us to consider the human conduct of questioning and that the latter then led us to study the being of negations. But before proceeding with our study, Sartre warns us not to interpret the term "question" as referring only to statements that man explicitly formulates in a question, such as "Is John home?" for questioning includes all human attitudes of expectation. All true expectations are about some disclosure or nondisclosure *in* being. If a mechanism, such as a watch, breaks down, Sartre notes that we expect not simply a judgment stating that it is broken, but some failure in its parts. Regardless of my judgment, there is an internal or necessary relation of the failing parts to the whole perfect watch. Of course, the broken parts, as parts, are things and thus are themselves *beings. Nevertheless, they are "failing" parts only in relation to the totality "watch," and since this totality is real—it functions as a real unity—the failing of the parts is real.* Still, we must not go to the other extreme and forget that the parts are revealed as "failing parts" only through man's attitude of questioning the watch, an attitude that ultimately not only reveals the watch's failure, but also brings this very failure to the watch without making this failure merely subjective.

An analogy may help. An artifact, such as a typewriter, comes into existence only through man and has meaning only in relation to man. But given man's original making-to-be of a typewriter, this artifact, while retaining a continual relation to man, exists independently of man's knowledge of it. In that sense, an artifact is not subjective.

---

1. Sartre notes that this explanation of negations does not logically require the existence of even mental realities, since the function of the term "not" is sufficient.

Analogously (but only as an analogy and not as an example), *nothings* arise within being only through consciousness' de facto upsurge (*le surgissement*) within being, but then these *nothings*, while always essentially related to man's consciousness, continue within being independently of man's awareness of them. Before this chapter is over, Sartre will reexamine this relation of nonbeing to man's consciousness in detail. At present, he further clarifies the nature of questioning.

Sartre notes that the true nature of questioning is obscured because we usually interpret a question as something asked of another person. The human reality, however, has an original (nonjudicative) relation of a questioning expectation directed to being on the basis of which qualities such as "destruction" and "fragility" arise within being. Of course, in the abstract, if there were no such reality as consciousness, destruction and fragility would simply be a rearrangement of being. Without consciousness, a mountain would not be "destroyed"; its parts would simply be redistributed. It is consciousness as a witness that impregnates being with the quality of "destructibility."

But it is important to realize that consciousness is a witness *prior to and independent of any knowledge of itself as a witness;* and reciprocally, nonbeing arises within being prior to and independent of man's knowledge of nonbeing.[2] There is thus a transphenomenality of nonbeing as well as of being; that is, nonbeing, as well as being, is not reducible to our awareness of nonbeing, or being. In the last section of this chapter, Sartre will reveal that nonbeing arises within being through the nonbeing that is consciousness.

The nonbeings we are referring to are the concrete nonbeings, such as fragility or absence, and not the abstract nothingness that terms such as "square circle" designate. An example may help in seeing the concreteness of nonbeing as absence. If we have been playing bridge for the past seven years with the same four persons, the same team, and then suddenly, without explanation one is missing, that non-being, for Sartre, is "real." To say then, "John is not here!" is not to announce an activity of the mind, but a concrete relation of absence.

2. In this sense, the term "witness" is a poor term because it connotes an external relation to that which is witnessed. But Sartre's point is that the very reality of consciousness is to be a witness to being-in-itself (and insofar as consciousness is an awareness, it is also a witness of itself).

The absence is due to an expectation, but this expectation is real and the relation it establishes is real. The empty chair is not a mere void. The entire room takes on a relation to this absence; the entire evening with all its activities is really modified by this absence. Sartre's distinction between an abstract and a concrete nonbeing resembles Aristotle's distinction between a pure negation and a privation. Classically, the term "not-seeing," for example, is considered a mere negation if it refers to something that cannot see, such as a stone. But when "not-seeing" refers to a man, who in general can and should see, not-seeing is considered a privation, blindness. Again, some would try to consider such an absence a mere negation. *But a blind person is a blind person; his entire being is modified by this absence.* The reality of blindness comes from the fact that this nonbeing exists in a certain kind of subject. It comes, therefore, from being.

In an analogous way—and only as an analogy, since privation implies a view of substance that Sartre rejects—Sartre maintains that besides abstract nothingness, there are real nonbeings both within and without us that are the basis of our concrete negative judgments. These nonbeings "haunt" being (*le néant hauté l'être*).[3]

Before attempting to "describe" these nothings (*négatités*) within the world and the nothingness (*le néant*) within the human reality, Sartre first considers Hegel's and Heidegger's approach to nothingness. Although the length and detail of these comparisons can obscure Sartre's main point, they are meant to reveal more clearly the distinctiveness of his own position. Confusion may also arise because Sartre briefly alludes to his own position before he is ready to examine it in detail.

III. THE DIALECTICAL CONCEPT OF NOTHINGNESS

Sartre approaches his task of revealing man's original relation to nothingness by examining Hegel's "dialectical" explanation of the relation of being to nonbeing. In general Hegel's dialectic is the movement by which both logic and reality develop and come-to-be. In

3. EN, p. 47.

its popular formulation, it consists of a thesis, antithesis, and synthesis. That is, the dialectic is a movement from a positive quality (thesis) to the explication of its negative aspect (antithesis) and then to the resolution of these two in a higher quality, in which thesis and antithesis are lifted up to form a new totality, or synthesis. For example, the medieval master craftsman is the synthesis of the Roman master aware of his mastery and the Roman slave whose skills give him mastery over nature but who lacks awareness of himself as master.

More to the point, however, being, for Hegel, is the most general of positive qualities and is shared by all things that are. It is thereby, however, the most undifferentiated of perfections. It has within itself no distinctions, for whatever would distinguish one being from another is still being. By this very generality and indefiniteness, being is close to nothingness. Indeed, nothingness is the negative aspect of being: being is whatever is; nothingness is whatever is not.

Being and nothingness, for Hegel, are resolved in a higher reality —becoming, or change. Becoming is a higher quality because it is closer to the concrete existent, which is always changing. Also, becoming is more definite and determined than either being or nonbeing, since becoming applies only to existing things, whereas being and nonbeing apply also to logical entities, such as a circle or a square-circle. The quality of becoming thus approaches in its definiteness the individual existing thing, such as a tree. A tree is neither pure being nor pure nonbeing, since while it is a tree, it is also becoming what is not, for example, coal.

For Hegel, the dialectic constantly repeats itself as it advances from the indefinite earlier stages to the more concrete later stages. The movement of history and being, as well as of logic, is from the abstract to the concrete. At each stage of the dialectic, some indefiniteness is left behind and reality approaches more and more the definite individual existent that is the goal of the dialectic.[4]

4. The term "immediate" refers, for Hegel, to the relatively undifferentiated stage of the dialectic, and the term "mediate" to the synthesized stage. Thus being is the most immediate of all qualities and is surpassed in the mediate, or concrete. Furthermore, the term "essence" designates the full meaning of the concrete existent. Thus Hegel can say that being is surpassed in essence, since the dialectic is always toward the more concrete. The concrete, or essence, as the goal of the dialectic, has the priority of a goal or purpose, for although the

To prepare us for his opposition to Hegel's understanding of non-being, Sartre now recalls an important result from the Introduction: being is not a meaning; the concrete existent is not a meaning. The phenomenon of being is indeed a meaning or essence, but the being (existence) of phenomenon is transphenomenal. Consequently, the true relation between being and nothingness is not on the level of meaning but on the level of existence.

But here Sartre mainly criticizes Hegel's view that being and nothingness are logically contemporary, since they function as true opposites. Thus, just as being is the empty concept that perfectly includes all that is, nonbeing is the empty concept that perfectly denies what is included in being. Nothingness would then be considered as an emptiness; and, in a sense, it must be said of this emptiness, as of being, that it is. For if nothingness is perfect emptiness, it is, as being, perfectly identified with itself. For example, a square-circle does *not* exist as a square-circle with the same undifferentiatedness as a tree *exists* as a tree. Therefore, nonbeing is what-is-not, just as being is what-is. Consequently, being and nonbeing function as true opposites and are logically contemporary.

According to Sartre, Hegel's notion of nonbeing is simply the abstract negation of being, which adequately accounts for empty notions, such as a square-circle, but does not account for the concrete nothings, such as absence. Rather, concrete nothing is always the emptiness *of something*. For example, Sartre states, when we tell someone, "Do not touch anything!" we mean anything *in this room*.

Thus Sartre sees concrete nonbeing as subsequent to being. It is the existing being that gives to concrete nonbeing its efficacy. Indeed, being has no need for nothingness, and if being were destroyed, there would not be nothings. Granting, however, the de facto concrete relation of consciousness-in-being, we must note that a "real" nonbeing in fact arises from being and "*exists only on the surface of being*." This nonbeing "haunts" being—in the sense that it is never *there*, as a void is there, but constantly eludes being.

---

accomplishment of a goal comes last in time, it is the first thing we intend. A book is not finished until the last word is written, but the last word is written only because a book was intended from the start. Thus, for Hegel, essence, as the goal of the movement of being, is logically and really prior to being, although essence temporally comes after being.

Heidegger, according to Sartre, approaches one step closer to seeing nonbeing as concrete and within the world.[5]

IV. THE PHENOMENOLOGICAL CONCEPT
OF NOTHINGNESS

Sartre now examines Heidegger's study of nothingness. He considers Heidegger's approach an advance precisely because it is phenomenological, that is, a description of nothingness as a concrete phenomenon. Nothingness, for Heidegger, is not an abstract concept, but rather is implied by numerous human attitudes such as hate, prohibitions, or regret. It is *Dasein*, or the human reality, that can, in the experience of anguish, confront nothingness.

According to Sartre, Heidegger claims that the "world" arises from the concrete tension between being and nothingness. An image may help us to understand how Sartre sees Heidegger's thought: if we imagine consciousness as a flame (an "ekstasis" in Heidegger's terminology) leaping from an absolutely uniform surface, this flame is (1) a being-in-the-surface, for the flame does not descend from above, but arises from the thermal conditions of the surface itself; and (2) the flame surpasses the surface, for it leaps upward from the surface. Definite relations of distances are now established between the tip of the flame and the various points of the surface. There are separations and nothings within which differentiations and specifications occur: this point on the surface is nearer or farther from the tip of the flame than some other point. Furthermore, the flame arises in a

5. In the text of *Being and Nothingness*, Sartre considers Hegel's interpretation of nonbeing as based, to a certain extent, on Spinoza's (Baruch Spinoza, 1632–1677) insight that all determination is negation. According to Sartre, Hegel interprets Spinoza's statement to mean not only that determination is negation, because determination separates a thing from everything else—a tree is a tree only because it is not everything else—but also because determinations (a tree) can be made only against, as it were, a backdrop or void. Thus, Sartre declares, Hegel was led to view nonbeing as a void. But, Sartre says, if we reverse Spinoza's formula, we can more clearly see the function of nonbeing within being. For if all negation is, in fact, a determination—we can deny only within the context of being—we begin to see not only the priority of being, but also that negations and nothings affect being.

concrete nothing, in the sense that the flame arises on the surface *here* rather than *there*. In fact, the concrete nothingness and the flame come-to-be contemporaneously, since, without the flame, there would be only an undifferentiated surface and, above it, an abstract nothingness. In an analogous way, man is a being-in-the-world, since, like the flame, he does not descend from above, but arises within being *here* rather than *there;* and from man's essential "thereness," there arises those concrete nothings within which the differentiation of a "world" comes-to-be.

Although Sartre sees Heidegger's understanding of nothingness as more concrete than Spinoza's or Hegel's, he still finds it too abstract. It is an emptiness that is still one with itself and thus a nothingness that is not truly within being. To return to our image: Although the distance between the tip of the flame and some point on the surface of the ground is concrete in that it is a relation from this point to that point, it is still emptiness. It is a nothingness neither within the flame nor within the surface. If we imagine the surface, or ground, as being and the flame as the human reality, then the nothingness is outside both the inner structure of being and the human reality. This kind of nothingness may be adequate to explain abstract negations, such as "square circles do not exist," but it is inadequate to explain concrete negations, such as "John is not here" or, indeed, the phenomenon of anguish itself.

Nothingness, Sartre notes, cannot arise from the surging up of *Dasein;* rather, in some way, nothingness must be within both being and consciousness. For Sartre, Heidegger leaves unanswered the question of what *Dasein* must be like to be able "to transcend" (that is, go beyond and establish relations of distance).

Returning to our image, we must first ask what is the nature of "flame" that it can arise from a surface and not be the surface. Whatever distinctions or nothingness result from that upsurge, it already presupposes a more fundamental distinction of the flame from the surface, a more fundamental nothingness.

Sartre concludes this section by calling our attention once again to negations that imply a nothingness within being itself, as opposed to those that simply imply an "ultra" mundane or abstract nothingness. The distance separating two points, for example, can be regarded either as a phenomenon in which negation is primary or as one in which the negative element is secondary. If we turn our attention to the space between the two points, then the space appears as a continuum and the points are the limits—the distance does not go beyond the points. In this sense, negation, for Sartre, is secondary, since it is consequent upon the intuition of the distance as a "plenum," or fullness.

But more properly, the relation of distance is primarily a negative phenomenon. It appears if we draw our attention to the points first. Then the distance appears for what it is, the negation of the fullness of being between the points. This negation cannot be reduced to a mere idea or the phenomenon of measurement; it is, in fact, the basis for these. This negative phenomenon is neither the points nor the space between the points, but a synthetic whole—a gestalt—a totality that is greater than the sum of its parts. Distance is the *negation* of being (space) *within* being (points).

There are, for Sartre, therefore, an infinite number of realities (otherness, regret, absence) that are experienced as having nothings constituting their internal structure. It is the origin of these specific nothings (*négatités*) coiled, as it were, within being that we must now investigate.

V. THE ORIGIN OF NOTHINGNESS

Section v is certainly one of the most important sections of the book. Here Sartre begins his own description of nothingness and consequently lays the foundation of all that is to follow. Since the entire book is a description of being and nothingness, Sartre is forced several times to refer the readers to subsequent chapters. But he does give some of those revealing concrete descriptions that are one of the strong points of the entire book.

It may be helpful to anticipate Sartre's discussion and briefly consider the main characteristics of his description of nothingness (*le néant*). There are two fundamental regions in which concrete nothingness is to be found: the world and the human reality. In the chapter on transcendence, Sartre will describe the "world," with all its distinctions of things, as arising from the happening of nothingness to being in-itself. And he will further reveal that these *nothings* within being-in-itself (the brute existent) come to the in-itself from the concrete nothingness within man.

We will now briefly describe the concrete nothingness within man:

1. The human reality's concrete nothingness is its consciousness.

2. Consciousness, or awareness, is a concrete nothingness because consciousness is not perfectly one with itself or its "object."

3. But consciousness is not thereby separated from itself by a void, for then consciousness would in no way be one with itself.

4. This concrete nothingness cannot be pictured, but an approach can be made to understand it if we repeatedly ask ourselves *what* we are. Am I an American? Am I a male? When I ask such questions, I recognize that, indeed, I am an American and a male, but only in the sense that the living of these characteristics is a free interpretive task. When I question myself in this way, I recognize that no characteristics define my existence; my existence precedes my essence. I am not one with myself in the sense that an apple is an apple. (Even my body is something that I can make into an object of study or more accurately, something that I live according to my choice.) This ability to question myself is a sign of a basic lack of identity with myself. It is a sign of a constant sliding from perfect identity, a sliding that, for Sartre, is the nothingness within me. *Concrete nothingness is the constant "elsewhereness" of consciousness.*

Because this section is long and involved, the following subheadings, which are not in Sartre's text, may further help in reading the original.

(A. A DISCUSSION OF THE NATURE OF THE QUESTION)

To return to our consideration of the text, Sartre notes that our procedure resulted from questioning the nature of being. This, in turn, led us to consider that particular being in which being itself could best be studied, namely, the human reality. We then recognized that this very question, "What is the nature of being?" is itself a being. We examined this question as a characteristic mode of human conduct and realized that every question is a being that implies a negation. Finally, we saw that negations require more than logical or psychological foundations.

Our answer to the question concerning the nature of nothingness must carefully avoid all the pitfalls already noted. Nothingness cannot be substantialized into an undifferentiated emptiness. It cannot be a void either outside or within being-in-itself, for then there would be the fullness of being surrounded or, as it were, punctured with clear emptiness—nothingness would be "there" and being "here." All the preceding views of nothingness leave it outside the very texture of being.

Rather, as the foundation for inquiry and negations, *nothingness must itself always be in question,* for otherwise it would have the stability and self-identity that characterize being-in-itself. Nothingness must have that borrowed brought-to-be being, that elusive being of not-being in the very act of its being. But this means that nothingness must come to being through a region of being other than the undifferentiated and perfectly identified being-in-itself.

Sartre is at first a little ambiguous about identifying the being that, in its reality, questions its own being; but it is clear that, in general, he is referring to the human reality, and in particular to consciousness as the pre-reflective cogito. Consciousness can question being because it has a "distance" from being. Every question is a certain attitude toward being, a light thrown on being from a certain perspective and thus from a certain distance. In popular expression, we refer to standing too close to something to be able to judge it correctly. Analogously, despite the obvious unity in knowledge of subject and object, Sartre reasons that a *certain lack of identity, a certain ontological "distance," is also needed for the subject to be aware of its object and not to be homogeneously one with its object, as in a solid mass.*

Thus, Sartre maintains, man could not adopt the attitude of questioning if he were united in a causal series with being-in-itself. Sartre, however, now parts company with his predecessors. For he insists that the ontological (that is, real) distance required for questioning is the concrete nothingness of the human consciousness. He sees that without this nothingness, there would be a continual causal series between the questioner and the reality questioned, as there is a continuous line of cause and effect among bodies: if I hit a billiard ball with a known force, its line of motion is determined and predictable. A line of cause and effect thus would establish a continuum or plenitude of being that would prevent that distance and differentiation needed for questioning.

In questioning, the questioner wrenches from being its continuity with itself, thereby "nihilating" (*néatiser*) being in relation to other aspects of being. Furthermore, the questioner himself must be separated from any continuity with being, for only thus can he await, by his attitude of questioning, the continual possibility of the presence or nonpresence of being. For example, when I ask, "What is a tree?" I remove, or negate, the tree from the totality of nature in order to question it as a distinct entity. Also, when I question the nature of a tree, I must have a certain "distance" within myself that allows the tree to reveal itself to me. It is this "nothingness" within myself that both separates the tree as this *thing* within nature and allows me to be aware of the tree.[6]

It is this break with a causal series, which would tie being in with being in a fullness of being, that is the nothingness within man and the source of nothingness within the world.

It may help us to understand the role of nothingness in Sartre's philosophy if we recall Aristotle's understanding of how knowledge is possible. For Aristotle, to know is to possess the form of a thing *as other*—the knower has within him the same form as the object, but in such a way that the form remains the form of the object known. Thus, in seeing red, the sense of sight does not become red, and in knowing a tree, the intellect does not become a tree. This acquisition by the subject of a form *as other* is possible because in some way the subject's own form is "immaterial." Although all forms, insofar as they are not matter, are, for Aristotle, "immaterial," the forms of knowing beings have a higher degree of immateriality than minerals or plants precisely because they can receive forms as other. The immateriality of man's form is of the highest degree because he can receive the forms of all beings without physically becoming these

---

6. Sartre uses the term "nihilation" (*néantisation*) to signify that the origin of negation is more than merely psychological or mental. We will see that, primarily, nihilation is that happening within being that is the "upsurge" of consciousness as a concrete nothingness.

beings. During the Middle Ages, this view of man's form was one of the proofs for the spirituality of the soul. For, it was reasoned, just as the sense of sight can see all colors because it itself is not colored, so too the intellect can know all material beings because it itself is not material. Without claiming that Sartre is "reasoning" to nothingness, it is still true that he sees that knowledge requires a *distance*, a lack of perfect identity of knower and known. Sartre's *being* and *nothingness* can be the more sympathetically understood if they are approached from the view of a man who sees the uniqueness of man in both knowledge and freedom and yet abhors any kind of substantiality or spirituality.

Nothings, that is, such concrete negations as "absence," which Sartre has termed *négatités*, consequently come to being through man. Sartre agrees with Heidegger that the nonbeing comes-to-be through the concrete relation of the self with being. But he insists that Heidegger stops short and allows nonbeing to evaporate into an emptiness between the full beings man and the world.

For Sartre, the being through which nothingness comes to being must itself be nonbeing in its very structure; only thus could it bring about a nonbeing within the very fabric of being.

But we must not imagine that the human reality is a union of nothingness and matter or a union of consciousness and a body. The entire Introduction was an attempt to avoid these dualisms, which miss the totality of man as a being-in-the-world.

The human reality (le pour-soi) *is matter* (l'en-soi) *as already completely metamorphosed into a new region of being, the for-itself. The human reality is being-in-itself as so completely affected by the happening of consciousness that this being-in-itself is no longer pure being-in-itself.* The for-itself is thus a new region of being, a region that has been so permeated with nothingness that, from every aspect, the original unity of the brute existent has been dispersed. The for-itself is a region of being in which everything is in question, even the fact of its own nothingness.

Throughout his book, Sartre will present man as that unique being who, from all viewpoints, is never one with himself.

It is this "delicate and exquisite" being that "nihilates." We are forced at times to speak as if pure nothingness acted on being, somewhat as a mind would act on its body. But it is only the being whose unity is its search for unity that "nihilates." The human reality, or the for-itself, can nihilate because it is brute existence as already nihilated. Being-in-itself cannot nihilate, since the in-itself is simply what it is (an apple is an apple). Nothingness cannot nihilate because nothingness is not an independent force or void, but the collapse of the identity of being. Thus, Sartre states, "nothingness [in the sense of a void] is not, nothingness 'is brought-to-be' [by the human reality that is its own nothingness]; nothingness does not nihilate itself [as a void or force], nothingness 'is nihilated' [by man who is his own nihilation]." (*Le Néant n'est pas, Le Néant 'est eté'; le Néant ne se néantise pas, le Néant 'est neantisé'.*) [7]

The fact that we can wonder and question our own nothingness or freedom proves, for Sartre, that this nothingness or freedom does not reside in us as a hole or vacuum.

(B. FREEDOM AND NOTHINGNESS)

Sartre is now interested in freedom only as related to nothingness.[8] It is already clear that freedom is not a property added to man's nature. The study of the pre-reflective cogito has revealed that in man, existence precedes essence. Man's free actions, for Sartre, are the sole origin of all his distinctively human characteristics.

Sartre sees that many apsects of contemporary philosophy show that in questioning, in doubt, in reflection, the human reality has the capacity of detachment from the world. Although this does not necessarily imply that freedom is the very structure of man, Sartre maintains it does show that human conduct cannot be enclosed within a causal series.

Man's break from a causal series is revealed by real absences within man and within things. These absences cannot be accounted for by first *imagining*, for example, a friend, John, and then realizing that he is not here. The very ones who give this explanation, Sartre argues, also insist that the image (for example, my picture of John) is a complete and full psychological entity, an internal "being-in-

---

7. EN, p. 58; BN, p. 22. (I have translated *est été* as brought-to-be rather than "made-to-be" to avoid any causal connotation in the French terms.)

8. Cf. Part Four, Chapter One, for a detailed discussion of freedom.

itself." But then, as complete and full, it could not account for the real perception of absence, but would at most justify only a logical and abstract judgment of absence: I compare my picture of John with the emptiness in front of me and I form the judgment "John is absent."[9] On the contrary, my *perception* of John's absence, as awaiting him to complete a fourth for bridge, can take place only if I have within myself a break with being, a "room" or distance (not to be visualized as a space or void, but rather, as we will see, as a sliding from being).

In our attempt to understand concrete nothingness as man's freedom, we must also take seriously the temporal character of consciousness. Nothingness must not be considered as a "thing" slipping between the present, the past, and future. This would not only destroy the temporal continuity of the psychic states and lead us to the problem of how instantaneous "nows" can add up to a continuous span of time, but would also destroy the very ontological reality of nothingness, since nothingness would degenerate into a mere void.

To repeat, nothingness *is not*, in the sense that it is never *there*, but rather is itself in question. As will be elaborated in Part Two, Chapter Two, "Temporality," the concrete nothingness of consciousness is, from its temporal aspect, consciousness' continual negating (nihilating), by which it simultaneously holds and suspends a past, negates this past as not now being the self, and then projects this negated-suspended-past to a freely interpreted future. According to Sartre, this temporality of consciousness, which is its concrete nothingness and freedom, is the *being* of consciousness and not the result of

9. Sartre refers us to his work *Imagination, A Psychological Critique*, trans. with an introduction by Forrest Williams (Ann Arbor: University of Michigan Press, 1962), where he maintains that the image is, in fact, not a complete entity, not an in-itself, that just happens to reside in consciousness rather than outside it. The difference between the awareness of the most perfect image of Peter and the perception of the existing Peter is not that the image resides in the "imagination," while the existing Peter is outside consciousness. Rather the image immediately presents itself as taking the place of the perceived Peter, of not-being the existing Peter. The image has within it nothingness rather than being the origin of nothingness. Furthermore, Sartre here continues, we cannot explain the perception of Peter's absence by claiming (as Sartre maintains Husserl does) that we have an intention of Peter that has been emptied of content. For the perception of Peter's absence—as in awaiting a fourth for bridge—is not simply of a psychic emptiness, but a real perception of not-being-there.

learning. Again, we are on the ontological level of being rather than of knowledge.

(C. FREEDOM, ANGUISH, AND VALUE)

If freedom as nothingness is at the very nature of consciousness, and if every consciousness is an awareness, then there should be a constant awareness of freedom. But we must always remember that consciousness, nothingness, and freedom must themselves constantly be in question lest they collapse into an identity with themselves and become an opaque, thick, fixed in-itself. With this in mind, Sartre insists that *anguish is that consciousness of freedom in which freedom itself is in question.*

In agreement with both Sören Kierkegaard (1813–1855) and Heidegger, Sartre distinguishes fear from anguish. Fear is immediately directed outward toward the object feared and is, consequently, unreflected. For example, I see someone tampering with my car and I fear being robbed. On the contrary, anguish is a reflected phenomenon, focused within ourselves. I am in anguish over how to live with the constant threat of being robbed. Stephen Crane's *The Red Badge of Courage* is an eminent study of the anguish before battle, as distinct from the fear of actual combat.

Sartre beautifully describes the difference between fear and anguish in relation to the possibility of vertigo. While walking on a ledge, I can experience fear of accidentally slipping. I can then adopt an attitude of care. But unlike, for example, my height and weight, this attitude must be constantly kept in existence by me. While adopting this attitude of care, I simultaneously recognize that it is only one of my possible attitudes, and I see myself relaxing this attitude, giving myself to the lure of the chasm before me. Further, no amount of reflections on my motivations will reveal a necessary causal sequence leading either to maintaining or relaxing my vigilance, for if this were the case, I would recognize that, in fact, I was about to maintain or relax my vigilance. But I have anguish precisely because I am aware that while I have not now chosen to relax my efforts and care, I can and might adopt such an attitude.

Despite my attempts to motivate myself to act in the future, there is a real nothingness between myself and the future that I would be.

This nothingness is not merely because the future has not yet arrived, but more importantly, it is because when the future is present, I may not want to be then what I wish to be now. My present state can never cause my future behavior, nor can any other existing thing determine the behavior that I may adopt. I can indeed slip and fall down the ledge by accident, despite my care. But this is not the point. I experience anguish because I am afraid of falling through my own will.

Thus Sartre says that the self that we are depends on the self that we are about to be precisely insofar as the self that we are about to be does not depend on the self that we are. The first part signifies that my present self depends on my future intentions—I am now painting because I intend to be one who will have painted a painting. The second part indicates that this present intention to be something in the future is in existence now precisely because I choose it to be so. Thus nothing forces me to choose to complete this painting; I choose it aware that I may falter and give up the very decision to do what I now intend to do.

Anguish is experienced not only in the face of the future but also in respect to past resolutions. For example, the gambler's past resolutions cannot cause his present actions, and he must resolve anew not to gamble. The past resolution is there, but as past. It is *not* the self that he is. There is a rupture, Sartre says, between this past decision not to gamble and the self that is now facing the gambling table; *nothing* prevents him from gambling now. I thus face the past resolution, as it were, asking it for aid; for although I recognize that this past resolution *is* *my* past resolution, I realize that it cannot now move me to action. I must decide anew and re-create the very motivations that led to my decision not to gamble.[10]

Again, Sartre warns us not to conceive of consciousness as a void separating motives from actions. Nothingness *is not;* it is brought-to-be (*est été*) by consciousness in its relation to itself. Nevertheless, nothingness is not made-to-be as a void. The pre-reflective cogito, as we have seen, is empty of all content and makes objects to exist for itself as motives by giving them their very weight and meaning as motives. Simultaneously, as consciousness makes an object to exist

10. For Sartre, psychological determinism is irrelevant at this point. Cf. pp. 196–202.

for itself as a motive, consciousness nihilates this very motive, causing it to be other than consciousness; consciousness now faces this motive impregnated with "nothings" as that which is not consciousness, as that which is its transcendent object.[11]

But why, Sartre now asks, is anguish so rare if it is intimately connected with the nature of consciousness and freedom? His answer is that the very nature of consciousness that accounts for freedom and nothingness also requires that this freedom and nothingness be in question. *We never directly face freedom or nothingness as a thing.* Freedom and nothingness are rather the very nature of consciousness that allows it always to question itself. Consequently, this very freedom and nothingness must itself always be *in question.* Thus there is both the permanent possibility of becoming aware, in anguish, of this nothingness and the constant possibility of avoiding this awareness. Sartre will elaborate the ways of avoiding anguish in the chapter on bad faith (Part One, Chapter Two), but for the present we will follow his lead and give a brief example.

Suppose that I am engaged in writing a long biography of President Kennedy. The project has been planned and approved, and I am resolved to complete it. As long as I continue with the book, not reflecting on my original decision to do it, I do not experience anguish, and I never face the question of the entire meaning of the

---

11. Sartre distinguishes three nihilations, or makings-to-be of nothings:

    1. the motive as impregnated with transcendent nothing, but this transcendent nothing is based upon two more basic nothings

    2. the nothingness of the pre-reflective cogito, for in its very being it is empty of all content

    3. the nothingness of consciousness' temporality that projects itself to a future that it is not, from a past that it is no longer. (In the chapter on temporality, Sartre will show that consciousness also "flees" the present.)

Sartre states that he will not now elaborate on these nihilating functions, but wishes merely to make clear that the description of negation is intimately connected with the description of self-consciousness and temporality that are to follow. He does, however, refer here with approval to Hegel's description of essence as that which man has been. In man, existence precedes essence, and consciousness constantly places the self, which it has caused by its past acts, behind it. Consciousness, or the pre-reflective self, is thus aware in anguish that it is not and never can become the self, which it has constituted by reflection; it is always separated from this self by a nothing.

work and my responsibility for it. However, when I was merely thinking about doing a biography, I was more apt to reflect on its meaning because it was then merely one possible mode of behavior. But in the act of writing, I discover my own concrete desire to write a book. As the work unfolds, it beckons to me for completion, organizing itself around me as part of the meaning of my life and world. Of course, the very moment I write a sentence, the sentence takes on an existence of its own and transcends, or escapes, the bonds of my consciousness, and thus I can always stop and reevaluate the entire decision to write. But I normally reject this possibility, realizing the anguish it would involve: is there really a need for such a biography?

Indeed, once I raise such questions in respect to the fundamental meaning of this particular work, I also attain a fleeting glimpse of the possibility of reevaluating the decisions on which my whole life is based: should I be engaged in studying the past? In a similar way, I have a fleeting awareness of the possibility of overturning my entire system of values. But normally my everyday morality is a way of escaping the anguish that would result from realizing that all my values are not "givens"; they are freely held in existence by my consciousness, and my consciousness itself has no foundation other than itself.

Values, Sartre insists, do not have an independent being. Objective norms, for example, do not grant respectability to those accepting them. Rather, we freely decide to allow ourselves to arise and become engaged in a respectable environment, to become invested with respectable morality, and finally, to accept as good and bad the blessings and taboos of the environment.

According to Sartre, every one of our actions is influenced and governed by our original projection of a general goal or manner of life. Following most classical analyses of choice, Sartre insists that our daily decisions are to a great extent directed by more basic decisions. A decision to go to Europe, for example, determines choosing some means of transportation and allotting some time and money for the trip. In a similar way, every ethical choice is already colored by our more basic conception of a life that is good and desirable for us. As long as we do not face the possibility of reevaluating our primitive goal—our original intention of what we want for ourselves—we attempt to escape anguish and avoid the nothingness that separates ourselves from every chosen value and way of life.

(D. ANGUISH AND THE FLIGHT FROM ANGUISH)

Nevertheless, not every reflection on our freedom results in anguish. There are, as Sartre will describe in the next chapter, on bad faith, patterns of flight whereby one adopts certain reflective attitudes toward one's consciousness so as to avoid anguish. For Sartre, psychological determinism is such an attitude. Thus, to consider that our intentions are in fact determined by a causal series—that our seemingly free acts are really determined by environment and history—is to consider ourselves as an in-itself, one of the fixed beings among many in the world.

For Sartre, psychological determinism does not itself attempt to deny the original *intuition* (experience) that we are free—for example, our immediate and pre-reflective awareness that we can lie or not lie in a given situation. Rather, it offers an argument that this original intuition of freedom is deceptive, since it claims that we are actually determined in our decisions. It attacks freedom not on the level of experience, but on the level of logic, by presenting to consciousness a purely possible hypothesis. But, according to Sartre, I am conscious of presenting myself to this hypothesis of psychological determinism in order to allow it to convince me. I adopt an attitude toward it and thus simultaneously I give evidence of my freedom.

In the abstract, many possibilities are merely objective possibilities, and I can indeed imagine a series of causes moving me to these. For example, the moment I envision the possibility of not writing a biography, as an abstract objective possibility, I can also conceive of causes that could lead me to adopting it; for example, perhaps I could better spend my time writing a more original book.

In effect, however, I am considering this possibility as outside me, as the possibility of "someone." In the concrete, the possibility of not writing a biography arises for me as my possibility the moment I reflect that a nothingness separates me from my original intention to write this book: I am writing as one who at each moment does not have to write. When I explicitly make this reflection, I bring about that nothingness that separates me from my writing; I cause there to be, for me, the concrete possibility of not writing. I experience anguish. In my desire to avoid anguish, however, I allow myself to be ruled, to be distracted from my concrete possibilities, and to yield to the lure and safe attraction of contemplating abstract possibilities as my own.

Just as there is both a freedom and an anguish in relation to the future, there is also a freedom and an anguish in relation to the past. Thus, rather than face anguish, I conceive that my past hides my true self. I then view my freedom as a property of this self giving me the liberty to be "true" to myself. Such a conception of the self, however, as we have seen, is nothing but the *object* formed by reflecting on our past behavior. The true self is the self-knowing-this-object, the pre-reflective cogito that arises *in* a situation but does not come as determined *from* a situation.

At each moment, the original upsurge of consciousness, the primitive, or first, intention of a way of life, is, for Sartre, ontologically separated from the reflected, or derived, ego (that is, my idea and whole perception of myself as a certain kind of person) by an ontological nothingness. But then consciousness tries to flee this very nihilation by attempting to take refuge in the very god it has created: *it hypothesizes that the pre-reflective self arises from the reflective self, that our actions come from a determined nature.* In this way, Sartre says, we conceive of our freedom as the freedom of another person (the "other"). For just as in meeting a person after a number of years, we are inclined to imagine a continuity in his consciousness similar to the continuity of a biological process—that he has changed by modifying a permanent substratum—so, too, we attempt to flee the freedom of our past by conceiving our consciousness as similar to the continuity of a biological process. In general, then, we attempt to flee anguish by considering our possibilities as produced by some internal or external object rather than accepting them as arising from the concrete nihilations from our past.

Nevertheless, the flights from anguish can never perfectly succeed. We are indeed the very consciousness of our freedom. But, by its very nature as nihilations, consciousness is itself always in question.

This means that consciousness simultaneously keeps in existence the permanent possibility of questioning our freedom in the very act of being free. For example, I now freely decide to go to Europe this summer, but I decide in such a way that I am in question about the very freedom of this choice. This is true because when I freely decide, I also wonder if my choice is a free one. Indeed, if we are free, we must be free to question whether or not we are free. Otherwise our freedom, as our nothingness, would exist in us as some given void or force. Further, what kind of freedom would it be that could not question its own freedom? Our freedom is not a given thing, but the nihilations of all givens, including freedom itself conceived as a thing.

Nevertheless, the flight from anguish is not the same as the facing of anguish. To understand this, we must now look into the nature of bad faith, which is essentially man's flight from anguish.

But before we turn our attention to the study of bad faith, it may be useful to recapitulate briefly our description of nothingness, or consciousness, and to *anticipate* some of Sartre's future descriptions.

1. Consciousness, for Sartre, is pure activity. And since the only type of activity is self-activity, consciousness, or nothingness, is pure spontaneity.

2. Since nothingness is a self-activity, it naturally tends to sustain itself. But we must remember that this activity is not a force or an energy. Rather, this self-activity is the continual *failure* of consciousness to be one with itself and its experiences. If I decide to go on a trip, my self-activity, or nothingness, is my constant attempt and failure to *be* the entire experience of the trip all-at-once.

3. This pure spontaneity, which is consciousness, simply "happens" to matter, and that happening "is" the human body at the stage of its human awareness.

4. Although there are no causal ties between consciousness and matter, we will see that consciousness manifests itself as the attempt to remove the contingency of matter. The human body is different from a tree because the human body is matter attempting to justify its brute existence through its awareness of existence. (In general, the "totality" of human beings, together with the history of human endeavor, manifests itself as the attempt of all brute existence [being-in-itself] to remove its contingency.

The "totality" of consciousness appears as providing reasons and explanation for the "totality" of existence.)

5. The goal of the for-itself, which is to be perfectly identified with its own reasons for existence and yet conscious of these reasons, is doomed to failure because consciousness of goals requires a lack of identity with those goals.

6. But, as we shall see in the chapter on the for-itself, the very failure of the human reality to attain its goals is also the very being of the human reality; it is the nothingness of consciousness. Thus I live my life attempting to give meaning to it by being a good person and a useful citizen. I strive to rest in this goal as something achieved and as something that defines me. But I *fail* to be one with my goal. This failure is also my success as a conscious being. For insofar as I fail to attain the goal of my life, I am at a "distance" from it and thereby am conscious of it.

It should be clear that Sartre finds it difficult to describe this concrete nothingness that is consciousness. There has been a great deal of criticism about his use of such terms as "to nihilate" (*néantiser*) and "nihilation" (*néantisation*) and the seemingly meaningless phrases in which nothingness is described as apparently acting on matter and on itself. But these terms and phrases must be understood within the entire endeavor of the book. If a philosophical work is a gestalt, the entire work "says" what individual sentences strain to say.

In the following chapter on bad faith, Sartre will show that we can successfully lie to ourselves because of the nothingness within ourselves. Reciprocally, the phenomenon of bad faith reveals the concreteness and the "meaning" of the nothingness within us.

2
Bad Faith

I. BAD FAITH AND FALSEHOOD

Man, Sartre says, not only directs negations outward toward the world, as in awaiting Peter's presence, but often directs negations to himself as well.[1] Rather than consider these internal negations in general, Sartre states that he prefers to study the particular attitude of directing negations toward one's self that he calls "bad faith" (*mauvaise foi*).

Bad faith refers to a certain fact or phenomenon of human experience. Not everyone would call this phenomenon "bad faith," and certainly not everyone would explain it as Sartre does. But it is important to understand the fact on which the interpretation is based. Although, as we will see, bad faith occurs within our everyday experience—for example, we accumulate evidence to believe that we are naturally incompetent in mathematics—the clearest cases are those for which one might go to an analyst for help.

For example, a person with a manic-depressive illness appears to be ignorant of the reasons for his extreme change of moods. He goes

---

1. Sometimes, as in anguish, these negative attitudes are an attempt to avoid facing the consciousness of nothingness, which itself is the being of consciousness. Otherwise they are a manifestation of this fundamental nothingness within man. Thus man, for Sartre, arises in the world as a *Not*. He is not, in his nature, what others and the world would have him be.

to an analyst asking for help to understand why he acts the way he does. Clearly, many psychoanalysts would not explain his illness as a phenomenon of "bad faith," but they would all agree that at the present time the person truly believes that he does not know the reason for his behavior, and thus he needs help.

Sartre begins his study of bad faith by comparing it with lying. There are three elements to a lie. First, one must believe something to be true. Second, one must express to another the opposite of what is believed. Third, for a lie to succeed, the other must believe in the statement expressed.[2]

While bad faith has some common elements with a lie, it is, Sartre notes, fundamentally different. Bad faith is lying to one's self, and thus the very difficult thing to understand is how, being conscious of our lies, we can believe them.

According to Sartre, the usual way of explaining how we can believe our own lies is to appeal to the unconscious, to have recourse, as did Freud, to some degree of division in the psyche.[3] The unconscious is then treated as the residue of hidden or forgotten realities, and the so-called censor allows some of these facts to pass to consciousness and represses others.

Freud's distinction between the "id" (loosely, the unconscious) and the "ego" (loosely, the conscious) results, for Sartre, in a fundamental division within the psychic whole. As a conscious being, I am not my id. The conscious *I* stands in a similar relation to its unconscious as to another person. When the *I* acts, the motives of the unconscious are not always the motives of my conscious ego. I may

2. Sartre describes the lie as a phenomenon of transcendence. The term "transcendence" has at least two meanings in this section. The most literal meaning is that a lie is transcendent because it is directed beyond, or outside, the subject to another. The second meaning is a specification of the first. The lie is said to be "transcendent" because the subjective truth on which a lie is based is a possibility of the subject, that is, the belief in this truth is outside the nature of consciousness, separated by a nothingness from consciousness. The entire structure of a lie is said to be a phenomenon of the transcendent because both the truth and its false expression are oriented toward convincing the other to accept the lie.

3. Sartre's treatment of Freud is clearly a simplification. Freud does not substantialize the "divisions" within the psyche, but Sartre's criticism is that Freud's approach to analysis implies a real division within the psyche. Nevertheless, Sartre will qualify this view of Freud in Part Four (see pp. 217–218).

steal a book, Sartre says, thinking it is because I desire this particular volume. In reality, however, there is a whole line of causal connections uniting this conscious motive to deeper, more real motivations, for example, to an Oedipus complex. The analyst then uses various constructs or theories to unite us with our unconscious self. For such an analyst, there is no bad faith, but simply a more subtle phenomenon of falsehood, the unconscious lying to the conscious. Thus we can easily understand how we believe our own lies, since the *I*, in its awareness, is effectively as separated from its unconscious as from another person.

Sartre has several objections to this explanation of lying to ourselves. First, he maintains that the analyst himself is aware that the id is not a thing or an in-itself. The id plays games with the analyst, who reports that the patient resists when the truth is about to be uncovered. But, Sartre asks, what can be resisting? The conscious, by hypothesis, is not aware of the real truth of its motivations, and thus it cannot know what it is hiding. Furthermore, the person is seeking help and has no reason to hide from the truth. In a similar way, the resistance cannot be accounted for by the possibly disturbing daily revelations about oneself. For if we admit that our resistance to the analyst results from wanting not to face the conscious knowledge about ourselves, then our original problem of facing our own truths is on the conscious level, and there is therefore no need to have recourse to the unconscious in the first place.

As a matter of fact, Sartre continues, the psychoanalyst explains this resistance as coming from the depths of the unconscious, as the result of the operation of the "censor." The censor, in effect, "knows" that the analyst's questions are reaching the truth. It parries these questions, attempting to throw the analyst off the track. But the experienced analyst knows some of the wiles of the censor. Analysis is thus the battle between two brilliant "minds," the censor and the analyst. The poor, simple ego awaits the results.

The censor then must be "aware," for how else could it repress only some things. It must therefore be capable of judgments, knowing what is to be repressed and from whom it is to be repressed. But then all that we have done is to push the problem of bad faith back to the censor. The censor is in bad faith, for while *conscious* of what it is repressing, it nevertheless presents itself to itself as distinct from consciousness.

The Freudian interpretation of lying to oneself, for Sartre, also results in a fundamental division within the self. This division would both destroy the unity of our experiences and be incapable of accounting for the phenomenon of anguish. (As we will see, anguish is, in some way, the consciousness of the totality of our experiences in the light of our freely chosen goals, which we sometimes attempt to avoid in all their demanding consequences.)

Furthermore, not only does the Freudian hypothesis not explain the phenomena which it was invented to explain, but also there are, in fact, many evidences of explicit conscious lying to ourselves. Thus Sartre refers to the Viennese psychiatrist Stekel, who reports instances of women who claim to be frigid and yet whose husbands testify to their manifestations of pleasure. Stekel, Sartre says, extracts from these women indirect admission that they consciously apply themselves to the act of being frigid. In advance of the sexual act, they turn their attention to other things. Clearly, these women consciously wish to be exactly as they complain they are against their will, namely, frigid. Thus the problem of bad faith must be faced on the conscious level.

Before Sartre gives his own answer to the very difficult question of how we can consciously lie to ourselves and still believe these lies—for bad faith is not cynicism; the "frigid" women believe they are frigid—he describes some instances of bad faith.

II. PATTERNS OF BAD FAITH

Sartre now gives several descriptions of bad faith. Since his work is phenomenological, that is, a descriptive as opposed to deductive approach to being, these descriptions are not merely examples, but are essential to his philosophy.

He begins with an example of flirting. A woman goes out with a man and knows that theirs is a mutual attraction. She also knows that at some time she will have to make a decision about their relationship, particularly about his imminent sexual advances. But she does not now wish to face the temporal development of their relationship and the consequent decisions. Sartre says that she does not know exactly what she wants: she requires attention to her person as a free and creative personality as well as to her body precisely as a body. She wants more than respect from this man but is repulsed by the brute fact of sexuality, preferring not even to name it. But now, Sartre says, if the man takes her hand, he upsets this delicate equilibrium. What does she do? She leaves his hand in hers as a thing. She attempts to neither consent to nor reject it as an advance and begins to talk of lofty and abstract matters, Life, Beauty, and so on. She focuses attention on herself as a pure consciousness, attempting to hide momentarily from her body. She is, Sartre says, in bad faith.

The woman is in bad faith because she knows her companion's action for what it truly is as well as she knows her own desire for that action. But she continues to perform in such a way as to avoid that which she knows. She realizes that their desires are not things, which can be contemplated independently from consciousness, but she consciously persuades herself that they are so; she consciously continues to maintain herself in bad faith.

The human being can maintain itself in bad faith because it is simultaneously facticity (*facticité*) and transcendence (*transcendance*). By facticity, Sartre here means that certain things can be said to pertain to us in a factual way.[4] These certainly include our body, its height, color, weight, and our entire past—when and where we are born, as well as what we have actually done. Facticity also includes what is actually happening to us. Thus it is a fact that the couple are holding hands and have sexual desires for each other.

But our consciousness is never perfectly identified with our facticities; we are more than our body, our past, or our environment. And we know this. By the mere fact that we can contemplate our facticities and examine them as "objects," we know that we are not identified with them. We can thus interpret our relation to these "facts," and in this sense, we transcend them.

In particular, at any moment, we recognize that what we are actually doing and how we are actually reacting to things are but one among many possible modes of our behavior. Thus our transcen-

---

4. A more technical meaning of the term "facticity" will be elaborated on in Part Four, Chapter Two (see pp. 203–204).

dencies are our possibilities in two senses: (1) what we might be doing or what might be happening to us; and (2) what we are actually doing, insofar as it is not necessary for us to have chosen this action. As the term is used here, however, "transcendencies" does not mean remote or farfetched possibilities, but believable ways of behavior.

For Sartre, we keep bad faith in existence by attempting to make our transcendencies into facticities and our facticities into transcendencies. Thus the woman tries to transform a transcendency into a facticity by attempting to convince herself that she is actually having an intellectual conversation: a purely intellectual conversation with a man is a real possibility for her, and she concentrates on this transcendency, allowing it to convince her that it is, in fact, what is actually happening. (We will see in the next section that evidence is crucial for the whole accomplishment of "self-deception."[5]) Nevertheless, at all times she knows what is actually happening but avoids this knowledge by simultaneously reversing the process, attempting to transform facticity into transcendence. She takes this concrete, factual holding hands as not actually happening to her as a person. After all, her body is not her personality, and what is *actually* an advance to her person in its sexuality she attempts to contemplate as a *possibility*, as happening to "another." Thus his hand is not in *her* hand, but in *a* hand.

Man, for Sartre, should, in some way, be a synthesis of facticity and transcendence. Bad faith, however, attempts to keep them apart. It "succeeds" precisely as bad faith because it separates them by constantly going from one to the other. When the woman attempts to contemplate the possibility of having an intellectual conversation with a man as being factual for her, she is again thrown upon the antithesis, namely, that she is factually being made love to; nevertheless, she then realizes that this lovemaking does not encompass her personality. She is more than what is happening to her; *she* is not her body. She can interpret what is happening as not happening to *her* but to her *body*, and believe that her real self is engaging in an intellectual conversation. But since both facticity and transcendence refer

5. "Self-deception" is Kaufmann's translation of the term "bad faith." See Walter Kaufmann, *Extentialism from Dostoevsky to Sartre* (Cleveland: World Publishing Co., 1956), p. 222.

to a true aspect of human nature, they each, for a while, can play the total role.

Furthermore, one can play this game of facticity-transcendence in regard to another person. Thus the woman knows that the man does indeed have respect for her, that this is one of his attitudes, and that, on another occasion, he might be interested in a mere intellectual conversation. But she also recognizes a temporal development of the situation—right now it is leading to more than conversation. She attempts, however, to fix the man's respect for her as an in-itself, trying to make of this factual temporal phenomenon an abstract unchanging attitude of pure respect.

In one of his famous paradoxical definitions, Sartre states that we have to consider man as "a being which *is* what-it-is-not and which *is not* what-it-is."[6] Man *is* what-he-is-not in the sense that man *is* his possibilities: he is freedom, which is the nothingness within his being; and he is his consciousness insofar as this is not a "what" or nature. Conversely, man *is not* what-he-is. Man *is not* his body, his past, his environment. In bad faith, man attempts to keep separate what he is from what he is not.

Bad faith, however, is not only metastable, or transitory, it can also become a way of life. To understand how this can happen, Sartre makes an interesting comparison between bad faith and sincerity.

Sincerity is usually identified with that honesty by which a person admits to be as he, in fact, is. As Sartre will say later, we merely wish the homosexual or alcoholic to admit that they are thus and then we will respect or at least "forgive" them. But is sincerity possible? Can *I* ever say I am really such-and-such? Of course, one can be sincere in respect to the past, insofar as one admits having acted in a certain way. But to say I *am* lazy is to make laziness a structure, an in-itself. Man, however, is not identified with himself in the sense that an inkwell *is* an inkwell. If he were, bad faith would be impossible; he could never truly succeed in deceiving himself.

Sincerity is thus not a state, but an obligation. We often conceive that we have the obligation to make ourselves be what we are called. Thus a waiter, Sartre states, attempts to play the role of a waiter. He attempts to live up to the model that the world presents to him. In a

6. BN, p. 58 (italics and hyphens mine).

similar way, most of us play roles assigned to us by society, and society expects us to stay within the limits of that role. The "good" teacher, student, and father are those whose actions say to the world, I am a student, teacher, or father. But, Sartre notes, the waiter knows that being a waiter is only a role for him and that his consciousness is not identified with his role.

For Sartre, our lack of identity with ourselves touches all our emotional and psychic states. I am sad, Sartre says, only in the sense of not being sad, since I "forget" my sadness when I am distracted from it, as happens in a sudden interesting meeting. This proves that I really invest myself with sadness, as with a role, and return to it as to something I need and want. Here Sartre hints at his theory of emotions, which is consistent with his understanding of the being of consciousness as empty of all content. We are conscious of our emotions; this consciousness makes-them-to-be, giving them their entire weight and value. Thus, for Sartre, emotions and psychic states are not produced by a causal series either within or without us, for then we would be connected with them in a continuity or plenitude of being characteristic of the in-itself.

Sincerity escapes us from all sides. We cannot even say that consciousness is what-it-is, since consciousness *is* only in the sense of continually nihilating its "object" as that which is not the *being* of consciousness. Even in relation to another, consciousness appears as a lack, as the dubious and questionable meaning behind the other's behavior: I can see Peter smiling, but I never know what his smile really means.

Thus true sincerity is impossible; I can never say without qualification that I am now this kind of person. Rather, I am a teacher only in the sense of not being one, only in the sense that at each moment I can freely divest myself of this role, which never encompassed me to begin with and from which I was always separated by a nothing.

Sartre maintains that we are well aware of the impossibility of sincerity. Indeed, we are aware that what is usually described as sincerity is, in fact, bad faith, for it is an attempt to escape the constant obligation of becoming and to rest in a state of stability.

The impossibility of sincerity allows for the possibility of bad faith, for it allows us to slide back and forth from facticity to transcendence, from what is actually happening to what could be happening.

Correspondingly, one who demands sincerity from others can himself be in bad faith. For example, one wishes the criminal to admit to being a criminal in order to forgive him. That is, one demands that the other person temporarily treat himself as stable and fixed and await the concession to change. The advocate of sincerity wants temporary custody of the other's freedom in order to give it back to him with his blessings. He wants to treat freedom as a thing.

Finally, sincerity can be bad faith not only when sought from another but also when directed toward ourselves. In our very admission that we are evil, we attempt to escape being evil. We know that one who admits being evil is now remote from it and transcends it. To the extent that we say to ourselves, "Look I am evil!" we are really patting ourselves on the back for our honesty.

Thus, for Sartre, sincerity, as an achievement, as an admission of an identity with my present mode of behavior, is itself bad faith. It is this impossibility of sincerity that allows for the possibility of bad faith and for that delicate state of mind in which we consciously believe ourselves to be as we know ourselves not to be. But this leads us again to the difficult problem of how we can manage to believe our own lies.

III. THE "FAITH" OF BAD FAITH

In bad faith, we actually manage to convince ourselves that our lies to ourselves are true. For Sartre, this implies that from the very outset we must be in bad faith even about the nature of bad faith, since otherwise we would know the lie as a lie and would not really believe it. The paradox is that we are conscious of lying to ourselves and yet believe (have faith in) our lies. To show how this is possible, Sartre briefly examines the nature of "faith."

Faith is concerned with a kind of evidence. Strictly speaking, I do not believe that two and two is four; I know it, and the evidence is convincing (apodictic). Faith, however, is concerned with the type of evidence that is not perfectly convincing. I believe, for example, that

Peter is my friend. His past and present actions seem to indicate this friendship, but this evidence can never present itself to me as apodictic, as proving his friendship in the sense that two and two is four.

Bad faith is distinguished from good faith precisely in its attitude toward this evidence. When I am in good faith, I first "decide" what is reasonable evidence to believe. Although this may be different for each person, nevertheless, the criteria are faced consciously and some attempt is made to be critical. In good faith, we are willing to allow ourselves to be convinced on the basis of what we consider to be a reasonable amount of evidence.

We are in bad faith, however, when we first decide to believe and then decide not to require too much evidence for our belief. Bad faith, Sartre says, is in bad faith about the nature of faith itself. It knows that in matters of faith no amount of evidence can perfectly convince us beyond a shadow of doubt, and, therefore, it is free to decide for itself what evidence is needed; it can choose to believe with almost no evidence.

For example, love can be in bad faith.[7] We know that we can never be absolutely certain of the love of another, that we have to believe in this love. In good faith, we would face the other's actions first and then try to decide whether these actions indicate love. In bad faith, we meet someone for whom we have an immediate attraction and decide immediately to believe that the other loves us. The slightest favorable action of the other is then interpreted as very meaningful, as an indication of love.

Again, we often decide in bad faith that we lack certain "abilities." Thus the child fails a mathematics examination and now faces the possibility of trying, with his best efforts, to pass the second examination. But suppose he should still fail? The child then may turn from confronting failure in the face of his best efforts—better for him to believe that he does not have ability in mathematics. But if he does not have ability, why waste time studying? Therefore, he does not study and, of course, fails the second examination, accumulating for himself the evidence to support his belief that unfortunately he has no ability in mathematics.

7. This is not Sartre's example, nor is it his technical explanation of love, which is given in Part Three, Chapter One, section I.

The situation, however, is not this simple. We have made a too clear distinction between good faith and bad faith. The person would surely know that he is in bad faith, and bad faith would collapse into cynicism. The truth of the matter is that bad faith is possible because perfect good faith is impossible; i.e., belief evaporates as soon as it is recognized as belief. When I face my belief as an object of consciousness, I know that I believe. Thus the immediate belief has within it the antithesis of nonbelief, knowing certainly that I believe. Pure belief is therefore impossible. But this should not surprise us: man is that being who is what-he-is only in the sense of not being it. Everything in consciousness must be in question, otherwise consciousness would have being-in-itself within it, and the perfect translucency of consciousness would be marred by the opaqueness of the in-itself. Thus belief can be maintained as belief only if it is always in question as belief, only if we never quite know that we believe.[8]

Bad faith and good faith begin from an awareness of the same inner disintegration (*désagrégation*), the same awareness that we are what-we-are-not and are not what-we-are. *But in good faith and bad faith, we face this lack of perfect identity with consciousness differently.* In good faith we start with the realization that we are freedom; we recognize, however, that we can exist only by tending in the direction of being, only by trying to become what we freely choose to be. We also recognize that our very flight toward being will never be achieved as an identity. In good faith we do not flee our freedom, and in particular, we do not flee the very fact that our good faith is always in question.

Sartre will elaborate on the distinction between good and bad faiths particularly in Part Three, Chapter Three, and in Part Four. In the present section, he is primarily concerned with bad faith as a negative attitude, and his main point is to stress that both good and bad faith reveal consciousness as lacking identity with itself. Consequently, the distinction between good and bad faiths is not here

---

8. Sartre states that we do a certain violence to language in speaking of the pre-reflective cogito as "knowing" (*savoir*). Basically, it is nonthetic, that is, it has no object in the sense of a delineated, reflected object, and thus in consciousness' original upsurge it does not "know" in the sense of forming judgments. Nevertheless, in its original upsurge, consciousness is an awareness of something, and thus consciousness is not "blind." See pp. 132–134.

emphasized, leading some to interpret Sartre as claiming that good and bad faith are not fundamentally different projects or choices of our being.

There is justification for this interpretation: first, in this section, Sartre portrays both good and bad faiths as originating from the fissure within consciousness that makes sincerity as a present state and as an ideal in the future an impossibility; second, in a footnote in this section and in Part Three, Chapter Three, Sartre indicates that good- and bad-faith attitudes toward other people have a tendency to slide into each other.

The apparent ambiguity of Sartre's presentation arises because good and bad faiths can refer both to a "metastable," relatively transitory behavior, as in the example of the woman flirting, and to fundamental projects or choices of our being.

As transitory attitudes, good and bad faiths are metastable and slide into each other. Even here there would seem to be a real difference between a good-faith attitude that will end in bad faith, and a bad-faith attitude that will end in good faith. Thus, although love as an ideal of good faith cannot succeed, Sartre himself claims that it is different from, for example, sadism, which must fail as an ideal of bad faith.

Sartre's point seems to be that, as ideals, both good and bad faiths must fail, since man can never be one with any of his ideals. Nevertheless, Sartre repeatedly states that bad faith is an attempt to flee from our freedom, whereas good faith is an attempt to face our freedom. To the extent that we try to achieve either our flight from freedom or our confrontation with our freedom, we will be unsuccessful: we will be either awakened to face our freedom or led to try to possess our freedom as a thing and thus begin to flee it.

Granting the failure of both good and bad faiths as transitory attitudes, we must still distinguish the radical difference between good and bad faith as initial projects of facing our freedom or avoiding it. Good or bad faith as an original choice of our being is a gestalt, and Sartre will make clear in Part Four that this gestalt allows modifications within it.[9] Thus, while we may not be able

9. Despite these qualifications, Sartre does seem doubtful about the ontological status of good and bad faiths. At times he refers to bad faith as a reflective phenomenon and at other times he hints that bad faith is an aspect of the being

always to avoid transitory bad faith, we can still be in good faith to the extent that we realize that our good faith must always be in question, that it must always involve a task of avoiding falling into bad faith, and that it must involve, as Kierkegaard would say, choosing to be what we think we are.

Furthermore, as a gestalt, which is the very being of the for-itself, good faith must be good in the sense of not being one with its goodness, and bad faith must be bad in the sense of failing to be one with its badness. Nevertheless, these failures, as the very being of the for-itself, are fundamentally different orientations to the world and others. In good faith, we begin with a realization that we are our failure to *be* one with our body, our environment, and our entire situation, but we still recognize the necessity of struggling toward the being that we would be. In bad faith, we attempt to see ourselves both as the product of our environment and heredity, and as "cursed" by not being able to be what we would wish to be. We then choose this failure and attempt to rest and enjoy it.

Sartre thus finds that bad faith seeks to flee the in-itself through the continual "elsewhereness" (*désagrégation*) of our being. He seems to mean that, for example, the person with an inferiority complex seeks to flee the accomplishment of being superior (in-itself) by using the very freedom that has given him this project. He wishes to be superior but knows all the sacrifices and demands required of uniqueness.

---

of consciousness. Our own distinction between bad faith as a transitory phenomenon and as the being of consciousness is more definite than the distinction expressed in Sartre's text.

Also, the concluding footnote in this section is confusing both in the French and in the English translation. (The footnote begins with a conditional sentence in which the antecedent seems to contradict the consequent.) In this footnote, Sartre seems to say both that it is indifferent whether one is in good or bad faith and that we can, by a self-recovery not to be explained in BN, radically escape bad faith. But if it is indifferent whether one is in good or bad faith, why should there be the question of a radical self-recovery from bad faith? Perhaps Sartre means that although we face our freedom equally in both good and bad faiths, there is nevertheless a way of avoiding the bad faith living of our freedom even though this living is consistent within its own gestalt. Or perhaps he is referring to the possibility of "conversions" which he calls attention to in Book Four (see p. 201). The fact that conversions are both needed and possible would seem to emphasize that good and bad faiths as the being of consciousness are radically distinct.

He chooses to believe that his efforts are useless because nature has cursed him with natural weakness.

Bad faith thus starts with a conception of a given self endowed with certain capacities and then tries to interpret its freedom in the light of these capacities. In its attempt to avoid the fullness of its freedom, bad faith pretends to attempt to escape the bonds of a "nature" that it itself has created.

Sartre concludes that bad faith is possible because it is a permanent risk in the very heart of consciousness.

We are led, therefore, to undertake a fundamental (ontological) study of consciousness. This study will begin with a somewhat separate description of consciousness as a being-for-itself and then gradually include a description of the human reality in its totality, that is, of the for-itself as simultaneously a being-for-the-world and a being-for-others.

BEING-FOR-ITSELF

In Part Two, Sartre begins to describe man (the for-itself) as that being who is so affected with nothingness that from all aspects his unity is fractured. This "fracturing," or dispersal, of the for-itself's unity is never so complete as to result in man disintegrating into separate entities, such as mind and body—entities that would then be merely externally related to each other.

Sartre, in this part, tries to achieve a delicate balance. Man is a flight from perfect identity with himself, but a flight that is always a search for unity and never an achievement of unity. This view of man would not be worthy of note except that, for Sartre, *this flight from ourself is our very being.*

In the first chapter, Sartre will show how this fundamental lack in man's being is his presence to himself, his "personality," his value, and his possibility. Further, Sartre will stress that our nothingness and our lack of identity with ourselves are not abstract but arise from definite conditions.

In the second and third chapters, Sartre will also show that man's lack of identity *is* temporality and that the temporality that is man's being is the origin of the world's time.

1

The Immediate Structures
of the For-Itself

In Chapter One, Sartre begins a detailed description of the being of the pre-reflective cogito. Some of the material repeats what has been said of consciousness in the Introduction. But the emphasis in this chapter is to show that from every aspect, the for-itself is affected with nothingness. The presence, facticity, value, possibilities, and very selfhood of the pre-reflective cogito are thus "nihilated" structures of the for-itself.

I. PRESENCE TO SELF

In section I, Sartre examines the awareness of ourselves that is a sense of presence to ourselves. His description of this presence attempts to avoid two extremes: first, to consider presence below the level of awareness as an instinctive and blind feeling about ourselves; and second, to consider presence as a reflection of a self-as-a-subject on a self-as-an-object. Sartre will claim that the original presence of the self is an awareness of oneself as a subject without making this self-as-a-subject into an object of study.

We have proceeded, Sartre says, from negation, to freedom, to bad faith. We recognized that bad faith is a permanent possibility within the being of consciousness and, consequently, are now led to examine more closely the very being of consciousness, the pre-reflective cogito.

Our initial approach to the cogito is crucial if we are to avoid earlier errors. Descartes began with the activity of doubting and thinking and was led to conclude that thought was substantive, that the mind was a spiritual in-itself. He remained locked within his mind; his thoughts were unable to achieve a valid connection with external existence. Husserl tried to avoid this trap by considering consciousness as intentional, as by its very nature related directly to something other than consciousness. But that to which consciousness was directly related was an objectivity that bracketed existence. Sartre claims that, despite Husserl's protestations, his phenomenon is close to the Kantian phenomenon, which hides rather than reveals the existent. Heidegger, indeed, tried to avoid describing essences stripped of existence by starting his phenomenology with the phenomenon of human existence. He viewed the human reality as a "pro-ject," or leap from being, and as an essential outwardness and openness that allows for the understanding and interpretation of the possibilities of being. Thus, the human reality arises fundamentally as a self-understanding of its own possibilities and as a concern and "care" for being.[1] Sartre does not deny that the human reality is a self-understanding, but he claims that knowledge must always be a consciousness of knowledge, and thus knowledge and "care" must have their foundation in the being of consciousness. Consequently, according to Sartre, Heidegger does not originate his phenomenology from a direct awareness of the being of the human reality, which is the being of consciousness.

To understand the human reality, we must thus understand more of this being of consciousness. More importantly, we must recognize that consciousness is clearly distinguished from the material existent, or being-in-itself. Only the in-itself (*l'être-en-soi*) is perfectly identified with itself—a chair is a chair.[2] Unity is thus not a goal of the in-

---

1. This care, for Heidegger, is the basis of all our sciences and traditions. For without this essential care on the part of *Dasein*, being would degenerate into a sort of blind instantaneous passage from one state to another. There would be no history of being and there would be no meaning in being, since history and meaning demand continuity.

2. Strictly speaking, being-in-itself is not an in-it*self* because it totally lacks selfhood.

itself, but a perfect achievement; there is no distance or nothingness within the in-itself. Consciousness, however, is not identified with itself; unity is merely a goal that consciousness never achieves, as is evident in our relation to our beliefs:

I am my beliefs, although I am never perfectly one with them; my beliefs, in fact, exist *for* me, and in this first existence, even before any act of reflection on my part, my beliefs stand as needing a witness, as needing my subsequent reflective awareness of them. Nevertheless, consciousness is not first a being that then directs itself toward belief as an object. Rather, in its first inception, consciousness, *from the viewpoint of its content*, is identified with that which it believes. Thus, if we ask *what* is consciousness-of-belief, the answer is that, as a "what," consciousness is totally belief. But in its being, in its existence, consciousness is not a "what," but the pure translucency and awareness of what is believed. Consciousness can be the awareness of belief only by "nihilating" itself from what is believed, that is, only by allowing nothingness to slip between itself and belief as a "what." Belief, then, in its original conscious existence is already not simply belief; it is a belief that can be questioned. It is "troubled" belief.

We cannot, according to Sartre, rediscover the identity of consciousness by claiming that consciousness-of-belief *is* consciousness-of-belief, since consciousness-of-belief becomes an object only on the level of reflection. Consciousness-of-belief, as an object, however, is not the original nonreflected consciousness-of-belief, but the personal, constructed *I* studying its beliefs. Furthermore, even on the pre-reflective level, consciousness-of-belief is not identified with consciousness-of-belief, since, in the very beginning, belief exists as "troubled."

Here we should recall that while the pre-reflective cogito is immediately a consciousness-of-an-object, it is also an awareness, and every awareness is a (self-) awareness. Thus consciousness is not blind. Nevertheless, this original (self-) awareness, or reflec*ting*, is nonpositional; that is, *it does not directly place a self as an object*. Consciousness is thus originally a reflec*ting* to itself that is not a reflec*tion* on itself as an object. Thus, while engrossed in playing tennis, I am immediately but *indirectly* aware of myself as a subject playing tennis and *directly* aware of my tennis playing. When I become directly aware of *myself as an object* (for example, as gracefully or ungracefully playing tennis), I begin to interfere with my playing.

According to Sartre, many philosophers (for example, Spinoza and Hegel) have been misled by the original nonpositional (self-) consciousness of consciousness to conclude that the essence of consciousness is to reflect on the self as an object and thus become aware and "present" to oneself. Sartre insists, however, that this reflected awareness of our "presence" is a derived knowledge of the self-as-an-object, and that in respect to this reflected awareness of ourself, the self is more properly termed "pre-reflective."

To understand the true nature of our awareness as a presence to ourself, we must remember that consciousness is never one with itself. This does not mean that consciousness is perfectly *not* a self, for then it would be as divorced from selfness as the material existent (in-itself). Rather, the "self" is consciousness-as-a-subject, in the sense of consciousness as a unity: the pre-reflective cogito, as a (self-) consciousness, lays the foundation for that struggle for unity in which the self attempts to synthesize and unify its experiences. But as soon as the self attempts to be aware of itself as a unity, it escapes this unity by the very fact that it is aware of it. *And ironically, this very escape of the self from itself (which is the attempted awareness of the self-as-a-unity) brings-to-be that very nothing or "distance" by which the self can be in its own presence.*[3]

Presence is therefore not substantive; it is not a property of a spiritual entity. Presence requires that a nothing has slipped between consciousness as an awareness and as a subject. But again, this nothingness that slips between consciousness as a self and as a subject is never *there*; it is not a void. Rather, it is always *elsewhere*.

There is, for example, no continuity between consciousness and belief. The consciousness of belief is the very denial that belief can ever be perfectly blind and untroubled belief; it is the denial that

---

3. Consciousness is a concrete nothing, and like every concreteness, it can be understood only in its "aspects." Presence, value, possibility, and time are among the aspects through which we try to understand the concrete being of the pre-reflective cogito. Nevertheless, these aspects are not the aspects of an absolute unity, and Sartre will note that it is through consciousness that multiplicity enters the world, because consciousness is, in its own being, never one with itself. See p. 106, n. 9.

belief can, as it were, be worn by consciousness as one wears a hat. The consciousness of belief is therefore the immediate presence of belief to the self. Thus, as presence, the pre-reflective cogito refers us immediately to the self and the self to the pre-reflective cogito. It is only later that we make of this movement a construct or idea and try to conceive of presence as a completed totality or substance.

Man is the region of being in which "matter" (the in-itself) perpetually degenerates and becomes *present* to itself. This perpetual nihilating within the in-itself is, for Sartre, an ontological act, an absolute event—the distinctive possibility of being. Nothingness is made-to-be by being. But this nothingness comes to being only through the human reality. Nevertheless, the human reality is human precisely as the original project of its own nothingness and as the attempt to be the foundation of its own nothingness within being. To understand how nothingness is made-to-be by being-in-itself, in such a way that the human reality is still the foundation of its own nothingness within being, we must first turn our attention to the relation of facticity to the human reality.

II. THE FACTICITY OF THE FOR-ITSELF

Although the human reality is not an in-itself, Sartre says that there is a sense in which the for-itself *is*. In particular, we cannot choose the circumstances of our birth and our entire bodily condition. These "facticities" appear to us as having no foundation or justification. Why is one person born blind and another born with perfect vision? Facticities are thus contingent, they present themselves as simply "there." Specifically, man's presence in the world appears as an unjustifiable fact.

According to Sartre, both Descartes and Heidegger try to avoid facing this absolute contingency of facticities and look for an explanation of existence. Descartes attempts to use directly this realization of contingency, particularly man's contingency, as a proof of God's existence. Heidegger, according to Sartre, tries indirectly to justify contingency by indicating his desire to lay the foundation of an ethics: he claims that the realization of contingency is the beginning of the call of consciousness to authenticity. Sartre, however, insists that the reflective awareness of our contingency leads neither to the existence of God nor to authenticity.

Nevertheless, it is true that neither being-in-itself nor consciousness can be the foundation for its own being. A foundation in being would require reasons and laws that would make being's existence totally explainable to itself; it would require a consciousness of one's being, as a totality and unity, in which everything appears as justified. But then, precisely as a consciousness of its necessity, this being would stand at a "distance" from its own necessity and thus be separated from it.[4]

This analysis of the foundation or justification of existence leads Sartre to speculate on the "origin" of the for-itself. According to Sartre, one can consider consciousness as the attempt of matter to provide a foundation for its existence because consciousness tends to give reasons for existence and, by its awareness of existence, to justify it. In particular, my consciousness of myself is my attempt to make my body appear as necessary to some extent, for insofar as I am aware of my body, it is more than a simple contingency.

While appearing to arise from matter (*en soi*), consciousness, on its part, tries to reestablish its connection with "things" by attempting to found and be one with its facticities. In particular, the human

4. Furthermore, according to Sartre, a foundation of being cannot be explained by attempting to go from the conception of necessity to the existence of necessity. First, because the very concept of a necessary being implies a contradiction: the total consciousness of perfection and the identification with that perfection. Second, because we can never pass from the logical to the ontological order (the ontological argument for the existence of God). Sartre refers here specifically to the attempt by Leibniz (Baron Gottfried Wilhelm von Leibniz, 1646–1716) to reason that the concept of a necessary being implies its existence —a necessary being, in its very possibility and definition as necessary, is one that *must* exist. But for Sartre, the level of knowledge always remains on the level of knowledge; possibility as an ideal is not the possibility of being. Real or ontological possibility, as Sartre will show, exists only insofar as being holds its possibilities in existence. Possibility follows existence and not vice versa. (Sartre's atheism seems particularly addressed to a specific "theism," namely, that we can have clear and distinct concepts about the a priori possibility of God. For to conceive of the impossibility of God is to claim to have clear concepts about the "nature" of God—we conceive that a square-circle is impossible because we have a clear concept of a square and a circle.)

reality, as that particular region of being in which the nihilation of being-in-itself occurs, tries to become reflectively aware of its facticities and integrate them into a totality. The for-itself then tries to become one with its totality of facticities but fails precisely because it is aware of them.

Consciousness is thus tied to the world in the very act in which it nihilates itself from being-in-itself. Consciousness is not a pure spirit that can choose its relation to being-in-itself. Furthermore, while the human reality must always "play" roles, such as that of a waiter or writer, these roles are not absolutely arbitrary. One's condition makes certain roles believable, as I can now choose to play at being a teacher because, given my background, this role is believable for me.

Although my facticities never give the meaning to my life—I am my birth and past only in the sense of not being them—they are not thereby to be viewed as a pure in-itself, resisting consciousness as a brick wall. *Facticities are the in-itself as already nihilated and as one aspect of the human reality.* My sitting in a chair, Sartre says, is never a simple "being there" in the way that a tree is there; consciousness will always discover motivations for its manner of presence to the world ("I am here because . . ."). Furthermore, facticities are only one aspect of the human reality. The for-itself has its own projects that, while never perfectly separated from facticities, are also never perfectly identified with them.

To the extent that consciousness has its own projects, consciousness sees its awareness as, in a sense, necessary; it realizes that consciousness can never *be* without being an awareness. To the extent that I am thinking, I am aware that I am thinking (and to this extent Descartes's cogito is correct). But consciousness is still contingent; it is still gratuitous, since there is no reason that it should be at all, no reason why the in-itself should degenerate into a for-itself.

There is also no reason for the original "attempt" of being-in-itself to found itself, thereby giving rise to the for-itself. But the shadow of being's attempt to found its existence remains in the for-itself as its facticities. Furthermore, while being's attempt at providing its own foundation gives rise to the factual existence of consciousness, consciousness, on its part, freely supports its presence to the world by its nihilating acts. Thus, while nothingness is brought-to-be by man's failure to justify his existence, it is man who sustains nothingness by continually nihilating himself from matter.[5]

III. THE FOR-ITSELF AND THE BEING OF VALUE

Although section III is long and appears involved, the outline of the argument is clear. The discussion falls into two main parts. First, Sartre describes the for-itself as lack; then he shows that the for-itself as lack is the foundation of value. The basic structure of the argument fits in with Sartre's earlier discussion of *négatités*, for again Sartre wishes to avoid the two extremes of idealism and Cartesian realism. Thus he shows that idealism is avoided because lack and value are shown to be not merely "subjective," and realism is avoided because lack and value are shown not to be realities existing independently of man.

If we turn our attention to consciousness as nihilation, we realize that the human reality is not enclosed within itself as is the Cartesian mind. Nihilation is intentional; that is, it is always originally the nihilation *of* something other than consciousness, namely, the nihilation of an in-itself, for example, an apple. The in-itself, however, is never expelled, leaving consciousness as a fixed emptiness.

From another viewpoint, the nothingness of consciousness is a continual failure of man to be identified with himself as a consciousness. Thus the for-itself immediately reveals itself from all aspects as a lack, as identified neither with being-in-itself nor with itself as consciousness.

"Lack" as the most fundamental of internal negations has, for Sartre, three aspects: (1) that which is lacking—for example, the arm of a chair; (2) the existing thing that lacks—for example, the remaining section of the chair; and finally, (3) the totality that would be the unity of the two and that would make the existing thing precisely that which lacks—for example, the total chair makes of this "section" a *broken* chair. Lack thus always includes a surpassing of

5. This very abstract description of the relation of the human reality to the in-itself will be made more concrete throughout this work, particularly in the chapters on transcendence and the body (Part Two, Chapter Three; Part Three, Chapter Two).

the in-itself toward a totality that it is not. Strictly speaking, all that exists is the in-itself of the section of the chair.[6] This in-itself is pure fullness; it is what it is, an arrangement of wood and material. It becomes a broken chair only when consciousness surpasses the section (in-itself) toward the totality "chair."

As with negations, lack arises in the world only through the human reality. But again, as with negations, this fact does not mean that lack is subjective.[7] For Sartre, the reality of desire is sufficient to prove that lack is not merely subjective. The desire to complete a book, for example, cannot be simply identified with the activity of typing a sentence. If it were, the sentence typed would not lead to a next sentence. For the first sentence, as a proposition, is complete and full; it is an in-itself, and as an in-itself, it would not have led to writing the next sentence. The writing of the first sentence is therefore a lack, for it was not the last sentence of the book.

Furthermore, this desire to finish a book cannot be identified with some kind of force or drive within me. For again, precisely as a drive, it would be positive fullness or energy. This fullness would be nothing else than the pure activity of typing, and there would be no reason for it to continue toward that which it is not. As a desire to complete a book, this drive must be viewed as lack, for otherwise the present activity would cease, as "typing" does indeed cease when an object such as a lamp falls on the keys of a typewriter. Thus the desire to complete a commentary surpasses what-it-is toward what-it-is-not.

As the foundation of all negations is the nothingness of consciousness, so too the foundation of all lack is the lack of the pre-reflective cogito. Man arises as a negation of identity with *any* particular thing or in-itself. *To be specific, man arises as a lack of identity of a self with a self.* Thus, in its original upsurge within being, the for-itself tends simultaneously toward identification with a self and consciousness of this self.

The very being of man is the failure of consciousness to attain this

6. Sartre notes that the process can be reversed and, for example, the arm can be regarded as the existent and the section as that which is lacking.

7. In this respect, "blindness," since it is not an artifact, might be a better example than a chair. Sartre uses the example of a crescent moon in relation to a full moon.

identification. But consciousness is aware of its own failure, and this awareness is also its very being. The pre-reflective cogito is a self only as lacking a self.[8]

The human reality is, therefore, by its very nature an "unhappy" consciousness. It is perpetually invested with the ghost of a totality that it can never be but that it must perpetually attempt to be. The very being of consciousness consists in its failure to be its original project of identity. Nevertheless, the identity that consciousness lacks is not an abstract identity with a self. Consciousness arises in a situation; and the self that consciousness lacks and would be is an original "situational" self.

We are now, Sartre says, prepared to examine more closely the being of the pre-reflective cogito. *This being is value.*

For Sartre, philosophers have the same problems with understanding value as with understanding lack. They tend either to hypothesize it as an independent being or to make it purely subjective. However, as with lack, value enters the world only through man, but it is not thereby dependent on man's knowledge.

As with lack, things can be said to have value only insofar as they surpass what they are toward what they are not. A book has value only as related to some end or purpose. The world has value only as viewed in relation to an end or totality. Value is, in fact, the surpassing of all surpassings. If I ask myself why I am writing, I can say to complete a book. But if I continue the questioning, I do not rest with a final answer unless I have arrived at what I consider the ultimate goal or "value" of my efforts.

All surpassings, all transcendings, are conditioned by value. Value itself is the unconditioned insofar as value is the very nature of the pre-reflective cogito. Even though it is unconditioned in respect to my other surpassings, I am still conscious of it as unconditioned and, consequently, nihilate it. In fact, I am conscious that the very nihilating of value as achieved is what gives value to value, for it is that which allows me to be separated from, and thus conscious of, my

8. Insofar as consciousness is aware of its basic imperfection as lack, Sartre says that Descartes's proof, that an imperfect consciousness demands perfection, is rigorous. Its mistake is to identify this perfection with God, rather than to realize that it is the original project of the pre-reflective cogito.

value. Thus value is the unconditioned as a failure to be unconditioned and as always "elsewhere."[9]

Although Sartre does not here elaborate the concrete aspects of
value, he is considering the specific value of the individual as it
includes the individual's original projection of a "goal," for example,
to be average or superior. This goal, however, is not on the level of
knowledge. It arises with the very upsurge of consciousness. Nevertheless, it is entirely free, since *nothing* causes this value and *nothing*
at each moment separates the pre-reflective cogito from this value.

Value is thus both absolutely necessary and absolutely free. It must
exist insofar as consciousness keeps itself in existence as the failure of
an unconditioned value to be unconditioned. Consciousness, however,
has no causal or necessary links with value and can freely change
them; consciousness is thereby "contingent" and is freely responsible
for keeping value in existence.

It is clear that values are not therefore merely subjective, since
they are the very being of the for-itself. They are not themselves
(conceptual) knowledge, although they can become known by reflection. Insofar as consciousness is also in the world, values can be
known by others and in fact have a relation to other persons (to be
considered in Part Three).

IV.   THE FOR-ITSELF AND THE BEING
OF POSSIBILITIES

The general argument in section IV is by now familiar. Briefly, Sartre
maintains that, as with lack and value, possibility enters the world
only through the human reality, although possibility is not thereby

9. Value, Sartre says, forms a dyad with the being of the pre-reflective cogito
as surpassing. He seems to mean that value and surpassing are "aspects" of the
being of the pre-reflective cogito and, further, that these aspects are not like
the aspects of an in-itself, such as an apple. For the apple is a perfect unity
that must manifest itself to consciousness in a series of aspects. The for-itself,
however, is a "fractured" unity, the failure of being to be one with itself. Thus,
lack, value, and possibility are more than mere aspects of a perfect unity and
yet not separate entities. They are the for-itself as constantly attempting and
constantly failing in its struggle to be a synthetic whole, a struggle that neither
perfectly succeeds nor totally fails.

merely subjective or a state of knowledge. Possibility comes into existence through the very being of the human reality.

The section is divided into two parts: first, an elucidation of the nature of possibility to show that it has neither an independent nor a subjective existence; second, a description of how possibility enters into the world through the human reality.

The introductory paragraph gives a brief sketch of Sartre's understanding of possibility. We have seen that the human reality is a being that is what-it-is-not, that it comes into being as a lack of coincidence with itself. The human reality opens up possibilities by always projecting beyond what-it-is to what-it-would-become.

But what the for-itself would become is a for-itself as a self. In relation to this projected self, the for-itself now has possibilities. We will soon return, with Sartre, to consider the description of possibility in more detail.

First, Sartre shows that Leibniz's and Spinoza's understanding of possibility is inadequate to explain the "real" possibilities that exist in the world. For Leibniz, something that does not exist can be said to be possible if it is not a contradiction and, consequently, God could produce it. Thus a square circle is not possible, while the creation of another Adam who did not sin is possible. According to Spinoza, however, something is said to be possible only because we do not know that it exists. Everything that *can* be is, in fact, already identified with the divine substance, and its recognition merely awaits our knowledge. Sartre considers that both notions lead to understanding possibility as a state of knowledge: for Leibniz, a noncontradiction that God knows and could, if he willed, cause to exist; for Spinoza, a state of ignorance about the world.

Possibility, however, Sartre insists, is a real state in the world. To say, "It looks like man may inhabit the moon," is not to refer to a mere logical possibility, but to a situation that points to an imminent coming-to-be. Our technology opens the horizon for this possibility and is aimed at this possibility as to a "lack."

Sartre warns us, however, not to interpret this to mean that possibility is thereby something like Aristotelian potentiality—a capacity arising from the so-called substantiality of things. As we have seen, being-in-itself, such as a rocket, simply is. Still, we must not go to the other extreme and conclude that therefore possibility is merely in man's mind. Possibility is a surpassing of the in-itself that comes to the in-itself only through the being of the human reality that is its own surpassing.

Again, as with negation, value, and lack, Sartre's point is that possibility comes into the world through man's being and not through his knowledge. Thus, while it is true to say that without man there would be no possibilities, it is not true to say that possibility depends on man's knowledge of something as possible. Granting the original upsurge and surpassing of the for-itself within being, there are, through this original surpassing, "real" possibilities in things—or more appropriately, things take on possibility in relation to the original possibility in man's nature.[10]

As with value, possibility is another aspect of the concrete nothingness that is consciousness. The very being of the pre-reflective cogito is to be a lack of identity of a "self" with itself. Man is present to himself as a self (totality) that he would be but is not. The human reality is conscious that its projection is to be a self conscious of a self; it would not lose its consciousness to obtain identity.

Nevertheless, this original self within the project of the pre-reflective cogito is not an "object" of thought. It is not the ego, or the reflective knowledge we have about ourselves, as when we consider ourselves to be temperamental or kind.

Sartre's own example may clarify what is meant. The original project of thirst is not to eliminate the desire of thirst, rather it is a desire to satisfy thirst as *desire*, that is, to have it satisfied and continued as desire. The pleasure and happiness we seek is an ever escaping achievement of pleasure and happiness in which we would still desire the pleasure and happiness we would have achieved.

In a similar way, the self projects itself to be a self that it still would *want* to be (a self that is an escaping or surpassing self). Consequently, it projects itself to a totality that is a nihilation. It is this nihilated totality (detotalized totality) that opens up the for-itself's possibilities.

Sartre concludes this section by noting that the pre-reflective cogito's original project of totality includes the self as a totality, a

10. In the chapter on transcendence, Sartre will elaborate on how possibilities enter *in* being through man.

circuit of selfness (*circuit de l'ipséité*), and the self's relation to other persons. Sartre considers this unique totality of the self in the next section, where he briefly indicates that all our actions are pre-reflectively a consciousness of ourselves as in some way "one." He will continually return throughout this work to describe how our pre-reflective awareness of ourselves includes an awareness of ourselves as an "ideal" or "total" self—although this "total" self is neither an ideal to be accomplished nor an object to be studied.

V. THE SELF AND THE CIRCUIT OF SELFNESS

In section v, Sartre clearly distinguishes the pre-reflective self and the self as a totality from the ego. The ego is a reflected construct whose function is to unite all our experiences into a unity; it is the *I* that we present to ourselves and to the world for study and recognition. *This ego cannot be consciousness because it is present to consciousness as an object to be studied and does not have the perfect translucency of consciousness.*

Sartre notes that we are not to conclude from this that the pre-reflective cogito is impersonal. The pre-reflective cogito is a nihilation that is a presence to itself, and it is this presence that is true "personality." For Sartre, the ego, or *I*, is a sign and product of this personal consciousness, or "personality," rather than the cause of it.

Further, the ego is not to be identified with the self as the original project of consciousness. This self is an ideal limit of our self-awareness-of-an-"object." It is projected as the limit of our immediate self-awareness, but it is projected as nonpositional. It arises simultaneously as consciousness itself.

Consciousness is thus the (self-) consciousness-of-an-object-in-a-self. But this "self" is, as we have seen, the self as the foundation of possibilities. It is a self as nihilated and surpassed. This self continually escapes us, not because it is like the ego, a thing hidden in us, but because it is affected with nothingness. After all, Sartre says, must not man have a free relation with himself?

But how does the human reality surpass itself and continually go out of itself, transcending itself, to future possibilities? Sartre agrees with Heidegger that it is only in the face of the world that the self surpasses itself. Consciousness does arise in a situation, in a "world," and the for-itself, on its part, attempts to be united with the world. The world is invested with possibilities, and the for-itself is the self-consciousness of one of these possibilities. In living, I attempt through my possibilities to make the world *mine*.[11]

Sartre concludes this chapter by noting that while the examination of negation has revealed some aspects of the being of consciousness, we have failed to focus attention on the temporality of consciousness. The cogito is not enclosed within an instant; it projects itself toward value and toward possibility, transcending itself in time. Thus we must now examine the nature of temporality.

11. In the following chapter, on transcendence, Sartre will elaborate on the for-itself's relation to the world.

2
Temporality

I. PHENOMENOLOGY OF THE THREE
TEMPORAL DIMENSIONS

Sartre's description of time, although involved, follows consistently the view of the for-itself begun in his Introduction. To recapitulate, Sartre's task is to provide a description of reality that avoids the extremes of idealism and Cartesian realism. He constantly attempts to avoid idealism by showing that negation, lack, possibility, and time, which appear to be merely aspects of man's knowledge, are in fact aspects of his being. Simultaneously, he attempts to avoid Cartesian realism by insisting that negation, lack, possibility, and time are not independent realities, but are brought to being through the being of the for-itself, which is its own negation, lack, possibility, and time.

Time thus comes to being only through a reality that is temporal in its own reality. Given the original nihilation, which is the upsurge of the pre-reflective cogito, a "world" is brought-to-be, not through the knowledge of this cogito (that is, not through the thematic role of consciousness by which it knows objects), but through the being of the cogito (that is, the nonthematic or pre-reflective consciousness).

As an aspect of the for-itself's being, time is a synthetic unity and, consequently, more than the mere addition of past, present, and future. Nevertheless, a somewhat separate study of the temporal elements is needed if we are to be led to the intuition of time as a whole.

A. THE PAST

According to Sartre, previous opinions have either given no reality to the past or have attempted to grant it some kind of honorary being. If we consider that the past has no reality, then everything is actually in the present, and the past is conceived as that which previously caused present modifications in things and in the brain. For example, to say of a bent nail that "we remember when it was straight" is only to compare the present mental image of it as having been straight with the (present) perception of it as crooked. The mind, or memory, then constructs, in the concept of the "past," the continuity between the mental image of the nail's straightness with the perception of its present crookedness.

Sartre rejects this description of the past for the same reasons that he rejected the notion of desire as the fullness of some force existing in the present. For, as desire is an intention to that which is lacked, the past is an intention to that which *was*. Furthermore, if my awareness of the past state of the nail is nothing but the comparison of an image present in the brain with the perception of the nail's present state, there would be no way of distinguishing the imagination of a nail from the memory of it.[1] Memory would then have to be either a "weak" image or a reasoned conclusion. But as "weak," the image would still be an image and not an intention to the past, and as a reasoned conclusion, the past would lose all its character as an immediate personal perception belonging to my history.[2]

Also, if the present is the only actuality, we are faced with the unsolvable problem of how to construct the continuity of time from

1. According to Sartre, the image is not a "picture" residing in the brain, for, as with desire, this view of the image would result in considering it as a being-in-itself, full and complete, with no intentionality.

2. Sartre also refers to Husserl's notion of retentions. Consciousness, for Husserl, has intentions to the past ("retentions") as well as intentions to the future ("protentions"). For Sartre, both retentions and protentions are locked within consciousness and cannot explain the true outwardness of time, either to the past as *my* past or to the future as *my* future.

the instantaneousness of "nows." For, as Sartre will elaborate in the next section, instantaneous nows cannot result in the continuity of time as duration any more than indivisible points can result in the continuity of a line as a length.

Nevertheless, we cannot go from the extreme that the past has no reality to the extreme that it has some kind of "suspended" or "honorary" being. The past, according to Bergson (Henri Bergson, 1859–1941), has a continuity of being in that the past is merely the cessation of the active existence of things but not of their being. Again, this account cannot explain why the past is perceived as *my* past; it cannot explain the intimate relation the past has to consciousness.[3]

All the preceding approaches to the past are unsuccessful because they begin by considering man as one existing thing among many existing things: man and the chair he is sitting on are viewed as contemporaneous because they both share the same "now"; and thus the past of man is viewed as the past of the chair and not as first and foremost *my* past.

The usual attempt, however, to explain my awareness of the past as mine is to consider the past the changing aspect of what is otherwise my permanent substance. For example, I am the same person who awoke this morning, since the intervening changes have not been so radical as to change the fundamental nature of my *I*. The past, according to this view, is thus simply the recognition of the duration of my fundamental, unchangeable substance. However, this explanation presupposes the "myness" of the past, which it is supposed to explain. For why and how does my present awareness of myself lead out of itself to my past? Also, as we will see in the next section, if I am fundamentally unchanged, I really do not have a past. In some way, then, we must restore the past as an aspect of the totality of the human consciousness.

We must begin with the realization that the past is *my* past and then consider how the past can be a totality of individual pasts,

3. According to Sartre, neither Descartes, Bergson, nor Husserl can explain this *myness* of the past, since they separate the past, present, and future from consciousness and consider these temporalities as beings-in-themselves. But, as beings-in-themselves, these aspects of time are only externally related to each other, and the synthetic unity of time both within and yet transcending consciousness has been destroyed.

rather than reverse the process.[4] For Sartre, the ontological aspect of the past is revealed in such expressions as "I was fatigued," "I earned that money," "I wrote that essay." A remark about our past hurts or flatters us because we are not disassociated from our past. *It is here clear that I am my past in the sense of being responsible for it; in some way I claim to carry it with me.*

Of course, it is true that I am my past only in the sense that my consciousness is not identified with this past. Thus the "content" of my consciousness, the "what" of my consciousness, is first and foremost my past.

By reflection and the consequent turning of this past into an object, I can explicitly state that I am not my past; *but in the original pre-reflective cogito, the past is that aspect of my consciousness that is the context of my pre-reflective actions.* The past is thus not an aspect of my knowledge; rather, the past is an aspect of my being. But while my being (or consciousness) is not identified with its past, the reason for this is not because my *self* is always in constant flux. The self continually escapes itself, not because it is a constantly changing substance, but because the self is always separated from itself by *nothing.* This nothing does not result in the past "slipping" behind me. I *am* my past in the sense that my consciousness can arise only as the nihilation of being one with *my* past. (Conversely, I must not be my past precisely in order for it to be *my* past, for it is only by nihilating myself from my past that I make-to-be that "distance" that is the consciousness of my past.)

The past is the human reality as it approaches the in-itself, that is, as it approaches the identity of a thing. Thus Sartre again quotes with approval Hegel's description of man's essence as that which man was.

We are now in a position to view the past as an aspect of the being of the for-itself.

Man "sustains" himself only by continuing as the failure of being-in-itself to found itself; in particular, he is the failure of his body to become a necessary existent. By this failure and nihilation, man

---

4. According to Sartre, Bergson indeed tries to establish time as an internal relation but fails because he starts by considering the past as past rather than as *mine.*

surpasses himself, although not totally. Being-in-itself, or facticity (in particular, the body), remains as the content for man's free projections and nihilations; facticity remains as a "haunting" of the being of the for-itself. (The past is facticity, but not every facticity is past; for example, my environment is facticity.)

Facticity gives the context and contingency to man's being, preventing him from becoming a pure spirit that could choose his relation to the brute existent. Facticity is what makes certain roles believable and others imaginary.

My past is the precise density to which my consciousness is condemned to be related. I pre-reflectively nihilate my oneness with *this* past; my past is the precise context for my surpassings of myself.[5]

The past and the present are thus not continuous or homogeneous relations within the continuum of time. They are ontologically different aspects of the human reality. The past is the for-itself as it has become an in-itself. For example, my past laziness is a laziness that is fixed and identified with itself but that I must now relate to as *my* past.

As facticity, the past is the opposite of value because value is always in the light of my future possibilities. Nevertheless, we can attempt to deceive ourselves by trying to find "ourselves" and our values in our past. But value lies in the future projects of the human totality, and to turn to the past for our values is but another attempt to flee anguish.

The past, however, resembles value in that the past "enters" within being only through the human reality and yet does not depend for its reality on man's knowledge. The past is brought-to-be by consciousness; the past is a modification of being brought to being by the for-itself.

In the chapter on transcendence, we will see how the past of consciousness impregnates being with the past of the "world." Sartre, however, is here still concerned with the temporality of the for-itself and now turns his attention to the problem of how man keeps his

5. This section is important, for it illustrates Sartre's attempt to avoid the Cartesian dualism of mind and matter in his own distinction of the for-itself from the in-itself.

continuity with his past, that is, how the present and future of man is the present and future of his past.

B. THE PRESENT

Sartre notes that the being of the present seems to be the being of things that are. Common opinion asserts that, in contrast to the past and future, the present *is*. Upon examination, however, the being of the present escapes us and finally is revealed as affected with nothingness.

The present cannot be regarded as the instantaneous now. An instant is that which has no duration, and time cannot be composed of an infinite number of durationless instances. Also, the reality of time, as a temporal duration, would thereby disappear, since the instants of the past are gone and those of the future have not yet arrived.

For Sartre, the being of the present is revealed to us if we realize that to be present is to be in the *presence* of something or someone, as the soldier answers, "I am present." The present is the presence of the for-itself to the world. The being of consciousness, as intentionality, is an outwardness by which consciousness is present to being. Thus the for-itself does not first exist as a quasi substance closed in upon itself, related only secondarily and externally to being; rather, the very nature of man is to be a presence to being. It is man who, by his presence to being, brings totality and temporality to being, organizing being into a world.[6]

But what precisely is the being of presence? Clearly it is not the simultaneous existence of two realities conceived as in-itselves. In this conception, two things simply are, and their presence is the witnessing of their simultaneity by a third being. But presence would then be a mere external relation between the two beings, and the

6. The for-itself is present to all of being, to a "world." The for-itself does not arise within being as a consciousness or presence of just this or that being. Of course, it is true that the facticity of the for-itself demands that it rise here rather than there. But this situational existence merely gives the for-itself a certain perspective on the world rather than exhausting it as a relation to only certain beings.

witness, as some sort of pure mind (God), would be merely externally related to the existing being. The being of time would then disappear into the mere subjectivity of the witness. Rather, the for-itself, by its very nature, is a witness of its own being; there is no need for a third term, such as God, to give man his presence to being.

The present, as *presence*, is rather the for-itself as the disintegration of being-in-itself; it is matter losing its identity to become present to itself. This disintegration, or lack of identity, is never accomplished, since "things" never succeed in facing and in being conscious of themselves.

The present is man's continual flight from identity, a flight that brings-to-be the presence that is the failure of being to be totally present to itself in a moment, or "now." Consciousness fails in its attempt to be totally present to itself in an instant, and this failure is the very temporal dispersal of consciousness, nihilating itself from a past and fleeing the present toward a future.

C. THE FUTURE

In discussing the future, Sartre first considers objections to accepting it as an aspect of the being of consciousness. He states that, unlike the present, most people will agree that the future depends on man, since without man or consciousness things would simply be. For Sartre, the error is to conclude from this that the future is merely an aspect either of man's knowledge or of his drives. The future, however, cannot be simply a representation in man's mind or an inclination in his nature, for, precisely as psychic entities, these are full and complete; they are in-themselves.

The future, therefore, must arise from a being that is its own future. My future is my very consciousness as it fails to be present to itself all-at-once. To be conscious, consciousness must be separated from itself, it must flee itself, to be present to itself. But, Sartre repeats, this flight of consciousness (which is the for-itself) must not be envisioned as an achieved reality, like, for example, leaving behind a hat. The for-itself fails in the very attempt to be a self that is present to its selfhood. The for-itself is thus present to itself as lacking itself.

The future is that aspect of the for-itself's lack that makes us realize that presence is never an achieved thing. The presence of the for-itself is always beyond itself. The future is possibilities opened by this presence-at-a-distance of the for-itself. The future is the "beyond-being" of the for-itself, which we must now further examine.[7]

It is because the for-itself is the original nihilation within being that a "beyond of being" is made-to-be. But it must be remembered that this nihilating is a nihilation within concrete being: the nihilation of particular facticities, arising from a particular for-itself trying to become present to itself.

Thus the future arises as the negation that a particular for-itself, with all its past, can ever *be* what it would become. My beyond is a beyond of *my* past. The *I* that I would be is the total reflective *I*, in which I am one with my past and future. I do not wish to lose anything of myself when I meet myself in the future, for I would still remain myself. I would thus be conscious of my future self, and the future toward which I run is not the destruction of my consciousness, but the maintaining of it. But as the presence of my consciousness to itself, my consciousness must flee toward a new self, for presence is flight from being (present) toward being (future).

The future that I would be, therefore, is not a fixed future, but a future of a future. We should note that, in a sense, both the present and the future are "future," for they are both flights from being toward a beyond. The difference is that the term "future" does not, strictly speaking, refer to that immediate flight from being that is the result of the nihilation of the for-itself. *Rather, the future is my projected meeting with a remotely distant self.*

My future is not the writing of a sentence, but the awareness of myself as having completed a book: I would be the person who has the past of having written a book.[8] However, as such, I already await myself in the presence of a self that is beyond my having written a book; I await myself precisely as one who, in the future, will have

---

7. The next few paragraphs in Sartre's text (BN, pp. 126–128) can be confusing, since he is simultaneously considering the Future and individual futures.

8. The example of writing a book cannot be taken too literally. My future is really the presence of myself as a totality to a future self as a totality. Thus, Sartre says, being-in-itself is dragged along by consciousness, for the self would lose nothing in its flight from itself.

fled that future as a past, as one who will "do something different," or who will then "rest." It is this future of a future that is the beyond-being of my present consciousness.

We must also remember that the original upsurge of consciousness is a pure nihilation. There cannot be anything within consciousness that is in any way an in-itself; everything must be affected by nihilation. Thus, as with value, lack, and possibility, the future of the human reality must be in question in order to be a future.

As an analogy, imagine a sapling to have a future not insofar as it is destined merely to become a fully grown tree at one with its growth, but rather as having a future precisely as a consciousness of its growth. But as a consciousness, the sapling would be "distant" from its growth; it would have to nihilate itself as identified with the *being* of its growth. This very nihilation would break the causal lines that would necessarily lead it to its growth, and thus freed from its facticities, it would not have to be *this* growth.

This freedom and "beyond," however, must be understood correctly: the tree could not replant itself or give itself a new past. Rather, it would have to be the nihilation of its facticities, such as the particular seed and soil from which it arose. Still, its growth would always be a task, and as a task, it could grow only by projecting itself toward a future to which it would be present. What would then be "possible" for this tree? All that we can say is that in the light of its negation of its facticities, it would grow as projecting itself toward a future in which a new kind of growth would still be possible. The future, Sartre thus says, is the "continual possibilization of possibles," that is, a concrete projection of ourselves that makes for ourselves concrete possibilities out of our facticities and that distinguishes our "future" from our daydreaming.

We have viewed time from its separate aspects as past, present, and future. We must now try to recapture an insight into time as a whole.

II. THE ONTOLOGY OF TEMPORALITY

Sartre now studies the (ekstatic) nature of time as a whole from two viewpoints. The first is a somewhat abstract or "static" consideration of time as an order of before and after; the second, dynamic, view is of time as an order of a particular before to a particular after.

A. STATIC TEMPORALITY

Sartre begins by noting that time, as an irreversible order of before and after, in some way separates the previous states of the self from its subsequent states. Yet there appears to be a unity to time as there appears to be a unity of the self. The problem then is to explain time in such a way that it keeps both the irreversible order and the unity of the self.

The usual approach, as we have seen, is to consider time as an even, or homogeneous, succession of "nows": the past, or before, is considered a "now" that *was;* the present, a "now" that *is;* the future, or after, a "now" that *will* be. The present instantaneous now, according to this view, is the only reality. Those who hold this view would agree that there is some basis for the "nows" to be considered as before or after. Thus the associationists would explain the basis of the ordering in time as an external one, the mere placing of one moment next to another, somewhat as one book is placed on top of another book. Time would then be merely external to being.

According to Sartre, both Descartes and Kant attempt to avoid considering time as a mere external relation by viewing it as the function of a witness. For Descartes, this witness is God; for Kant, it is the a priori structure of the human mind. But whether the unity of time comes from God's or man's mind, it is still a unity external to being.[9]

Both Leibniz and Bergson react, according to Sartre, against this notion of time as a succession of "nows" and emphasize its continuity. For Leibniz, the only reality of time is the continual duration of things, and the instantaneous moment is a mere abstraction. (Just as one draws a line by a continuous sweep of the hand, so, too, time is a continuum.) But for Sartre, this is to forget that *before* and *after* are real aspects of the temporal, as well as to avoid facing the problem of

---

9. For Sartre, it does not help to consider time as a potential unity that comes-to-be as a unity with a future succession. Besides the vagueness of the concept of potentiality, each state would still be an in-itself, and we could not explain how the mind could impress true temporality on being.

who or what enables the being to endure. As a line must be produced by the sweep of the hand, the production of the continuity of time must still be explained.

According to Bergson, a past clings to and penetrates the present. But this notion too does not explain the continuity and diversity of time. For even Bergson admits that the organization of time is accomplished through the memory of a present being, and for Sartre, it is not clear how the multiplicity of both before and after can be explained by the so-called unity of memory.

The inadequacy of the preceding views makes it clear that we must keep in mind both the multiplicity and the unity of the temporal. If we start with the multiplicity of before and after, we will never arrive at the unity of duration. Conversely, if we start with the unity of duration, we will never arrive at the reality of the before and after. Thus we must realize that the temporal, as a thing-in-itself, *is not,* but rather that time must be made-to-be by a temporalizing being.

Our previous phenomenological study of past, present, and future reveals that the for-itself can exist only as a temporal being. By its very nature as nihilation of the in-itself, the for-itself arises as diasporatic, that is, as dispersing itself in the three dimensions of time.

Although the in-itself is perfectly simple and identified with itself, the for-itself brings about a quasi multiplicity in being by these original temporal relations of itself to itself.

To be more specific, *each temporal dimension reveals itself as a necessary aspect of the nihilating act of the for-itself.* The past dimension is that which man has to be from "behind"; it is the given that man attempts to found. But in his very attempt to give foundation to his past, man arises as a nihilation and surpassing of his past, *leaving it unfounded and gratuitous.*

Since the for-itself must always have a past, we must take a new look at the question of birth. Sartre admits that there is a *metaphysical* problem concerning the origin of the for-itself, that is, *why* it arose from this in-itself. This problem is, for him, probably unsolvable. The metaphysical issue, however, has no bearing on the ontological description of the for-itself's origin. It is indeed true that the for-itself must arise as the nihilation of a fetus or a body. Nevertheless, we are inclined to create problems for ourselves, according to

Sartre, by imagining a universal time preceding the birth of the for-itself. "Before" comes-to-be only through a for-itself. The continuity that is the world comes-to-be only by the for-itself providing the horizon or ekstasis in which the states of the in-itself can be compared as "co-presents" with the for-itself. For example, a tree is an organic, growing totality that has meaning, as growing, only because of the for-itself's horizon of past, present, and future in which it can unfold. Thus the fetus is a fetus only because there is already a horizon of time brought to being by the being of the for-itself.

We create further problems for ourselves by viewing the past only as an object of study. Although the past can become an object of knowledge, it arises, for Sartre, nonthematically (that is, not as an object of study), as the very being of consciousness. Without my knowing the past as an object (but not without my being aware of it), the for-itself arises as a surpassing of that particular facticity that is its past. The past is that which continually and pre-reflectively orients the for-itself to the world.

Thus the for-itself is condemned to live its past by renouncing and negating the past is its past. But the for-itself is also condemned to the gratuity of renouncing *this* facticity, *this* past, *this* birth.

In the dimension of the present, the for-itself flees itself in its attempt to be presence to itself. In the dimension of the future, the for-itself is present to itself as lacking the self it would be. *From all its temporal directions, the for-itself is thus elsewhere, and conversely, the diverse separations of the self from the self are the for-itself's temporal ekstasis.* Vainly would the for-itself attempt to repose in one dimension of its being.

The for-itself disperses itself simultaneously in the three dimensions of time. Yet, in opposition to Heidegger, who puts the emphasis on the future, Sartre declares that the present is the focus of the synthetic unity of the temporal dimension; it is in the light of the for-itself's attempt to found itself as a presence to itself that it nihilates its past and surpasses itself toward a future self that it can never achieve.

B. THE DYNAMIC OF TEMPORALITY

Sartre now considers the problem of duration, i.e., why the for-itself arises from a particular past and becomes the present of *this* past.

The general argument is clear and basically familiar, although the arrangement of tenses and long sentences make for difficult reading. Again, Sartre insists that duration of the for-itself is due neither to the for-itself's permanence nor to a witness measuring the for-itself's instantaneous states. Duration, for Sartre, is not due to the measurement of change; rather, change itself comes to be only through that temporal aspect of the for-itself that is duration.

Sartre begins by rejecting Kant's and Leibniz's notion that duration is permanance within change. It could be argued that change implies something that changes, and thus the duration of the for-itself would be due to a permanent aspect of the human reality. For Sartre, this approach to duration reduces the for-itself to an in-itself and reduces the reality of time to that of change. Furthermore, this approach does not explain change, since real change requires a total change of the entire being, as, for example, an animal dies when it completely ceases to live.

Our previous study of time has shown that the temporal dimensions are of the very being of consciousness. Thus duration must be an aspect of this temporal being of consciousness and not a permanence within the for-itself or the measurement of so-called instantaneous states of the for-itself by some witness.

For Sartre, the problems concerning the for-itself's duration, namely, how its present becomes a past and how it arises into a new present, are really part of the same problem. Man (the for-itself) arises into the present only by being the nihilation of a past, or to be more accurate, a man continually renounces his present into a past, since he is never completely present to himself.

The present of man, we must remember, is always a flight from his self as a thing and, simultaneously, a bringing-to-be of his self as a "thing" that is the past of his self. That is, the present is the using up of freedom and thereby the bringing-to-be of the for-itself into the in-itself as a past.

The past of the for-itself retains the character of having been the past of *this* for-itself's present. The past and pluperfect tenses indicate that each remote past is connected as the past of a former present, as, for example, "I had already answered your letter when I was surprised by your telegram."

Similarly, the future is affected by the pastness of the original upsurge of consciousness. Depending on whether the future is the immediate or remote future, it is differently related to the present and past. In the first case, the present is the being of the immediate future (of some past). For example, "Here is the package for which I was waiting." But simultaneously, as I am aware that the package I was waiting for has arrived, I am no longer the one waiting for it. *Also, I am aware that I was, in fact, never one who was identified with the mere waiting for this package.* The arrival of the package closes the episode of "waiting," but it closes it as *my* waiting; it settles into the past as an in-itself, but an in-itself that had always been *my* lack.

Furthermore, as the former future becomes the present of my past, I am aware that my future is not my former future. For example, with the arrival of the package (former future become present), I, as one who had awaited the package (present of my past), must now decide what to do next (make-to-be a new future).

The far future, on the other hand, retains its character as future as long as it is the possibilization of possible, that is, as long as the possibles are still possible for me. The far future can become a mere abstract future in the light of past actions; for example, yesterday it was possible for me to make certain arrangements to go on a trip next week, but now it is impossible.

We can now understand something of the being of the for-itself as that spontaneous total change into a new present from a previous present that becomes a past. Again, we must recall that contrary to popular opinion, the past is not what does not exist or what merely exists in the memory. The past, rather, is that aspect of man's being that he *is not*. The past is a specific kind of in-itself. It is the former present of the for-itself become the in-itself, and it is within the continuity of a former presence to being that the for-itself settles into the fixity of the past as a being-in-the-midst-of-a-world.

On the other hand, it is only in relation to man's former present that being retains its character as a "world." The past is thus the history of the upheaval of the for-itself within the in-itself, of "man" within the being of brute existence.

The duration of the for-itself is nothing but its perpetual flight away from the in-itself, a flight that is not instantaneous or homogeneously continuous. Rather, it is a flight of a *diasporatic* or ekstatic being, *spreading* itself simultaneously to the three temporal dimensions. This flight, this arising of nothing within being, continues until the final victory of the in-itself in the death of the for-itself. At death, man is completely his past and the totality of a "thing."

The duration of the for-itself is thus identical with the very being of consciousness. Furthermore, this ekstatic or diasporatic nature of consciousness must simultaneously be a spontaneous change. The spontaneousness of consciousness, Sartre says, must be allowed to define itself. This means, however, that consciousness must deny what it posits itself to be and must transcend itself by simultaneously making a past of what it posits itself to be. Furthermore, it must separate itself from what-it-is by being present to what-it-is. Finally, fleeing the presence of itself to itself, it must project itself to a future. *Thus spontaneity must be temporal, and temporality must be consciousness.*[10]

Sartre concludes by noting that this same result can be reached by recalling the function of the pre-reflective cogito. The immediate self-reflection that is consciousness would become a given, a completed emptiness, unless there were a continual denial and flight from the self as a totality. If the nihilating act of consciousness were in an instant, consciousness would collapse into an in-itself. The for-itself must be, as continually having-to-be, as continually attempting to found itself, and as continually rejecting its past, the foundation of its being.

The totality of time is indeed continually aimed at, since the for-itself would be itself all at once. But this totality is continually missed. The for-itself is the failure to be all-at-once. This failure, however, is not an abstract failure; rather, it is the failure of a historical for-itself, using its freedom in its attempt to found itself. This concrete historical failure of the man to be himself all-at-once is the temporal duration of this for-itself.

III. ORIGINAL TEMPORALITY AND PSYCHIC TEMPORALITY: REFLECTION

Sartre is concerned in section III with the relation of the original temporality of the pre-reflective cogito to that temporality that is a

10. In the text, Sartre opposes Kant on this point.

derived knowledge of ourself as an enduring ego.[11] But before examining the relation of the pre-reflective cogito to the ego (that is, the conception of ourself as enduring with such psychic states as love, hate, and anger), Sartre engages in a lengthy discussion of an important subsidiary problem, the nature of *introspection* (non-positional or "pure" reflection). The reason for this long digression is that Sartre realizes that the ego is revealed to consciousness only by reflection and that there are two kinds of reflection.

First, there is that immediate reflection of the self to itself that we have termed "introspection" or intuitive reflection (pure reflection). Second, there is a more deliberate and, therefore, a more cognitive reflection that is directly related to the ego, a positional, or impure, reflection.

Sartre realizes that, to a great extent, his entire ontology is here at stake, for reflection is the only means by which the nature of consciousness and the entire ontological descriptions of the for-itself are revealed to the for-itself. Indeed, our knowledge of the pre-reflective cogito is not the pre-reflective cogito. Also, since the duration of the self is not the sum of instances of the self, Sartre rejects Descartes's and Husserl's view that the certitude of reflection is due to reflection's grasp of the instantaneous state of the self. Nevertheless, he also realizes that reflection cannot be on past states of the for-itself, for reflection would then reveal the for-itself as a past or as an in-itself. Furthermore, reflection, in this latter sense, would be merely probable knowledge.

11. There is some ambiguity in Sartre's usages of the French terms signifying "to know" (*connaître, savoir*). Generally, he is aware of the Cartesian and Kantian distinctions between knowledge and being. In this context, "knowledge" is always of an object, always positional; it always consciously delineates an object from other objects. From this view, Sartre is forced to say that the pre-reflective cogito is precognitive and that the intuitive reflection that we are about to examine is also *pre-* or *quasi*-cognitive. Nevertheless, he does not wish to imply that either the pre-reflective cogito or intuitive reflection is blind or unconscious. They both totally reveal or reflect, as in a perfect mirror, the content of consciousness; and they are both an awareness of themselves as not-being this content. Thus true introspection and the pre-reflective cogito, insofar as they are an awareness, are an immediate reflecting back to themselves in a non-positional way. They are a "reflect-reflecting."

Sartre begins his study of reflection by considering reflection in general, but it soon becomes clear, and he himself makes explicit, that he is first considering the immediate intuitive awareness of ourselves that is "pure reflection."[12] Reflection (intuitive) is, in some way, a self-awareness of our self-awareness. The idealist's position, Sartre claims, would attempt to reduce this self-awareness of our self-awareness to the first "self-awareness," that is, to a mere subjective state, and consequently, we would not be truly in contact with ourselves.

Cartesian realism, on the other hand, to be consistent, would have to maintain that we know ourselves by a representation of ourselves, and consequently, we could never be certain that this representation truly represented the self. Sartre concludes that the only way to guarantee the certitude of this intuitive reflection of ourselves on ourselves is to realize that pure reflection is not a knowledge, but a bond of being.

Nevertheless, this bond of being cannot be a perfect identity of the self-consciousness-reflecting with the self-consciousness-reflected-on, since reflection would lose its character as reflection. The unity of the self-consciousness-reflecting with the self-consciousness-reflected-on is, like everything in consciousness, the unity of a nihilation. But this does not mean that the nihilating act of reflection is identical with the nihilating act of the pre-reflective self-consciousness. In the pre-reflective cogito, the nihilation is a "reflect-reflecting" in the sense that the "content" or "aspect" (the side of an ashtray) is perfectly revealed (reflect), and simultaneously, this nihilation is a nonpositional awareness of itself (reflecting) as not identified with its "content."[13] In reflection, however, the content of consciousness (1) is consciousness itself (2). Thus we have: (1) a content, which is self-consciousness as the pre-reflective cogito (itself a reflect-reflecting); and (2) consciousness as the very pre-reflective cogito immediately aware of

12. Thus, in BN, p. 155, Sartre begins the last paragraph by claiming that reflection is a knowledge, but concludes by maintaining that pure reflection is not a knowledge in the usual sense of the term.

13. The awkward term "content" is used, rather than the term "object," because of the crucial distinction of positional reflection (self-as-an-object) and nonpositional reflection.

its "content," which in this case is itself. Nevertheless, the self-consciousness-reflected-on (1) is not identical with the self-consciousness-reflecting (2). The first (1) self-consciousness (reflected-on) is a *direct* awareness of a content (the side of an ashtray) other than consciousness (reflect) and a secondary, but simultaneous, awareness of the self as not being that content (reflecting). Here the self and its content are made-to-be only in that original upsurge that is a nihilation, that is, the being of consciousness arises as not perfectly one with the being of the in-itself (side of an ashtray).

In reflection, however, there is a deeper nothingness between the self-consciousness-reflecting and the self-consciousness-reflected-on than between the first self-consciousness and its original nonpositional content. For in reflection, the self-consciousness-reflecting and the self-consciousness-reflected-on are each a revelation of themselves (reflect) and a witness to themselves (reflecting). They each tend to that self that they would be but are not. Reflection comes-to-be as the nihilation that a self-consciousness-of-a-self can be, identified with the self-consciousness-of-a-self. But let us take a closer look at the relation of reflection to the pre-reflective cogito.

For Sartre, as we have seen, the coming-to-be of reflection is closely connected, but not identical, with that original upsurge that is consciousness itself. Reflection arises not as a new consciousness but as an internal modification of consciousness itself, a modification in which the original consciousness is kept as a primary inner structure. Sartre sees, in the original failure of consciousness to be identified with itself, the reason for the coming-to-be of reflection. In its failure to identify with itself as a self, consciousness comes-to-be as fleeing itself, as dispersing itself in the temporality of its being. Reflection, for Sartre, is a second attempt of the for-itself to capture its unity.

Thus the very reflect-reflecting being of consciousness provides the permanent possibility for the being of reflection. Furthermore, this being of reflection is precisely the failure of consciousness to again establish its identity with itself. *But insofar as it fails to found itself, it succeeds precisely as reflection.* That is, its "failure" to found itself, which is its flight from itself, gives reflection the temporality to be aware of the for-itself as a temporality. Reflection arises as a failure of the for-itself to *be* a for-itself, and it becomes invested with the very nihilating being of the for-itself. Reflection thus arises not as a new for-itself, but as the nihilation within a nihilation.[14]

For Sartre, (pure) reflection is not, strictly speaking, a "knowledge," since it does not posit (self-)consciousness as a clearly defined object separated from other objects. Yet insofar as reflection is the human reality's awareness of itself, reflection is indeed an *awareness:* it is a "recognition" (*reconnaissance*).

The for-itself's recognition of itself is, for Sartre, always apodictic, always certain. In the recognition of reflection, the for-itself is concerned not with its remote past, but with the present as it is being made past by consciousness' flight from it. This present-made-past is the very nihilating of the for-itself, and reflection arises within this very nihilation.

For example, if I am now reflecting on my playing tennis, I am aware of myself as playing tennis; I am certain that the self-that-is-playing tennis is the self reflecting on my tennis playing. Nevertheless, I am also aware of the difficulty of continuing to play tennis while reflecting.[15] When I reflect on my tennis, I am aware that I can never perfectly *be* the self that is playing tennis. But this very nihilation (which is reflection), namely, that I can not-be a self that is identified with my tennis playing has its origin within the act of tennis playing, within the *being* of the original pre-reflective awareness that the being of consciousness is not identified with the being of tennis playing.

For Sartre, impure reflection is distinguished from pure reflection in that impure reflection is not on the present that has been made

14. Sartre notes that the being of reflection and the being of consciousness-reflected-on are profoundly altered by reflection (BN, p. 152). But clearly, this profound alteration is not the alteration of "impure" reflection on the ego, which is yet to be explained. He seems to be referring to the fact that reflection reveals consciousness' character of "otherness" to consciousness. To some extent, we become aware of ourselves as an "other." Thus reflection gives evidence of the relation of consciousness to the "other" that will be elaborated in Part Three.

15. In a similar way, we can reflect on the naturalness and ease with which we perform a certain acquired skill. I can thus momentarily become aware of myself as one-who-swims easily and naturally. But if I continue in such reflections and try to unite my explicit awareness of myself with myself as swimming, I interfere with the naturalness of my swimming.

past, but on a remote past.[16] It is the reflection on ourselves as a succession of states: for example, yesterday we were tired; this morning we felt rested. Impure reflection is a knowledge of myself. But as a knowledge, it fixes the for-itself as an in-itself. When we reflect on ourselves in our past, we consider ourselves as an in-itself that has behavioral patterns within a "world." This self, or ego, which we know by reflection, is not totally indifferent to the for-itself. Further, impure reflection appears as the decision to take a point of view on the for-itself become in-itself and usually to affirm that the for-itself is related to this past as to a nature. Thus, for Sartre, impure reflection is in bad faith. It is true that impure reflection realizes that it is taking only a point of view of the self, but it attempts to affirm that the self-reflected-on is more than this point of view, that there is a hidden ego that has had these past states and that in some way is the cause of the present actions of the self.

For Sartre, the psyche is the transcendent ego, the self that we present to ourselves and to the world for study. The psyche is the organized totality of our past states and, as such, is the natural object of psychological research. It is our love, hate, and anger that have become objects of study rather than possibilities within the temporal ekstatic being of consciousness. Within the psyche, there is, indeed, a real distinction between a present, a past, and a future, for we can view these states as the successive states within the duration of the ego. The psyche is thus made-to-be by consciousness, insofar as consciousness sustains it in being by adopting an attitude toward its past. Sartre says that we keep our psyche in existence by a sort of inertia.

In the psyche, we find all the characteristics and problems of psychic time. The entire attempt to explain how a "past" penetrates a "now" (Bergson), or how time is the measurement of change, comes from impure reflection on the psyche. Finally, it is within this impure reflection on the psyche that many novelists, such as Proust, try to

16. The entire section (BN, pp. 158–170) should be read in full, particularly for those who are interested in Sartre's psychology. I have concentrated on pure reflection because it is more important for showing the basis and possibility of a descriptive ontology. This commentary is here basically a summary of this section, in which Sartre himself states that his approach to the psychic is given in an "a priori" manner.

understand the actions of their characters as coming from a nature and explainable in terms of this nature.

Although the psyche is made-to-be by the attitude the for-itself takes on its self, we must not conclude that this attitude is arbitrary or that the psyche does not carry "weight" into the present. The psyche is the transcendent ego, the particular in-itself in light of which I interpret my present. While I am not welded to my psyche by causality, I do refer to it as the context of my actions. For example, I know that John annoys me, and so I decide, now, not to visit him. Furthermore, insofar as I am aware that I have appeared to John as one-who-was-annoyed, I am aware of my psyche as the canvas on which I understand myself as having an "outside." But, Sartre concludes, the "outside" of consciousness is not perfectly realized by impure reflection. This realization will come only when we consider the for-itself as a being-for-others (Part Three).

3
Transcendence

I. KNOWLEDGE AS A TYPE OF RELATION
BETWEEN THE FOR-ITSELF AND THE IN-ITSELF

Sartre has already warned us that our separate study of the for-itself and the in-itself should not close our eyes to their true synthetic unity, which will be considered in its totality at the end of this work. For the present, we must be content to add another aspect to our study by examining the relation of the for-itself to being-in-itself that is transcendence.[1]

Although we have devoted considerable time to the description of negations as the being of the for-itself, Sartre recalls that the original purpose of this study is to describe the relation of the two realms of being, the for-itself and the in-itself, in such a way as to avoid the

---

1. While both the for-itself and phenomena, apart from being-in-itself, must be considered abstractions, Sartre warns that being-in-itself is not an abstraction. For although the entire being of the for-itself is an internal relation to being-in-itself, the being of the in-itself is not determined by its relation to the for-itself. (It is as if Sartre has inverted the usual understanding of the relation of God to the world. Traditionally, the being of the world is determined by an internal, or transcendental, relation of dependency to the being of God—but the converse is not true.) But the in-itself as a "thing" is indeed determined by its internal relations to the for-itself (see section III of this chapter, particularly p. 141, n. 6).

extremes of idealism and Cartesian realism. We are now in a position to begin our answer by describing how and why the for-itself arises as a knowledge of the in-itself and how this knowledge gives rise to that diversity of things that is the "world." It is here that we meet Sartre's strange realism. The world arises not because man conceptually knows a world exists, but because man's *being* is such as to bring diversity and organization to reality.

For Sartre, deduction and argumentation are merely instruments of knowledge and means of attaining that immediate "seeing," or intuition, of an object. For example, in a mathematical proof, the purpose is to "see" a relation that was previously hidden: that one side of an equation is indeed equal to another. In a similar way, true knowledge (*connaissance*) occurs when there is an immediate presence of consciousness and being. This presence has usually been interpreted as the presence of reality to consciousness, but our previous study of the for-itself reveals that only the for-itself can be a presence. Consequently, knowledge is the presence of the for-itself to being, and it is this relation that we must now study.

From the Introduction until this section, Sartre has made a distinction between knowledge and being. But it is clear that he has been referring to empirical and reflective knowledge. Now, however, he is concerned with the human reality as essentially a knowing being.[2] The for-itself comes-to-be as the pre-reflective awareness of something other than itself; that is, consciousness is consciousness of being-in-itself. Consciousness can arise as an awareness of being-in-itself only by that nihilating act in which the being of consciousness is negated as identified with being-in-itself. By that very negation, which is that the for-itself is not the in-itself, the for-itself makes itself to be in the presence of the in-itself. This presence must not be understood as two beings-in-themselves facing each other, for then we would be back to Cartesian realism. Rather, this presence is the flight of the for-itself

2. For a discussion of Sartre's diverse usages of the term "knowledge," see above, p. 126. But there is a further ambiguity in this chapter, for Sartre seems to be considering "knowledge" as the transphenomenal being of the knower and also as that which results from this transphenomenal being, the in-itself as known. In reality, Sartre is stressing that knowledge, as a bond of being, reciprocally results in the in-itself as "revealed."

from the in-itself. Thus the for-itself comes-to-be as a presence and a knowledge of the in-itself.[3]

The for-itself's presence and knowledge is an internal relation to the in-itself. Unlike an external negation (a table is not a chair), an internal negation ("I am not good-looking") refers to a modification in being. The in-itself is the "term-of-origin" of the internal negation, since the for-itself must be that-which-is-not-being-in-itself. The for-itself must thus be a transcendence in order to be an inwardness; that is, the for-itself must be that internal negation that is an "outwardness." The being of the for-itself is the concrete nothingness that is the consciousness and revelation of the in-itself.

The phenomenon of fascination reveals, for Sartre, the immediacy of the for-itself to the in-itself. When we are truly fascinated by a movie, we are nothing but the consciousness of the movie. This does not mean that we are united in substance with the movie in some kind of pantheistic unity; rather, we are the pure revelation of the movie as the nothingness that is a presence to the movie. We thus *realize* the in-itself by knowledge. The knowledge that we are concerned with here is not an abstract or conceptual knowledge, but that knowledge that is simultaneously an awareness and an intention to do something. I *realize* the world by my lived intentions. Without man, a mountain would never be "realized."

In the sense that our presence *realizes* things and, as we will see in the subsequent sections of this chapter, makes them to be distinct as "things," Sartre says, *the real is realization.*

The known is thus a pure solitude; it is the pure revelation of the in-itself by the for-itself.

In the for-itself's diasporatic (temporal) flight from the in-itself, the for-itself realizes the in-itself; the for-itself makes the in-itself to

---

3. This same conclusion can be seen by recalling the nature of consciousness as a reflect-reflecting. As we have seen, consciousness is a pre-reflective cogito that immediately and perfectly reflects the in-itself as phenomenon. The in-itself, however, does not reside in consciousness. The phenomenon (or the in-itself reflected) is made-to-be by the for-itself negating that it is the in-itself and thereby making-to-be that nothing that, in turn, reflects or reveals the in-itself. Simultaneously, however, as the for-itself reveals and reflects the in-itself by being a presence to it, the for-itself makes itself to be a (self-) *awareness*. It is a *reflecting* of the for-itself to itself nonpositionally, that is, a reflecting to itself through something other than itself, the in-itself.

be "there" and, simultaneously, makes itself as the negation of that which is "there."

The internal negation that is the being of the for-itself as knower and that realizes the in-itself as "there," as a "thing" in the world, is *transcendence.*[4]

II. DETERMINATION AS NEGATION

We have seen that pre-reflective knowledge is the for-itself's bond of being to the in-itself. We must now investigate the origin and significance of the for-itself's knowledge of particular things ("thises") in the context of a "world." Again, we must remember that the task is to avoid both idealism, in which the being of things would consist in their being known, and Cartesian realism, in which knowledge is merely the correlation of representations with external realities.

Sartre maintains that a particular being is revealed as "this" only in the totality of a world and, conversely, that the totality "world" appears only as the unity of particular beings. Nevertheless, being-in-itself is neither a this nor a world; it simply is. Thus, as with negation, lack, value, possibility, and so forth, the "this" and the "world" come-to-be only through the human reality. Until now, however, we could quickly add that idealism was avoided because these modifications came to being through the for-itself's *being* and not through knowledge. But then we were treating knowledge in a secondary and derivative sense as empirical knowledge, such as the sciences and the knowledge attained by impure reflection. Now, however, we are describing the aspect of the being of consciousness that is the revelation of the in-itself. It is this change in emphasis that makes it difficult to follow parts of this section.

Sartre's argument seems to be this: De facto, the for-itself arises as the nihilation of this particular being. Although it is clearly an over-

---

4. Sartre illustrates this solitude of the known (brought about by the knower) by the analogy of two curves that are tangential to one another, that is, for part of their paths they appear to be one line. The two curves are always *two* curves, even though where they meet they appear to be one. They are, in fact, separated by *nothing*. In an analogous way, the knower adds *nothing* to the in-itself as known but a *nothing* that makes the in-itself *there*.

simplification, let us assume that the for-itself arises as an awareness of its body and thus a lack of identity of its consciousness with its body. This negation is radical in two senses. First, it is the negation of negations: from every aspect it is a denial that the for-itself is ever an achieved nihilation, a denial that the for-itself ever succeeds in not-being its body *all at once.* Thus the for-itself arises as a temporal spread. Second, this negation is radical because the for-itself is not *any* or *every* being-in-itself. In the very act of not being its body, the for-itself arises as not-being a table, a tree, or any *this;* and thus the for-itself arises as not-being *all* being-in-itself.

Conversely, since the for-itself arises as the negation of its facticities and past, the "all" arises not as an empty all, but as a "world" resulting from the union of "thises." While the "this" and the "world" come-to-be through the original upsurge of the for-itself, the for-itself, as intentional, becomes aware of itself as a failed totality only in the face of the transcendent ambiguous totality of the world.

Sartre declares that the world is knowledge in the sense that the world is being-in-itself precisely as revealed by the ekstatic nothingness that is consciousness. This revelation no more adds anything to being-in-itself than a perfect mirror would add anything to what is reflected. It merely invests being-in-itself with those internal and external negations in which a "this" and a "world" are made-to-be. But we must now take a closer look at those internal and external negations that realize the "this" and the "world."

There is clearly a fundamental distinction between those external negations that distinguish one thing from another and leave the things untouched in their being, and that internal negation in which the for-itself is distinguished from the in-itself. Nevertheless, these external negations are related to and arise from the original internal negation that is the upsurge of the for-itself.

Sartre's reasoning seems to be as follows: in the original nihilation, which is that the being of the for-itself is not the being of the in-itself, the for-itself arises as not-being the in-itself as exterior and, in particular, as not being that exteriority of the in-itself that is extension. But since the for-itself is not *any* in-itself, the in-itself manifests itself with a certain indifference in its extendedness.

Thus in its appearance as "exterior," the in-itself does not appear as having to be "here" as opposed to "there." It is temporality that provides that horizon in which a "here" and "there" have meaning. By temporalizing itself, the for-itself invests the in-itself with those ends and purposes that make it a "this" that is "here" or "there."

Furthermore, the for-itself attempts to be co-present with all of being, and thus the for-itself brings to being that ideal totality that is space. Space, however, does not enter within the fabric of being as time does. It is merely the idealization of the indifference of the in-itself to be in a particular place and the idealization of the for-itself's attempt to fix relations within this indifference. When this indifference of the in-itself to be an extended being here rather than there is hypostatized by a secondary or reflective act of knowledge, it becomes the object of geometry.

Thus the external negations (such as a table is not a chair) that distinguish one thing from another, within a totality "world," are based on that internal temporalizing negation by which the for-itself nihilates its being from the being of any in-itself. But this internal negation of the for-itself from the in-itself is in a context; it is also the concrete failure of the for-itself to be identified with its past and future selves. Consequently, the indifference that would result in an empty all rather brings about a world in which, as the next section will reveal, there is quality, quantity, potentiality, and instrumentality.

III. QUALITY AND QUANTITY, POTENTIALITY, INSTRUMENTALITY

Section III is particularly difficult because Sartre wishes to show that distinctions of things come to the world through the being and freedom of the for-itself and also that these distinctions are to some extent characteristics of the in-itself.

(The following subheadings are not in the original text.)

(A. QUALITY)

Quality, such as the yellow of a lemon, is the being of the lemon as the lemon is considered distinct from other things. Consistent with his rejection of idealism and realism, Sartre maintains that qualities are neither subjective states of the for-itself nor realities totally independent of the for-itself.

The for-itself comes-to-be as the concrete nihilation of the in-itself. One of the specific ways in which the for-itself comes-to-be is as that which is not the being of quality; for example, for-itself is that being that is not the being of yellow. Nevertheless, quality is not the in-itself, since quality comes-to-be only within the temporal horizon in which the world comes-to-be. A lemon has meaning, as a lemon, only within the temporal dimensions that can allow it to unfold with that permanence and continuity of being that are required for it to be a lemon (perhaps in this case the example of a flower unfolding would be easier to see). But as we have seen, temporality comes to the in-itself only through the being of the for-itself. Thus, while the for-itself comes-to-be as that which is not quality and "this," quality and "this," conversely, come-to-be through the for-itself. We will soon elaborate on this mutual relation.

The precise problem that Sartre considers in this section is the relation of quality both to a "this" and to the for-itself, for example, the relation of yellow to the lemon and to the human reality. Since the yellow in some way appears as a "profile," or aspect, of the total lemon, we are also faced with the problem of abstraction and the reality of an abstracted yellow.

Sartre is again not easy to follow. First, we must recognize that qualities interpenetrate one another: I see the sourness of the lemon through the yellow and taste the yellow in the sourness. This interpenetration of all qualities, Sartre says, is the "this"; it is the lemon. The qualities are not manifestations of some substance nor are they held together in their unity by the mind.

Nevertheless, in perceiving the yellow of a lemon, a priority of the yellow over the sourness and coolness of the lemon is also perceived. I am not free to avoid perceiving the lemon as yellow, although the perception of the yellow as the yellow of sour-cool is indeed related to my free projections. This seems to contradict what has been said of qualities interpenetrating one another. In effect, however, we are on two different levels of the for-itself's relation to being.

Abstraction, for Sartre, is not a mere psychological process but an aspect of the for-itself's ekstatic being. The lemon is the concrete revelation of a sour-yellow-cool, and the for-itself comes-to-be as not-being the yellow of sour-yellow-cool. Furthermore, the for-itself also comes-to-be as not-being the *yellowness* of the lemon, thereby revealing and making-to-be the yellowness of the lemon. *Yellowness is that fullness of yellow projected by the for-itself's temporal being and, simultaneously, negated as not-being the kind of totality that the for-itself could ever be.* The for-itself is the negation of a negation, a negation never achieved; but yellowness is the fullness of a negation, that yellow the lemon would have to be in order to be perfect yellow.

Abstractions are thus neither beings-in-themselves nor representations in the mind. They both come-to-be through the for-itself's projections and, reciprocally, make the for-itself *be* as that being that can never be an achieved totality. Thus "this," "quality," and "abstraction" are the in-itself as affected by negations. And in turn, the for-itself makes itself *be* as not-being the in-itself as "this," "quality," and "abstraction."[5]

When the for-itself reveals itself as not-being the totalized quality yellowness, the synthetic unity of the lemon "sour-cool" is left behind as having an undifferentiated relation to yellow; yellow does not have to be the yellow of a lemon. If I now consider the lemon to be the "content" or massiveness that has yellow, this is my free project. Thus qualities both interpenetrate each other, becoming the "this" and, as totalized, leave the "this" behind as their "content."

(B. QUANTITY)

While the for-itself arises as the concrete nihilations of not-being facticity, it simultaneously negates that it is *any* in-itself. As was noted, there thus arises a certain indifference of the for-itself to being and of being to the for-itself. In not-being this chair, I also establish that indifference by which I am not a table and, consequently, that indifference that distinguishes a table as *here* from a chair as *there*.

Without the for-itself, there is neither "this" nor "that," but simply being, as that which is what-it-is. This does not mean that being-in-

---

5. There appear to be two (related) senses of "abstraction": (1) to consider something as separate when in fact it is united in a synthetic unity; and (2) the totalizing of a quality.

itself is one, but that the very distinction of the one and the many come-to-be only through the for-itself.

We must keep in mind that to be a this or that, a chair or a table, for example, requires time in which the chairness or the tableness can unfold. We will return to this point when we consider the notion of potentiality. For the present, Sartre wishes to focus attention on quantity—the hypostatizing of negations that results in distinguishing one being from another as "here" or "there."

Quantity, for Sartre, is pure exteriority as idealized. Number is thus not a synthetic unity but a pure external negation, neither adding anything to being nor revealing anything in being. It is being's pure indifference to be a second, third, or fourth.

Although the absolute negation of the for-itself from the in-itself is reified into that indifference of the in-itself that is space and quantity, it is still true that the for-itself, from other aspects, is necessarily related to these facticities. Indeed, the negation of the for-itself is a unity-multiplicity negation rather than an undifferentiated absolute negation. It is because the for-itself cannot negate itself from the in-itself by any one great stroke that it disperses itself in time and brings to being both internal (necessary) and external relations.

The for-itself is a negation of a negation, a lack suppressed, a future never attained, a nihilation that is never achieved. It is a failure not only to be a totality, but also to be able to aim at a particular goal as a totality. Space and quantity, however, as idealized totalities, as definite projections over the horizon of time, enter within being precisely as the idealizations that the for-itself can never be. Conversely, the for-itself comes-to-be as the failure to be the definite totalities of space and quantity. For Sartre, the "world" is the ambiguous unity of the for-itself with these reified nothings, space and quantity.

(C. POTENTIALITY)

From another aspect, the for-itself, as noted, has internal relations with the "this." For example, the "potentiality" of a tree to grow and remain a tree comes-to-be from the temporality of the for-itself, and conversely, the temporality of the for-itself is the result of the for-itself's failure to be a tree all at once.

We must remember that each temporal dimension has its meaning in the other. Thus the potentiality of a tree to remain a tree comes-to-be only because the future is never an abstract future but always the future of this past: it is an engaged future. And thus the permanence of the tree comes-to-be because the for-itself projects itself toward a future from a definite past, such as, for example, the past of not-being a tree.[6] Furthermore, insofar as my past was never the simple negation of not-being a tree, but the negation of not-being an entire world, the world comes-to-be with a permanence or potentiality from the engagement with my entire past negations.

We can now take another look at the relation of essence to existence.

Essence is the perfect totality that, for example, the budding tree aims at but never achieves—the simultaneous possession of all the stages of the tree's growth with itself. *In this sense, the aimed at but never achieved union of essence and existence is beauty.*

Beauty is thus the constantly aimed at but never achieved union of the states of the world with itself that reflects the failure of the for-itself to be all at once. But unlike the internal ever-escaping failure and lack of the for-itself, the unattainable union of the world's essence and existence is a definite external failure.

Although the ideal of beauty arises from the for-itself's internal lack, beauty is first apprehended as a transcendent ideal, an ideal within being by which being itself lacks its aimed-at perfection. This apprehension of beauty as a transcendent ideal arises because consciousness is directly a consciousness-of-the-world. It is only in pure reflection that the absences in the world are seen as arising from the internal lack that is the for-itself.

(D. INSTRUMENTALITY)

We must now qualify what has been said of the relation of essence to existence. The in-itself can be projected differently according to the lived purposes of the for-itself. Thus the permanence of a chair, as a

---

6. The "tree," in this sense, comes-to-be as a "thing"—an in-itself with meaning, an in-itself as a plant of a certain species. We must therefore qualify the statement made earlier in this chapter (p. 132, n. 1) that the "in-itself" is not determined by its internal relations to consciousness. Throughout *Being and Nothingness*, Sartre seems to refer to the in-itself in two different ways: (1) matter as it would have been without the advent of consciousness; (2) matter as now intrinsically altered by the advent of consciousness.

utensil to sit on, requires my lived, as opposed to abstract, intention to use the chair in this way. If I need firewood, the chair now becomes a utensil for keeping me warm. The in-itself is thus revealed with a certain indifference in use to the for-itself, and this indifference is its "instrumentality."

Sartre maintains that we must modify Heidegger's interpretation of instrumentality. Heidegger, according to Sartre, views instrumentality as leading us to that self-awareness that is the escape from the worldliness of things to the authentic life. Rather, instrumentality reveals the world as a future-projected-world, and this projection is nothing other than the reflections in the in-itself of the for-itself's concrete future or possibilities. Further, it is through living in the world that I make "known" to myself those future projections that are, in fact, the ekstatic nature of the pre-reflective self.[7]

Nevertheless, we must not unduly stress the indifference that is instrumentality. Space, quantity, quality, permanence, and instrumentality are all different ways of trying to grasp the identical coming-to-be of the in-itself as a "thing." Thus the indifference of the in-itself as instrumentality must always be weighed against the permanence of the in-itself—a permanence that comes to the in-itself from the fact that my future projections are always the future of some definite past, which I would carry with me into the future in order to be united with it.

Sartre illustrates the relation of the indifference and stability of "things" to our own projections—a relation that results in the in-itself as "meaningful"—by the example of an ass trying to get hold of a carrot. The carrot is held before the ass by a stick tied to the cart that it is pulling. Every step forward to reach the carrot advances the entire ensemble. In a similar way, we run to meet our own projections, which our very running continually creates. Thus, Sartre says, there both is and is not a meaning in man's flight from the world as a

---

7. Sartre is not that clear on this point. He says that we cannot know, *as an object*, the instrumentality that is the projection of the for-itself's internal possibilities but, rather, that we adapt ourselves to this image by living. Nevertheless, it is clear that perfect reflection reveals our internal possibilities, and it would also have to be present as the "content" of the pre-reflective cogito; that is, we would "know" these instrumentalities pre-reflectively, insofar as "knowledge" is a bond of being.

transcendent ideal (that is, as an ideal that is not subjective or merely psychological).

IV. THE TIME OF THE WORLD

The constant theme in this chapter on transcendence is that the internal negations, which are the being of the for-itself, both result from and bring-to-be the transcendent nothings of quality, quantity, potentiality, and instrumentality. Indeed, it is as transcendent that nothing is first and unreflectively apprehended by the for-itself, since consciousness is immediately *of* something-other-than-itself.

These projections of the for-itself's true internal negation add *nothing* to the in-itself. They provide the horizon in which the absolute identity of the in-itself appears as fractured. Fracturing, or appearance of diversity, is the failure of the in-itself to found itself— a failure that is the for-itself. Nevertheless, we must also keep in mind that the relation between these transcendent nothings and the internal negations is an ambiguous one. These transcendent nothings come to the in-itself from the being of the for-itself and, reciprocally, bring the for-itself to-be insofar as the for-itself is not these transcendent ideals or nothings. But since the being of the for-itself is always in question, the for-itself's relation to the in-itself must always be in question. In particular, the for-itself's relation to the time of the world is ambiguous.

In this section on the time of the world, Sartre tries to account for that immediate awareness of time as *in* the world and of our understanding of "things" existing in time.

A. THE PAST

Although we must again consider each dimension of time separately, nevertheless a "this," such as a chair, appears to us all at once as a permanence existing in time. Indeed, we simultaneously apprehend the temporal and atemporal character of things, their passage through time as well as their identity in permanence. Thus a moved chair still appears both as a chair and as that which *was* in a different place.

The reason for the temporal and atemporal character of things is seen from the very relation of the for-itself to itself. Man, as that very dispersal of being that is temporality, must reveal the in-itself as in time. Nevertheless, insofar as the in-itself simply is what-it-is, it retains an indifference to time. Man never succeeds in making the in-itself a man; and the in-itself, although affected by the upheaval that is consciousness, retains an indifference to consciousness and to its temporality.

Temporality, Sartre says, is only a means of viewing the in-itself. The chair is a chair and does not appear as the synthetic unity of its past, present, and future, but simply as a chair. Time appears as external to it. But I also recognize that the chair has a past (it was "there"), although the chair is not its past. When I reflect in this manner on the relation of the chair to its past, time appears both as instants separated by nothings and, simultaneously, as a permanence. This apparent contradictory revelation of time is again nothing but the revelation of the ambiguous relation of the for-itself to the in-itself.

Again, we must not overemphasize being's manifestation of permanence. Things do appear to come-to-be, as a flower comes from a bud and steam from water. Sartre terms these passings-away and comings-to-be of beings as "abolitions" and "apparitions." He maintains that abolitions and apparitions must be accepted as givens and that they do not seem to result from the nature of the for-itself or the in-itself. They must be accepted as contingent facts that an ontology can only describe and that a metaphysics, perhaps, could investigate for reasons.

Since the in-itself is what-it-is, the passing-away and coming-to-be of things, even as givens, must come-to-be only through the for-itself.[8] As with the question of birth, we must not first visualize a world in which there are abolitions and apparitions and then a for-

---

8. Sartre seems to be maintaining (1) that "abolitions" and "apparitions" appear simply to "happen" to being as a result of the original "happening" of the for-itself, and thus, unlike time, there appears to be no internal relation between the happening of the for-itself and the coming-to-be of such changes as a bud becoming a flower; (2) that, nevertheless, they are meaningful as changes only in relation to the for-itself; and (3) that the precise interpretation of an apparition, a *bud* changing into a *flower*, somehow results both from the brute in-itself, and from the for-itself's free projections.

itself witnessing them. The very being-beyond-being that is the world comes to the in-itself only through the original upsurge that is the for-itself. Within the for-itself's temporal spread, things can now appear as coming from what they were not. These passings-away and comings-to-be, such as a budding flower, are, in relation to the in-itself, *nothings*, but they somehow come to being from the for-itself, the being that is its own nothingness.

The passing away of a thing has meaning only to man who was co-present with the former states of the thing. To say that a flower was a bud has meaning only because the for-itself was a witness to the budding. The for-itself is fixed in the past as that for-itself that was co-present with being.

Without man, as a former co-present with brute existence, there would be no past world. Further, my past is the past of the world insofar as I am now that fixed former co-presence in the world. I *am* the person who was born in this city, met these friends, and made these decisions. By my past, I belong to history, but I flee this past, in the face of my presence to being, toward a being that I would be but am not.

B. THE PRESENT

The present, as the for-itself's ekstatic presence to being, is related to the transcendent present of universal time through motion. It is through the awareness of moving bodies that the for-itself becomes aware of itself as presence to being. As with abolitions and apparitions, motion must be accepted as a contingent "given" that an ontology can only describe but not justify.

If we try to understand motion, for example, the moving of a red billiard ball on a table, as something passing through a place, as if the billiard ball passed through the place AB to the place BC, then for Sartre, we will arrive at all those paradoxes of motion indicated by Zeno.[9] Rather, we must recognize that both place and motion are different relations of the for-itself to being and of being to the for-

9. Zeno reasoned that while a moving arrow appears to be in motion, the arrow cannot be really in motion, since at each moment of its flight it is at a definite place (AB). But to be at a given place at a given time is to be at rest.

itself. Place or space indicates that aspect of a thing (*ceci et cela*), such as a red billiard ball, that is its indifferent and external relation to other "thises" and to the for-itself. Motion, on the other hand, is a new advent in being and a different relation of being to the for-itself.

When a red billiard ball is at rest, its red is what it is. On the other hand, when the red billiard ball is in motion, its red both is and is not what it is. A moving red is not a red at rest, nor is it a change to another color. A moving red is always beyond what it is, always exterior to itself. Motion is that which is always exterior to itself.

As motion is the in-itself as always *exterior* to itself, the for-itself comes-to-be as that which is not motion, namely, as *internally* a self that is always beyond itself. Motion, conversely, comes-to-be as a continuity of that which is always exterior to itself by arising as that which the for-itself continually is not.

Thus, for Sartre, there is a perfect correspondence between the transcendent present of universal time and the present of the ekstatic being of the for-itself. The for-itself projects the continuity of its present with its own past as that continuity of the present with the past of objective, or universal, time. For example, the past, as a state of rest of the billiard ball, is projected as the origin of the continuity or trajectory of the billiard ball. This "projection" occurs by the very being of the for-itself and not by a reflective act.

V. KNOWLEDGE

We are now in a position to outline some of Sartre's conclusions about the problem proposed in the Introduction, the problem of the relation between knowledge and being. Since the entire task of this work is to find a solution to this problem that avoids both idealism and Cartesian realism, the solution as presented here can only be a sketch of the full answer.

Knowledge, Sartre declares, is the presence of the for-itself to being-in-itself. By the nihilation of the in-itself, the for-itself becomes a presence to being-in-itself. Knowledge is thus not a property of man, but a relation of man's being to existence. Man can know himself only as "nihilation" (that is, only as that ontological separation that is not a void). Still, the being of the human reality does not consist in being known. The idealists are right, Sartre declares, in emphasizing the subjectivity of knowledge, but they erroneously conclude that knowledge is the measure of being. Like the for-itself, knowledge is ekstatic, but it is an ekstasis *in* being.

Man is that absolute event that is the failure of a self to be identified with itself. Through man, the absolute event of the world takes place in the in-itself. The in-itself simply is what-it-is. But through the presence of man (the for-itself) to the in-itself, there arises that "affirmation" that is the "thereness" of the in-itself. That *there is* a "tree" comes to the in-itself through the for-itself's internal negations, which are its flight as presence to the tree.

Further, the relation of the in-itself to the for-itself brings about an affirmation of the in-itself as a quasi totality that is *being*. Being-in-itself would be affirmed and this affirmation neither adds nor detracts from being. It comes to being only through the nothingness within man. Affirmation is the absolute happening of the for-itself within the in-itself.

The realists are thus correct in asserting that knowledge adds nothing to being, although they are wrong in considering that being is thereby merely known by some representation within man. Being is not known through the mediation of representations, but by the internal negation in which man is in the presence of being.

Sartre concludes that we should not be surprised that the body was not considered in this description of knowledge; for whatever the role of the body, it first appears as the known rather than as the knower. Furthermore, the body is precisely that which is known by the other. In fact, we first know the body of the other and view our own body through the eyes of another. The body therefore demands that we consider the for-itself insofar as it is fundamentally a being-for-others. The human reality's being-for-others brings us a step closer to seeing the for-itself in its true synthetic unity as a being-in-the-world-before-others.

PART THREE
BEING-FOR-OTHERS

In Part One, we approached the human reality as a synthetic relation, being-in-the-world. Questioning, as a mode of being in the world, focused our attention on man (the for-itself) as the starting point of our description of this totality. We saw that man could question reality and himself only because he had a nothingness within his being. In Part Two, we described how the concrete nothingness within the for-itself is the origin of all its distinctively human characteristics, and that the world itself, came-to-be from the original "happening" of consciousness within existence (the in-itself).

Now, in Part Three, in agreement with Heidegger, Sartre sees that the human reality is *in* the world *with* others (other persons). In Chapter One, Sartre considers the question of the existence of the "other." In Chapter Two, he describes the body as not only our past but as our being-for-others. Finally, in Chapter Three, he describes our concrete relations with others.

1
The Existence of Others

I. THE PROBLEM

Our study of the conduct of negating, Sartre notes, has led us to consider the human reality as those internal relations of not-being the in-itself. The human reality is thus its own time and possibility; it is for-itself. Nevertheless, pure reflection reveals that we are immediately and nonpositionally a consciousness before somebody. For example, shame reveals that we immediately view ourselves as before the "other." Shame, Sartre maintains, does not come about by a secondary, or "impure," act of reflection, but by immediately recognizing that we are as other people see us. Thus, when we perform some vulgar or awkward act and are surprised to see someone viewing us, we are *immediately* ashamed.[1]

Shame indicates both our responsibility for our actions and the immediate relation of our actions to "others." The awareness of shame brings us to consider the two questions of the existence of the other and of our relation to the other.

II. THE REEF OF SOLIPSISM

Sartre believes that both the realist's and the idealist's attempt to establish the existence of the other lead to solipsism, in which only

1. This will be elaborated in section IV, "The Look" (see pp. 159–168).

the existence of the self is taken seriously. In fact, by a strange irony, realism becomes idealistic when it faces the problem of the other's existence, and idealism, in its turn, becomes realistic.

Realism postulates the existence of the external world and emphasizes that the external world acts on consciousness, but it does not seriously consider the problem of how one consciousness can act on another. The realist admits that I can be certain only of the other's body and that I reason to the existence of the other's consciousness by analogy. Thus, since the other's body exhibits behavioral patterns that are analogous to my bodily behavior, I reason that within the other's body there is a consciousness analogous to my own.

Such an analogy, however, can at most give us only probable knowledge of the other's existence; it remains possible that the body before me is a robot.[2] But the realist truly wishes to assert the existence of others as well as the existence of bodies. Consequently, he is led to abandon his realist position and affirm with the idealist that other minds exist but that they are known only as measured by our knowledge.

Critical idealism fares no better in its attempt to account for the other's existence. Kant himself was concerned with the ideal, or a priori, conditions of the subject that make all experience possible and not with the existence of empirical persons. Nevertheless, Kant should have treated the other as one of those very a priori conditions that make the experience of others possible. Such an expanded Kantianism would, however, lead to inconsistencies. In particular, it would place the problem of the existence of the other as a noumenon hidden beneath phenomenon.

Indeed, even within a Kantian framework, the other would function as a regulative principle, as that which does not have to be but which helps me to organize my experiences. A regulative principle, however, would not account for the very phenomenon of the other. I experience the other as having a unity of experiences that, precisely as other, is *not* mine. Although I can predict some of the other's behavior, the concept of other is not limited to merely regulating my

2. Sartre here reverts to the usual meaning of the term "knowledge" as a secondary and conceptual awareness distinct from being.

experiences with the world. As we will see, there are phenomena such as shame that seem to exist only in relation to the other.[3]

Also, I see the other as one who sees me, and because he sees me I would affect him in his emotions and ideas. I simultaneously recognize, however, that his consciousness is not and cannot be mine. Thus, Sartre says, I as subject (immanence) attempt to determine the other as object, although I recognize that he as subject (immanence) denies me as subject and tries to determine me as object. The other is an immanence that is transcendent to me.

The immanent-transcendent paradoxical character of the other cannot be accounted for by the principles of critical idealism; thus the idealist becomes either a realist, postulating an immediate communication between two consciousnesses, or a solipsist, trying to show that the other is unimportant for experiences. Indeed, a solipsism (such as the behaviorism of Watson) in which the other is simply not important is logical.[4]

Nevertheless, since the existence of the other seems to be demanded by our deepest inclinations, most post-Kantian idealists continue to insist on the reality of the other. Ironically, they again end in adopting a realist position in regard to the existence of the other. They assert that all our conceptual schemes, while closed within themselves as quasi in-itselves, are mutually *representative*. My anger and gestures represent the other's anger and gestures. Consequently, the idealist has adopted a Cartesian realist's position with respect to the existence of the other by demanding a correspondence of the ideas of his behavior to the behavior of others.

This paradox by which idealism and realism mutually lead to each other arises, for Sartre, from the very perspective that the idealist and the realist take toward the problem of the existence of the other. They both consider the relation of the self to others as an external relation. The realist considers consciousness within a body and sees

3. Further, Kant's concept of causality cannot bridge the gap between the self and the other. Causality is meant to unify the phenomena of one and the same experience and cannot unify the temporal flow of my consciousness with that of another. Also, universal time is a mere concept and cannot connect my empirical, temporal, conscious states with the empirical, temporal flows of the other; for example, that my consciousness of anger is related to my gestures, as the other's anger is to his gestures, cannot be assumed.

4. According to Sartre, extreme solipsism, which denies the existence of the other, is purely gratuitous.

the bodies of the self and the other as separated by the external relation of space. The idealist considers each mind locked in on itself and thus views the distance between minds as the external relation between two fixed or given nothings.

The view that the self and the other are separated by a real or quasi space leads the idealist and the realist to consider the other as an object of knowledge and as known only through some representation. They are both faced with the problem of whether our representation of the other truly corresponds to the other. But only a "third" mind—God—could guarantee this correspondence. The concept of God, however, is contradictory. The only way out of the problem is to realize that the self and the other are related in an internal relation. We must now consider some interpretations that approach this view.

III. HUSSERL, HEGEL, HEIDEGGER

Most of the philosophers of the nineteenth and twentieth centuries, Sartre states, have realized that the self must be internally related to the other. The weakness in their positions is that they interpret this internal relation to be one of knowledge rather than one of being.

In particular, Husserl claims that each object in our experience is immediately given to us as intersubjective. For example, the very objectivity of an apple, as the synthetic unity of all possible appearances, depends on its internal relation to other minds. But according to Husserl, the self to which the objectivity of things is related is not the empirical self but the transcendental self. The transcendental self, as we have seen, is the result of the phenomenological reduction in which existence is bracketed and in which being is revealed as an essential meaning.[5] Even if Husserl could establish the relation of the transcendental self to the other, this relation would be on the level of meaning and would not guarantee the empirical existence of the other.[6]

---

5. See "Background," pp. 7–8.
6. In fact, according to Sartre, even at the level of meaning, Husserl has problems. For truly to know the other I would have to know the other as he knows himself, which is impossible. Thus Husserl admits that the other is known by an absence, but an absence that is my empty intention and not an internal relation of concrete nothings.

Although writing approximately one hundred years earlier than Husserl, Hegel puts the problem of the self's relation to the other on the level of being. The self, in its very determinations as selfhood, is established only by an internal necessary relation to the other. The stages, or "moments," in the Hegelian dialectic indicate a progressive realization of the self precisely as that which is not the other. The very being of consciousness as a *self*-consciousness is constituted by consciousness thrown back to itself as not the consciousness of the other. The other, in fact, becomes for me the very objectification of the self to which I would be identified. In order for there to be the *truth* of my identity with myself (I am I), I must discover myself in the other as an object. I can become myself only to the extent that I recognize the other as a me-as-an-object.[7]

Although I recognize that the other is a self-consciousness, with his own right, I also realize that I can establish my right only in opposition to him. Indeed, the self as *elsewhere* can never truly face the self-as-an-object, and the subject-object dichotomy is now formed by impure reflection. Hegel's insistence that the other is related to the self by an internal necessary relation is, Sartre maintains, an advance, but the problem still remains on the level of knowledge rather than being. For Hegel, there is an identity of being and knowledge; but even granting this identity, we are led to serious problems. Hegel's view of knowledge, and thus of reality, is of a consciousness as a subject-in-itself opposed to an object-in-itself, and that which separates the subject from the object is a given void or nothingness. The subject and the object are presented as definite "givens."

We have seen, however, that consciousness can be a self-consciousness by never achieving its nihilation; and to the extent that the subject-object relation ("I know myself") represents determination,

---

7. Thus the master-slave relationship develops: the other must become the slave, an object without a unique interiority, in order for me to discover in him the content of my own consciousness and in order that I can regard the other only insofar as he is aware of me. But I need his recognition of me in order to become a consciousness as a *self*. Thus my own value depends, and is constituted by, the value the other has of me: he must recognize in me a value as a self that is not tied to empirical existence, and I must thus manifest myself as one who is willing to risk my life (for example, the Roman master). But simultaneously, I wish the death of the other, for I do not wish to depend on his acknowledgment of me.

it is the result of a secondary act of reflection and not the pre-reflective awareness of ourselves. In fact, whatever the relation of man to other people, this relationship (just as our primary relation to ourselves) is *not* a subject-object relation. The for-itself cannot conceptualize its primary being-for-others, and it cannot conceptualize the other person as a for-itself. We must recall, Sartre notes, Kierkegaard's insistence that Hegel has forgotten the true, unique interiority of each individual.

Sartre sees Hegel's idealism as leading to an epistemological and an ontological optimism. First, Hegel optimistically assumes that the knowledge the other has of me can correspond to how I see myself as an object in him. Second, although I may recognize, in the other, myself as an object, this cannot be his view of me as an object.[8] To "know" how the other sees me would be to "know" him as a free subject. But I "know" the other only in the light of my own free subjectivity.

Heidegger, in *Being and Time*, accomplishes what Husserl and Hegel failed to do. The existence of the other, for Heidegger, is a false problem, since I discover in my own being a transcendental, or necessary, relation to others. The human reality is part of that synthetic relation being-in-the-world and is related to the instrumentality of things and the world only through a more primary relation to other human realities. This ontological relation to the other is conditioned by our freedom and consequent responsibility for how we are related to the other. Inauthentically, I realize my "being-with" as an impersonal relation; authentically, I realize my "being-with" as a personal "we" relation.

For Sartre, Heidegger has indicated the solution of the self's relation to the other rather than given it. He has defined, rather than justified, the human reality as part of that synthetic unity, being-in-the-world. Furthermore, Heidegger's approach remains on the level of the universal and not the concrete empirical. His Kantian view

8. Rather, I know myself and the other as a totality within the transcendent time of the world. But as we have seen, the time of the world comes to being-in-itself through the ekstatic being of the for-itself. We are then on the level of the unique being of the for-itself and not on the subject-object relation. However, it is clear that I cannot know the other in his own ekstatic being, and thus there is an *ontological separation* between the self and the other.

does not provide the foundation of my empirical relation of friendship with Peter and the consequent determination of my being in relation to Peter. The general difficulty of passing from the universal to the concrete, in Heidegger's philosophy, is here insurmountable. For, while the freedom and possibilities of the self can, to some extent, be understood as constituting the "world," the freedom and possibilities of the self can in no way guarantee the existence of the "other" persons.

Indeed, Heidegger's description of the self as ontologically related to the other makes unintelligible concrete (ontic) relations with others. For Heidegger's general description is not the result of an induction from concrete cases. Rather, his approach is Kantian; it is an a priori description of a universally necessary condition of the transcendental subject experiencing the world regardless of what exists. But this universally valid, or transcendental, relation to the other cannot guarantee the empirical or noumenal existences of John and Ann.

Sartre concludes that the basis for this failure is that Heidegger's concept of transcendence is in bad faith. In Heidegger's view of the self, we remain on the level of selfhood; there is no intrinsic, immediate relation to a reality *other* than the self, no true transcendence, as in the for-itself's relation to the in-itself.

On the basis of the analyses of Husserl, Hegel, and Heidegger, Sartre now formulates necessary and sufficient conditions for a valid theory of the existence of the other.

First, we must recognize that we cannot prove the existence of others. It is impossible, in principle, to imagine any experiment or criteria under which the existence of the other would be guaranteed, for solipsism remains a logical possibility. I can therefore only affirm the existence of an other in the way that I affirm my own existence in the cogito. *My active and lived resistance to solipsism can only be accounted for by finding that the existence of the "other" de facto essentially modifies my awareness of myself and the world.*

Second, we must recognize that we are looking not for reasons for the other's existence, but for the other as a concrete being who is not me.

Third, the other must be revealed as a concrete being concerned with our being and not as a mental representation conforming to the other with some degree of probability.

Finally, the other must be revealed within the cogito as having an internal relation of not-being me. Because of this internal relation, there results the synthetic unity of self-others—a totality in which I and others are internally related. But we must avoid the error of Hegel and realize that we cannot be outside the whole; the whole (the "we"), like the for-itself, can only be a detotalized whole whose very totality is always in question and never achieved.

With these observations in mind, Sartre now proceeds to answer the question of the existence of other persons and their fundamental relation to us.

IV. THE LOOK

The ultimate purpose of the study of the look (*le regard*) is to reveal the existence of other persons (the "other") precisely as free subjects. Sartre begins this study by showing that there are distinctive characteristics of our knowledge of the other as an object. These distinctive characteristics of our knowledge of man as an object prepare us for our realization of him as a subject.

Although our preceding discussion has shown that our awareness of the other cannot be reduced to the knowledge of his presence as an object, nevertheless "objectness" is clearly an aspect of this presence. It is true that if we remain on the level of perception, then the other's existence appears as merely probable. Still, this very probability indicates a more fundamental relation to the other as a person. (This fundamental relation to the other as a person should not be understood as esoteric; it is part of our everyday experience.) In fact, a close study of the way the other appears to us as object should lead us to see the fundamental everyday experience of the other as a presence and subject.

For Sartre, our perception of someone as an object and as a man indicates a regrouping of the entire environment toward the man. To be aware of a man walking in the park is to apprehend the benches, grass, and trees as forming a new relation of distances to the man as a focal point. If the man were perceived as a thing among other things, we would view him and the other things as having a relation of distance *to us*. Like the tree and bench we perceive as several yards ahead, he too would be perceived as an object five or ten yards from us. Rather, to perceive this object as a man is to perceive him without distance from us and as a new origin of distances; the tree and bench are so far away from *him*.

Our apprehension of an object, "man," is fundamentally different from our perception of other objects. True we are still on the level of "knowledge," and we may thus be mistaken about the existence of the other. The probability of this knowledge, however, does not contradict the fact that we first apprehend man as an object by apprehending a new totality in which he is a new center toward which things turn.

For example, although I remain present in the park, the *other* causes to appear a negation and disintegration of the grouping of things toward me and of their distances from me. I am aware that I can never know the way this park appears to him, the way the trees and grass present themselves to him. With the apprehension of this object, man, there appears to be, for Sartre, a hole in the universe toward which things are flowing.

What we apprehend, therefore, in the other-as-object is someone who sees what we see, someone who is a subject for other objects. We recognize that we too can be an object for him and that we have an aspect of *being seen*. Further, we become aware that our objectivity can unfold only before the other-as-subject, only before the other's look.

The phenomenon of the look does not refer immediately to the organs of sight. When the color or beauty of another's eyes strikes us, we are aware of looking rather than of being looked-at. On the other hand, to be aware of being looked-at is to be conscious of being seen, of being immediately thrown back to ourselves as having a body and as being visible to the other. When walking on a dark, lonely street we suddenly hear footsteps behind us, we become immediately aware of ourselves as being seen, as having a body that occupies space and is vulnerable. Thus, in the pre-reflective cogito, we become aware of ourselves *as seen*.

The phenomenon of shame, for Sartre, helps us to apprehend the meaning of "being seen." If, driven by jealousy, we are intently spying through a keyhole, we are at that moment taken up by the scene and are totally the nonthetic self-consciousness of what we are perceiving. We exist not as a self who then perceives a spectacle, but rather, we exist as a way of losing ourselves in the world. The keyhole becomes an instrument for seeing because I am my possibility as one who is jealous. This complex of keyhole, door, and room has become a "situation" because of my freedom and facticity: there is something to be seen because I am jealous, and my jealousy is nothing but the fact that there is something to be seen. (Nevertheless, I am not a situational being, for I am my jealousy only as not being identified with it.)

Now, states Sartre, if I suddenly hear footsteps, I am immediately and pre-reflectively aware of myself because I am aware of being seen by another. My pre-reflective cogito becomes essentially modified as revealing my consciousness to *myself* as an object for the other.

The *my*self now "haunts" consciousness not as an object of thought but as an originative and essential escape of consciousness toward the other-as-subject. I am immediately aware of myself as a being-in-the-world and as having an aspect of transcendence that is the ego. It is true that I am not identified with my ego, but neither am I totally divorced from it. I recognize it as my own while not knowing it; it is myself as "over there," as known by the other. The other, however, as a free consciousness, never totally reveals myself to me as I am seen by him. I escape myself, not in the usual sense of not-being what I am, but in an essentially different way: my objectiveness, my being seen, depends on the being-there of the other-as-subject, and yet, because he is a free subject, my objectiveness escapes me.

The presence of the other-as-subject rivets and engulfs my freedom and transcendence. In his own freedom, he interprets my jealousy and turns my freedom back to me as shame. I immediately experience shame; I know that at this moment I am for him nothing but a being spying through a keyhole. While *I* know that I am this being only in the sense of not-being it, only as surpassing myself toward future possibilities, I simultaneously recognize an "outwardness" of my possibilities: my immediate presence before the other. Further, insofar as the other is looking at me and not I at him, I recognize myself as an object transcended by his possibilities. I have become a transcendence-transcended, a freedom engulfed by another freedom.

The existence of the other means that I have an outside or "nature." The other is my original fall. The other, as the look, alienates me from my possibilities, removing me from that original innocence by which the instrumentality of things is an embodiment of my freedom. By the other's look, I am fixed within the world; things no longer have a simple relation to me; rather I and my situation are related to him as his instruments. Further, I am aware of this and recognize myself as now being in the world with my possibilities objectified and fixed by him.

Since my possibilities become transcended by his freedom, they enter the world as an object among other objects, as one probability among other objective probabilities. Through the appearance of the other, I recognize that my possibilities can never return to me as simply my possibilities and that henceforth my freedom is threatened by his freedom.

Through the other's look, not only is my transcendence transcended, but my spatializing and temporalizing are spatialized and temporalized. When I am the look, as spying through the keyhole, things are given to me in space and time (although I am not thematically aware of myself as in space and time). However, before the other's look, I am a looked-at look. The door and the keyhole are still related to me, but they now are related to me by him as forming a whole, which is his object. Also, by fixing me as co-present with him at this scene, I find my presence as a presence "out there," as the present of universal time. I both recognize myself as now part of universal time, since the other cannot be removed, and still recognize an alienation from this time as not my time. Finally, the other's look reveals me to myself as the object of unknown appraisals. Thus from all directions, the other's look makes me aware of a permanent modification within my consciousness; I see myself "out there" and in danger.

This recognition of ourselves as having objectiveness is not on the level of knowledge, since then the other would be known only as an object and, therefore, as a probable existent. It is through being aware of the other-as-subject that we are aware of our own objectiveness as unfolding before his free ekstatic temporality. This awareness, as we have seen through the description of the look, is *on the level of the pre-reflective cogito*. As the cogito reveals my own existence, it also reveals my consciousness as essentially modified by the presence of the other.

The other is thus the one who is looking at me, the one who reveals me to myself as being seen. The other is a direct experience of a freedom that is not my own. To be aware of a prohibition, such as not to leave the house, is to acknowledge an obstacle to our own freedom radically different from that of things that get in our way. We can always relate ourselves differently to things, but a prohibition presents us with our own freedom as now surpassed and fixed.

Further, only through the other-as-subject can I be revealed as having a self that is a myself, that is, a self that is not the self of the other. Thus, within the cogito, I experience the other as a fact that cannot be deduced from my own consciousness; I experience the other as an essential modification of my own consciousness. The other is not first *perceived* in the world; rather, he is first experienced as the alienation of our possibilities and the objectiveness of ourselves.

The preceding phenomenological description of the look, Sartre notes, may still leave questions about the existence of the other. First, it may seem that the other is merely the reification or projected *meaning* of my objectification. But the "me" that is revealed by the look is not a me that is my possibilities; it is a me as essentially modified by the other. The me is "out there." I both acknowledge it as mine and am alienated from it because it is not totally under my control or understanding. For example, my awareness of myself as "evil" or jealous is an essential modification of my consciousness, brought about by the factual awareness of a freedom that is not my own.

Thus the nothingness that separates my consciousness from me is a strange nothing, a nothing that is not completely made-to-be by my consciousness. Consequently, although the other is the origin of my objectiveness, this objectiveness is for him. In fact, since I cannot separate myself from my consciousness, the only objectiveness that I can have is my appearance to the other and the revelation to myself as a foreign self seen by the other.

Second, someone may object that we could be mistaken that the other is looking at us. For example, I may think that someone is looking at me and de facto experience shame, and then realize that no one is there. But at most, this proves that the existence of *this* other (the other as object) is probable. In fact, even if *this* other is not there, our experience of shame or fear has revealed ourselves as capable of being seen. Indeed, realizing that no one is now there, we may continue to relate ourselves differently to our environment because of the sudden awareness of ourselves as visible.

The phenomenon of absence also reveals that the presence of the other is not identified with his factual presence before us. I experience the absence of a friend only because of his continual presence to me as a subject. It is through him that distances arise within the world; he is so many miles away, gone for so many hours. It is only by a fundamental mode of presence to me that he can be absent from this spot. Even if I think that I perceive him at a distance and find that I am mistaken, his fundamental presence remains and ceases only with death.

Thus our relation with others again reveals to us the concreteness of nothingness.

The other's look is therefore the occasion of experiencing within the cogito that fundamental aspect of our consciousness that is being-seen. Even if *this* other happens not to be there, we still experience the reality of our being-for-others as a factual modification of our consciousness that cannot be deduced from the nature of the for-itself. *Nevertheless, although our being-for-others is factual, it is still an internal relation to the other.* However, this internal relation is fundamentally different from that which relates consciousness to the in-itself. Consciousness is internally related to the in-itself as its nihilation, but the in-itself is not reciprocally related internally to the for-itself, and thus the in-itself manifests an indifference of exteriority to the for-itself. Consciousness, on the other hand, is both internally and mutually related to the other.

The in-itself is not what consciousness has to be, and thus consciousness can negate that it is the in-itself. But the other, as a consciousness, is what the self has to be. In the cogito, consciousness is aware that its consciousness appears as an object for another to examine. In recognizing the other, consciousness simultaneously both refuses to be a self-as-object and recognizes the other's similar refusal.[9]

My recognition of the other-as-object is a secondary and, in a sense, *a degraded awareness of him as subject.* In shame, pride, and fear, my first awareness is of a foreign freedom. On the basis of the other's intruding freedom for which I am not responsible, I then become explicitly aware of my freedom as *mine,* of my consciousness as a *my*self. But, recognizing myself as not-being the other, I also recognize him as related to my freedom and as capable of being limited by my possibilities. He then becomes, for me, a transcendence-transcended, an object within the world.

It is because of our emotions such as fear and shame that we attempt to turn the other-as-subject into the other-as-object. Our original awareness of the other is not a matter of judgment but an unreflective response to a foreign freedom. Thus, for Sartre, fear is fundamentally the awareness of our possibilities as transcended by the other's freedom. We continue to acknowledge this transcendence by the other, but then we fix his very transcendence of our possibilities, transcending it in turn by our freedom. We attempt to make of his freedom a property that our own more fundamental freedom can cope with and understand.

In a similar way, shame is the awareness of being fixed as an object by the other's subjectivity. We stand stripped of all our possibilities, of being more than this-one-before-the-keyhole. *Shame is the awareness of being before the other in such a way as to need the other to recapture the very consciousness and freedom he has stolen from us.* Again, I attempt to recapture my original innocence by viewing and attempting to manipulate the other's subjectivity as a property within his objectivity. I thus view his subjectivity and knowledge of me as only a reflection of what I allow him to see of me. Consequently, my shame becomes simply his relative and subjective knowledge of me, and I no longer feel ashamed before him whom I have now fixed as an object.

9. On the other hand, my very being, as not-being the other, demands that I assume this me-as-object in order to negate it and, conversely, that I bear witness that my simultaneous assuming and negating of myself as an object before the other is the very condition of my objectiveness.

Pride, which is based on the original shock of ourselves in shame before the other's freedom, attempts immediately to turn the other into an object. When I am proud, or vain, because of some personal quality or accomplishment, I recognize that I need the other to constitute my qualities and accomplishments as being objectively mine. Without the other, I would have no objectivity. But then I attempt to have the other freely acknowledge that these qualities are intrinsically mine and that I do not need him for the objectivity, or "objectiveness," of my accomplishments.

Pride, or vanity, thus is a mode of bad faith and is distinguished from the authentic modes fear and shame (my original awareness of the other-as-subject) and from the authentic mode, arrogance (my direct confrontation with the other's freedom).

It is clear that I turn the other into an object-in-the-world by degrading his subjectivity. This is the result of a lived, rather than speculative, encounter. In living, I discover the other's freedom either as a full freedom encountering or engaging the world or as a fixed freedom having its place in my world. His gestures and behavior are indeed part of the totality of the world; they do not refer to any hidden meaning, although I can always know more and more about them, since I understand their relation to the world as a whole, a whole that is an inexhaustible object of investigation. On the other hand, the other's subjectivity is forever removed from me, and his true transcendence and freedom are never revealed in his objectification.[10]

We must remember that through the look, I am aware of myself as objectivized and of the other-as-a-subject. This awareness, however, has the character of an absolute experience, an irreducible fact that cannot be deduced from the objectivity of the world or from the nature of the for-itself.

To assert that the for-itself as a being-for-others is an irreducible fact is to border on metaphysics. (Metaphysics, for Sartre, concerns itself with the "why" of existents, whereas ontology is limited to a description or explication of the structures of being as a whole.)

10. According to Sartre, the behaviorist's position must be reversed, for it is only because there is first consciousness as a subject that things have a relation to an end. Thus if the other can be compared to a machine, it is because a machine is already human.

Sartre rarely engages in metaphysics, but here he gives some metaphysical speculations concerning the existence of others. It is difficult to determine how seriously Sartre views his brief speculations concerning the origin of the self and the other. It may be useful, however, to summarize these metaphysical speculations.[11]

We have already noted that our own consciousness appears as the attempt to capture the escaping unity of ourselves. Our pre-reflective awareness of our existence appears as the attempt to remove the fundamental contingency of our existence. If I am aware that I exist, then to some extent, I take hold of my existence, I *ground* it, I make it to be, in some way, necessary. This is what Sartre calls the first ekstasis of the for-itself, the "leaping out" of consciousness by which consciousness *realizes* existence.

However, I fail in my attempt to be immediately conscious and at one with my existence. I am separated from myself by a nothingness.

Reflection, as the second ekstasis, appears as another attempt to justify my existence. When I reflect, I attempt to become aware of my awareness; I attempt to know and realize myself. But, again, the I-reflecting is not the I-reflected-on; I cannot capture my subjectivity.

Finally, the other, as the third ekstasis, appears as the last attempt to be that perfect unity of consciousness with itself that is the impossible synthesis of God. The other appears as the self whom I would know as I know myself. But again, this subject whom I now face is not myself. And in knowing the other, I fail to know him as a subject.

We can express this more accurately, although somewhat more abstractly, as follows:

1. Being-for-others appears as the third ekstasis of the for-itself. In the first diasporatic nihilation, the for-itself is the very failure to be a self-all-at-once, and thus the for-itself comes-to-be in the three temporal dimensions. The for-itself then attempts to recapture its fragmented unity by reflection, but this attempt also fails, since the for-itself never succeeds in becoming a self facing a self. Reflection thus appears, not as a separate reality

---

11. It is not clear whether Sartre believes he is actually giving metaphysical speculations or merely preparing the way for the meaning and possibility of such speculations.

added to the for-itself, but as another dimension of the for-itself's original nihilation from the in-itself. By reflection, the for-itself makes itself to be "dispersed" by a deeper nothing than its original nihilation from the in-itself, since the consciousness-reflecting and the consciousness-reflected-on tend to become independent. Finally, the for-itself attempts to recapture reflection's failure to be a self-aware-of-a-self by becoming a self facing the other-as-a-self. Once more the for-itself fails and causes a still deeper nothing to appear as a structure of its being. Now the for-itself is separated from the other by a mutual internal negation.

2. *The for-itself's relation to the other would seem to imply an upsurge of consciousness as a totality.* In one sense, Sartre agrees that this must be admitted. The multiplicity of for-itselves, as *my*selves, must be viewed as a synthetic unity: they have their being only by a mutual relation; and by their being-for-others, they reflect the attempt of being to be a consciousness. But as the other appears only as the further failure of the for-itself to be a self-consciousness-of-a-self, the totality "others" is made-to-be as a failure: the other is not the self-consciousness I would know. Also, the plurality "others" cannot be mediated by any higher mind or reason, since this mind would have to be included in the plurality that is being totalized.

3. *Thus the for-itself and the other both are and are not a part of the totality of being.* They are being's total effort and failure to be its own foundation. In a similar way, the for-itself has a contradictory relation to the other that cannot be resolved: either the for-itself through the look meets the other in certainty or through conceptual knowledge faces the other as a probable object in the world.

After these metaphysical speculations, Sartre concludes this chapter by noting that we must now study the body, since it is through the body that the for-itself is manifested to the other.

2
The Body

Throughout his work, Sartre has drawn our attention to the for-itself as a nihilation of the in-itself. Until now it has not been clear that, primarily, the body is the in-itself as nihilated. The body is not merely matter added to consciousness, nor is the body an obstacle to consciousness. Rather, the human reality, as a being-for-itself and as a being-for-others, is, simultaneously, totally consciousness and body. Nevertheless, there is an order of priority in the body as a being-for-itself and as a being-for-others. We will see that: (1) the body, as our past, is the concrete way of existing our facticity; (2) our attempts to objectify the other, by treating his body as one object among many objects, lead us to understand our body by an analogy with the other's body; and (3) our objectification of our body and the other's body is often an attempt to escape both from the fundamental alteration of our consciousness and from the radical alteration of our relation to the in-itself caused by the factual existence of others.

Thus, while in the abstract our body is primarily a being-for-itself, in the concrete our body is also our alienated outwardness, and it is our consciousness as the concrete center of possibilities in the midst of a world of other centers of possibilities. Consequently, Sartre describes the body as ontologically a being-for-others, while first noting that it is both a being-for-itself and an object of knowledge for ourselves and others. Sartre will generally follow, in his three sections below, the three propositions given above, although he realizes that each proposition is related to the others.

I. THE BODY AS BEING-FOR-ITSELF: FACTICITY

The body, as the specific nihilated in-itself, is the concrete source of quality, quantity, instrumentality, objective time, and all those transcendent nothings that make the in-itself a world. Clearly then, the world as a system of relations is directed toward the body as to their point of reference and origin of meaning. It also follows that consciousness cannot be viewed as surveying the world from some absolute vantage point or as witnessing the world as a system of absolute relations.[1]

Man, by his very nature, is a there-being, and conversely, the *there* comes-to-be through the diasporatic nature of the for-itself's nihilation of the in-itself. Once the for-itself is given as the nihilation of the in-itself, the for-itself must exist somewhere and a world must come-to-be in which things present some particular perspective to man's body.

A study of the senses will help us better understand the body as a being-for-itself and as facticity. For Sartre, the realist's model of the senses is contradictory. The realist first views his senses, such as sight and hearing, through his understanding of the other's senses. Anatomy teaches him to picture the eye as a very sophisticated camera. The eye, unless diseased, accurately records the objective colors and configuration of things. But since it is well known that subjects respond differently to "identical" stimuli, the realist concludes that

1. For Sartre, recent advances in physics also indicate the impossibility of an observer merely recording objective events in nature. Heisenberg has shown that the scientist can never be the uninvolved observer of the subatomic, since the light he uses so crucially affects the observation that he can never know the exact position and momentum of a particle. Indeed, he can never know whether he is observing a particle with an exact position and momentum, or a packet of waves. (The "position" of the particle would have to be revealed by light of very small wave lengths and, therefore, of such very high intensity as to move any particle that might be there.) For Sartre, this indeterminism does not indicate any failure in knowledge, but rather, that the original structures of space and motion have meaning only in relation to man's body.

the subject interprets the results recorded by the eye. Perception becomes a subjective response to objective information; the colors are merely in-itselfs that are subjectively interpreted. But then, Sartre objects, how do we know that all our observations about the other's and our own sense organs are valid? How do we guarantee our very contact with the world, since our sensations may be merely subjective states locked within a consciousness lacking intentionality?

Following his view of knowledge as consciousness' mode of presence to the in-itself, Sartre maintains that sense knowledge must be understood as an aspect of that original upsurge of consciousness by which the for-itself is not the in-itself. The sense of sight, for example, is the for-itself as not-being color, that is, the precise way that consciousness arises as being aware of color by not-being identified with color. In the for-itself's original upsurge as not-being color, this nihilation reciprocally brings to the in-itself the determination of color.

We have seen that not only is every determination a negation, but every negation results in a determination. It is the for-itself's internal negations as not-being color, sound, or odor that bring-to-be transcendent determinations of color, sound, or odor; for simultaneously as the for-itself arises as not-being color, the determined field of "things-to-be-seen" arises and a "world" comes-to-be.[2]

As aspects of the for-itself's being, the senses are facticities and thereby exhibit both necessity and contingency. First, there was no necessity that the for-itself arise as not-being color. Second, given this nihilation, the field of things-visible necessarily arises. But here again, there is a necessity-contingency relation. Things must appear to sight to be somewhere, although it is not necessary that they appear to be here rather than there. Furthermore, the for-itself can freely choose to look here or there.

The facticity of sense knowledge does not mean that the knowledge is relative. "Relative" can have meaning only in respect to some absolute possibility that is here completely lacking. Rather, a color-blind or totally deaf person is present differently to the world, and colors or sounds have a different relation to his body as centers of orientation and action. A color-blind or a deaf person is not merely a

2. See Part Two, Chapter Three, "Transcendence."

healthy person who lacks the ability to see or hear. His entire body and his presence to the world are modified by these absences; he is a *color-blind-person* or a *deaf-person*.

As is true with the senses, the whole body exhibits a twofold contingency-necessity relation, that is, a contingency-necessity-contingency relation: (1) the for-itself is contingent since it does not have-to-be; (2) granting the contingent upsurge of the for-itself, it is necessary that the for-itself be the nihilation of the in-itself, which is the body; (3) nevertheless, the body is then the very context of our free presence to the in-itself and our free projections to the future. The body is the primary contingency and unjustifiable "happening." But this pure event, if it is to remain a consciousness, must continue as that unmotivated nihilation that is the failure of the in-itself to be founded.[3]

The nature of action can also help us understand the body as being-for-itself. As with sensation, we usually attempt to interpret the nature of our own body as a tool by an analogy with another's body. Just as a cane and a hammer are instruments for the body's action, we look upon the other's legs and arms (and then our own) as the soul's instruments for walking and handling.

But if we conceive the body as one instrument among many, we face paradoxes similar to those we faced in the realist's interpretation of sensation. We must either explain how an immaterial soul can use a body or admit to another instrument between the soul and the body. The first approach leads us back to Descartes's unsuccessful attempt to solve the mind-body problem; the second leads us to an infinite regress. Furthermore, we are aware that only as an exception do we view our body as an instrument: if we had to pound a nail with our fist, we would indeed be aware of our hand as a tool.

Rather than first being aware of our body as an instrument and as an object, we live our body as the center of reference to which, and from which, the world has its concrete order. Things in the world form a complex of references in which the instrumentality, the place, and the perspective of things are essential. For example, each re-arrangement of furniture in a room results in certain things being

---

3. For a discussion of facticity as a contingency-necessity-contingency relation, see above, p. 204 and pp. 211–212.

more useful than others and in manifesting certain surfaces and perspectives. But to whom or to what are these references primarily ordered? If they were related to some pure mind that could know all the uses and surfaces of things at once from some absolute viewpoint, then their very reality as relations in the world would vanish. On the contrary, they must be ordered to something that is both the origin of their relations and that retains their reality as relations in the world. It is to the human reality as a body that the instrumentality, the place, and the perspective of things are ordered; and it is because the human reality is a body that these relations are transcendencies in the world and not merely ideas in the mind.[4]

Thus sensation and action lead us to understand what Sartre calls the "nature-for-me" of my body. It is because the for-itself arises as a body that the complex of references that is the world comes-to-be, and it is because I arise as this body that the world arises for me in this or that way. Again, the world arises for me in a particular way because the body-for-me is my immediate past from which my concrete possibilities arise; it is the origin of my concrete surpassings, the center of references and the point-of-view that distinguishes my daydreaming from those future projects that are my being. The body is my finitude and the origin and reality of the world's finitude. The body is my necessity of arising as always the future of a past, the nihilation of a fetus through birth. The body is my primary facticity and thus my primary way of being my contingency-necessity. It is the very way I "exist" my failure to be the foundation of my own being. We never apprehend this primary contingency of the body in its brute form. Even if we are born blind, we immediately assume our blindness as an obstacle to be overcome, something to be given in to, or something of which to be ashamed. Indeed, our body, as our very finitude, means that we must always be in some particular way and cannot choose ourselves "all at once." But since we cannot choose

---

4. If we read the earlier chapter on transcendence together with this section on the body, it seems that Sartre views the relation of the world to the body somewhat as the relation of pure formless matter to an *incarnate* Platonic form: the world is the in-itself as participating in that pure nihilation that is the body. But this analogy must be qualified since the body is also our being-for-others.

ourselves all at once, we must choose ourselves many times from many perspectives.

The body as our past is the very being of the pre-reflective cogito as it surpasses itself toward a future. The body is thus not known as an object; it is the origin of my point of view, but an origin on which I do not have a point of view. Things within my point of view are objects, but the body is not an object. Thus, while there is an objective relation between myself and other things, there is an existential relation between my consciousness and my body.

Sartre says that in describing the body, it would be best to indicate this immediate and nonreflective awareness of our body as the context for all our awarenesses of things by using the verb "to exist" (*exister*) as a transitive verb, saying that we "exist our bodies" (*existe son corps*).[5]

We "exist our body" in the sense that our body is our immediate past from which we flee the present toward our concrete possibles. As our immediate past, the body is neither an object of consciousness nor the nonthetic self-consciousness of the pre-reflective cogito. Rather, it is that which is "silently passed over" (*passe son silence*) as the mute origin and habitual context of our future.

The body, of course, can become an object of consciousness. Sartre illustrates the difference between the original unreflective awareness of our body and the derived, reflective awareness of it as an object by the difference between pain and illness.

The first awareness of pain is indistinguishable from the immediate awareness of the way we exist our body. This "coenesthesia," or immediate awareness of the affective quality of our body, is then immediately surpassed and engulfed in a project. For example, if our eyes are "paining," this pain is the very contingent way our consciousness exists our eyes.[6] But just as our immediate past is surpassed toward some future project, this pure pain is surpassed toward some goal of the for-itself, such as reading. This "surpassing," however, must not be understood to be on the level of reflection. Rather, just as our immediate past forms, by its internal relation to

5. EN, p. 394; BN, p. 329.
6. This pre-reflective awareness of pain or pleasure is often experienced when we are engaged in some activity and suddenly become aware that we *have been* in pain or pleasure, that is, that we have been doing this activity painfully or pleasurably.

the present and the future, a totality of the temporal ekstasis, so too, pure pain becomes united in the nonthetic totality, consciousness-of-painful-reading.

Nevertheless, in its very attempt to flee pain by nihilating it as a pure given, the givenness of pain reappears as an aspect of the in-itself. For example, the letters on the book become difficult to read. It is precisely on this level of consciousness existing its body that we see the reciprocal relation between the for-itself and the in-itself—the for-itself nihilating the in-itself and in turn being appropriated by the in-itself.

Now we are ready to consider the way reflection turns pain into "illness" (later we will see how further reflection turns the illness into "disease"). When I stop reading, I reflect on the fact that it is my eye that is hurting. I conceive of my eye as an object suffering or bearing the pain. I become aware of the pain, as "pulsating," as "sharp," as being on the "surface" of the eye or somewhere "deep" in the eye. The pain takes on a structure that is projected on the body as an in-itself. The body then becomes a psychic space in which such phenomena as pain or joy take place. The psychic space thus conceived is not arbitrary; it seems to come about by a kind of natural reflection of the for-itself on the body as an in-itself. It is the body as psychic, Sartre says, that somewhat justifies psychological theories of the unconsciousness.

But reflections on the body's affective states are primarily the for-itself's attempt to flee the immediate awareness of the body as my contingency. This awareness of my absolute contingency, or *coenesthesia*, reveals itself as "my taste," as my "nausea."

II. THE BODY-FOR-OTHERS

The body is also a being-for-others. We have seen, in the section on the look, that the for-itself is related to the other by an internal, mutual relation. This mutual relation enables me to understand how my body is a being-for-others through an examination of how the other's body is a being-for-me.

We must keep in mind that the other's body is not the primary manifestation of his being-for-me. It is through the look and my consciousness of being seen that the other's existence is revealed to me. On the contrary, the other's body is, for me, an aspect of my objectification of him.

But we must not conclude that the other's body is known as one thing among other things. Sartre, it will be recalled, began his section on the look by examining the distinctive characteristics of knowing the other as an object. Thus the man in the park was seen to be a point of view. And although I can transcend his body as a point of view, things as instruments still retain a secondary and oblique order of reference to him. In my pre-reflective point of view of the park bench and the trees, I am aware that they present a face away from me toward the other's body. The material nature of things, their multiplicity of aspects and utility, indirectly point to bodies other than mine. In turn, the totality of things with their relations to other bodies indicate my body to me. In this way I become reflectively aware of my body precisely as a point of view in a world of points of view.

Just as my own body is the necessary way in which I exist my contingency, the other's body-for-me is a revelation of the necessity of his contingency, the manifestation of the facticity of his transcendence, and the synthetic relation of the other as a body-in-a-situation. But this is not yet the other in his flesh and blood.

When Peter enters his room, his presence is no longer indicated indirectly by his chair and pipe; he is directly present in the way he exists his contingency, in his taste for himself that becomes for me his flesh. Sartre implies that there is a twofold awareness of the other's flesh. In the casual acquaintance of everyday life, the flesh-and-blood presence of the other would seem to be, for me, his explicit facticity and contingency known as an object. But in a long intimate acquaintance, there comes a time, Sartre notes, when there is an immediate apprehension and affective awareness of the precise taste of the other, the absolute contingency of the other that is his nausea.

Nevertheless, even in my reflective understanding of the other as an object, his body never becomes for me a thing. The body is the other's past, and as such it becomes for me the facticity of his transcendence and the context of his freedom as objectivized by me. As the other projects his own future from his immediate past, I project his body in terms of the objective future of the world and in terms of my own future.

The other's body is thus meaningful. According to Sartre, meaning is freedom as fixed and objectified. An aspect of this objectification of the other's freedom is to understand him as having a certain "character." In this way we give unity to the ensemble of his behavior. The other's character is his body-for-us, and although it is nothing mysterious or hidden, its complexity does not allow it to be easily known.

Strictly speaking, however, the other's body is not his total character or complete objectification by me. The other's body is the facticity of this objectivity; the body is the context of my transcending of his freedom. For example, I consider Peter to have a pleasant character because I view him as having a certain behavior pattern. This behavior pattern is a synthetic relation of his past and present bodily actions and gestures, together with my understanding of his possible future changes. His body, as his immediate past, is thus the facticity of the totality of my objectification of him; it is the given in the light of which I interpret his freedom. And what is true of the other's body in relation to me is also true of my body in relation to him.

III. THE THIRD ONTOLOGICAL DIMENSION
OF THE BODY

In the first "dimension," consciousness exists its body as its facticity, as its immediate past, as the necessary mode of its contingency. In the second dimension, our body is known and used by the other just as we know and use his body. But these two dimensions are intimately connected. Consciousness is radically affected by the existence of the other, and this change in consciousness affects the way we exist our bodies. Thus in the third "dimension," we exist our bodies as that which is known by the other.

It is in the relation of our consciousness to our body-for-others that Sartre sees some foundation in the traditional distinction between an "inner" and an "outer" of the human reality and in those theories that call attention to the unknown or unconscious aspects of man. But we must be careful to understand this correctly lest we see in it a betrayal of the phenomenological method.

Sartre's thesis seems to be as follows: Primarily, consciousness is for-itself and the body is the precise way in which consciousness exists its facticity. On this level, there is no hidden outwardness, or unknown. The human reality is for-itself. But because of the existence of the other, a radical and essential modification occurs in consciousness. Through the look, we are aware of ourselves as being seen, and there surges up within consciousness the awareness that we have an outer.

But our outwardness escapes us for two reasons. First, the other, who sees and knows us, is a subject with a freedom that we can never know and see. And with his freedom, he transcends our freedom and future projections in a way that we can never know. Our outwardness thus escapes us, but not completely, since we acknowledge that it is *our* outwardness and that we are responsible for it. Second, we recognize a multiplicity of others and a complexity of relations between these others. We recognize that we exist in-the-midst-of-the-world, which we can never fully know.

At first, the existence of others seems to radically modify only my consciousness and to leave my body as that which is existed by me and merely known by the other. But this is to fail to remember that our body is the very facticity of our consciousness. Insofar as the other intimately touches our consciousness, he affects the way we exist our body. We exist our body for-ourself, but as that which is known by him. There thus arises an outwardness and an unknown aspect to our body.

The body's outwardness arises on two levels. Pre-reflectively, we experience our body as the precise mode in which we exist our being-for-others. It is our body that is seen and judged by the other's freedom; nevertheless, we are simultaneously aware that it is not a mere thing that the other sees as our body. He sees, as we do, the lived body, the flesh, that is the absolute contingency of a free subject. We then become pre-reflectively aware of being alienated from our body, since it is our exterior as judged by innumerable freedoms that escape us.

Through language, I attempt to regain something of my alienated body. Language is the means by which I attempt to relearn my body as it is for-others. This occurs only after I have first learned to know the other's body through language. Thus, Sartre insists, we reflectively know our own body only after first knowing conceptually the other's body. Before this, my alienation from my body was lived without any concepts intervening. Then, as we learn to know the other's senses as organs for knowing and his body as an instrument of his consciousness, we likewise learn to understand our senses and our body in this manner. The attempt, therefore, to understand our body as an instrument is not wrong, although it must be placed as a derived act of knowing and not the prototype of understanding our body.

Sartre concludes this section by returning to his discussion of pain and illness. Pain is the immediate way we exist our body—for example, our stomach. We then reflect on the recurrence of these pains and understand them as caused by an illness. But now our conceptual knowledge of the other turns this illness into a being-for-others, a disease. We learn to interpret our pain in the stomach as an ulcer by picturing the structure of the stomach—the stomach not as lived by us but as objectivized by the other. Even when we do not feel the pain, we conceive of our stomach as a thing-in-itself that can be injured and damaged by eating wrong foods or by worry. We comport our life in relation to our stomach as to some mysterious given that others must reveal to us.

Because the knowledge of our body as an instrument and as capable of illness is reflective, this does not mean that we should abandon the analogical studies of the body; rather we should realize that these are derivitive apprehensions of the body that never give us the lived body as we exist it but as it is a being-for-others. In a similar way, the difficulties that arise from the fact that our body can, at times, be an object for us must also be put in their proper place. The fact that we can see and feel our hand does not mean that we begin our study of our body as an object of knowledge. Indeed, there is no reason why a living organism must have senses that can be turned on its own body. This is purely the contingent way in which consciousness exists its facticity. But even when the right hand touches the left hand (or if the right eye could see the left eye), the one hand is always a knower and the other the known.

The body is thus the concrete facticity of our being-for-itself as affected by our being-for-others. The body is the context of our concrete relations with others, a subject that will be examined in the next chapter.

3

Concrete Relations with Others

Chapter Three is one of the most readable chapters in the book. Here Sartre's descriptive genius is most evident and telling, and the reader is urged to consult the rich nuances in the original text.

According to Sartre, we can have two opposed relations with the other. We can either attempt to assimilate the other's freedom into our freedom while simultaneously trying to preserve his freedom and our otherness; or we can attempt to reduce his freedom into an object. Both projects fail because each implies the other. Thus, in the very attempt to preserve the other's freedom, there is the danger of making this freedom into an object, since *we* wish to preserve it. On the other hand, if we make the other into an object, we recognize in this objectivized freedom the freedom of a subject.

Each basic relation with the other is subdivided by Sartre, and further relations exist between these subdivisions. In general, the basic relations exist either in good faith or in bad faith, and the for-itself must constantly use its freedom to continue in either relation. The immediate reason for the instability of these relations is that our relations with the other are always a conflict. Sartre, as we will see, does not deny that we often engage in cooperative enterprises, but he sees our efforts at cooperation both as based upon the more basic attitudes of conflict and as unable to eliminate conflict totally. Sartre's insistence on conflict does not result from a historical analysis of man's inability to cooperate with his fellowman, but on his insistence that each for-itself is freedom.

I. FIRST ATTITUDE TOWARD OTHERS: LOVE, LANGUAGE, MASOCHISM

It is, Sartre notes, entirely arbitrary which basic attitude we examine first, and love must not be considered to have any priority over the basic attitudes to be examined in the next section. Each attitude is the very being of the for-itself in its original upsurge as a nihilation and as a relation. The for-itself is relational, and the ideal of love is another attempt by the for-itself to found its being and remove the absolute contingency of its existence.

We have seen that in the first ekstasis, the for-itself is the very failure of a self to found its being and the failure of a consciousness to be totally aware all-at-once. This failure is the for-itself's temporal "spread." Reflection is a second attempt and failure of the for-itself to capture its diasporatic being and be a consciousness at one with its being. In the third ekstasis, the for-itself again attempts and fails to found its being by arising as a *my*self facing a self-as-other.[1] *Love, as a system of projects, aims at the ideal of overcoming this last failure of man to make, in some way, his existence necessary.*

In love, I aim at obtaining from my beloved a free and absolute acknowledgment of my being. For my beloved, I would not be a contingent, unjustifiable upsurge; I would have my facticity canonized and my total being acknowledged—as by God—as that-which-was-meant-to-be.

In love, I desire the beloved freely to return to me my very objectification that came-to-be by my relation to the other. The beloved will redeem me from my original fall, which is my exteriorization before the other; and the beloved, as the other, will unite me with my alienated self, freely returning to me the free and hidden evaluation of my exteriorized being. Because of the beloved, I am not a tool. The beloved's look makes me into that unique center and origin from which all things have their meaning and value.

1. See pp. 167–168.

The project of love is to possess the very freedom and subjectivity of the beloved in such a way as to keep it free; it is only by a freedom totally dedicated to my freedom that my absolute contingency can be removed. The project of love is therefore to be loved. But how can the lover obtain the beloved's free love?

Since two subjectivities can never meet, it is only through the lover's objectivity that the lover can beguile and seduce the beloved's freedom and subjectivity. The lover thus attempts to become for the beloved the object of fascination: the perfect in-itself revealed by the captured nothingness and freedom of the beloved. In love, fascination aims at eliciting from the beloved the free surrender of freedom and transcendencies.

It is clear that the ideal of love carries within it the seeds of its own failure. Since to love is to wish to be loved, the beloved can love only by wishing to be loved. Thus the beloved also aims at seducing the lover's freedom; and the beloved seeks to be the same unique center of meaning and value as the lover. The project of love can continue because the lover does not realize that the beloved has the same project.

The seduction of the beloved's freedom is, for Sartre, one manifestation of language. Language, in this basic sense, is not a pattern of terms; it is our behavior and gestures as a proof of our being-for-others. By the look, our immediate awareness of ourselves as being seen, our acknowledgment of and reaction to our externalized self spontaneously arises. Through language, I attempt to learn how I am objectified before the other and thus regain my alienated self. Through language, I attempt to cope with a self that is no longer the simple nihilation of the in-itself, but which is now the nihilation of the in-itself before the other, the arising of a self as a *myself* in-the-midst-of-the-world.

Masochism, for Sartre, may arise from the realization that seduction, as a language, can never succeed, since the beloved is using the same mode of language on the lover. This realization can lead to the despair of possessing the freedom of the other and a new project of relinquishing our freedom before the other's freedom.

In masochism, we reverse the attempt of becoming an object of fascination before the other and attempt to become an object of fascination for ourselves. We attempt to become identified with our own objectification before the other. We wish to be nothing but our objectivity and would totally surrender our freedom to the other. We willingly acknowledge the other to be truly free and ourselves to be the other's mere instrument. Masochism, Sartre declares, is a type of vertigo before the other's freedom.

But as with love, the ideal of masochism also fails. First, I recognize that my objectivized self remains alienated from me precisely because it is myself as before the other's freedom. Second, I am aware that I am using the other in my attempt to make him acknowledge me as a mere thing. I am thus thrown back upon my own subjectivity and upon my masochism as an original project of my own transcendence.

Although both love and masochism result in the for-itself's failure to be united with the other, and although each is a conflict of freedoms, nevertheless, Sartre hints at fundamental differences between the two. The masochist, from the very beginning, is well aware of his failure to lose his subjectivity in the other. It is this very failure that he then begins to seek and enjoy.

It is as an enjoyment of failure that masochism is a vice and distinguished from love, which, as a goal, seems to be a project of good faith doomed to failure because of the nature of the for-itself as a nihilation and failure.

II. SECOND ATTITUDE TOWARD OTHERS: INDIFFERENCE, DESIRE, HATE, SADISM

The origin of the second attitude toward the other is the attempt to confront the other's freedom directly rather than to try to appropriate it within our freedom. But we are immediately disappointed in our attempt to engage the other's freedom directly. To reach the other at the moment he is directing his freedom to us, we must look at the other's look, thereby converting that look into the object of a looked-at-look. We then find ourselves in the position of confronting the other's freedom only through his objectivity.

In the attitude of indifference, however, we do not attempt to engage the other's freedom directly; rather, the original project of our being is to treat the other as an object. In this "blindness," my being and original choice are identified in the project of ignoring the other's subjectivity. I attempt to become a practical solipsist.

Although indifference, as a state of bad faith, can continue for years, its self-contradictory nature will lead not only to rude awakenings but also to an uneasy struggle with unacknowledged freedom. For to the extent that I make others into objects, I am all the more thrown back upon myself as pure freedom and as totally responsible for my being. Nevertheless, I am simultaneously aware that I have been born and that my birth is before the other. Furthermore, while I have immediately made the other's look into a looked-at look, I am still implicitly aware of being seen by other subjects. *I am thus led to anxiety, which I attempt to cope with by explicitly turning the other into an instrument of my freedom.* But now I have endangered my delicate state of indifference to the other.

As indifference is the original attempt to eliminate the subjectivity of the other, sexual desire, according to Sartre, is the original attempt to get hold of the other's subjectivity in his objectivity. "Sex" is, in the sense of sexual desire, thus an ontological structure of the for-itself's relation to the other. The fundamental nature of sex does not mean that it can be deduced from the abstract being of the for-itself. Sex is indeed facticity, but it is not thereby a secondary structure added to consciousness. Just as the factual existence of the other radically modifies consciousness, the de facto arising of consciousness as desire radically alters our relation to the other.

Sexual desire is therefore more fundamental than sex organs or particular sex behavior, and therefore sex exists in the very young and the very old. Sex is our very desire for the other and our awareness that we are desirable before the other.

As a mode of consciousness, sexual desire can be examined as an intentionality, that is, reciprocally, as an *awareness* and as an *object*. From the viewpoint of its object, desire is neither toward a sexual act nor toward pleasure. Pleasure is the reflective and learned awareness of the relief and reward of desire. It is learned that a pleasure is connected with this act and the pleasure now reflectively becomes the object of desire. Desire thus reflectively becomes its own object as that which regulates pleasure.

From the viewpoint of its *object*, desire, however, is originally a mode of the pre-reflective cogito and is the desire of a body. The body is pre-reflectively desired not as a mere thing or machine but as the facticity of a consciousness. We may desire a person who is asleep, but normally not one who is dead.

From its viewpoint as an *awareness,* desire is a particular way of existing our body. Normally the body is existed as the facticity and context of our future projections; it is existed as that which is "silently passed over" and nihilated in the upsurge of consciousness as pure translucency and concrete nothing. In desire, however, we "exist our bodies" more intimately with our consciousness, and consequently, we exist our consciousness itself as "troubled." Consciousness is sluggish and heavy, and no longer the clear flight toward the future. Rather, consciousness chooses itself as body. Desire is indeed an appetite toward the other's body, but it is lived as a vertigo before our own body.

We can now begin to understand desire as a totality. It is, Sartre says, the very attempt to make ourself *flesh* in the presence of the other's flesh. Usually the body is not experienced as the pure contingency of presence, but rather is normally absorbed in that organized totality, the facticity of the for-itself in a situation. Desire, however, attempts to strip the body of its relation to a more-than-presence that is the freedom of the other.

The language that desire uses to lead the other to choose its body is the caress. Through caresses, the lover attempts to draw the beloved to choose its body as flesh; and further, the lover uses the beloved's becoming as flesh to draw the lover further into its own body as flesh.

We are now in a position to understand desire as an original way in which the for-itself chooses itself before the other and in relation to the other. First, we must recognize that although desire is primarily a relation to the other, it is not therefore an incidental structure of consciousness but the way consciousness chooses itself in the world before the other. We therefore return to desire as a consciousness existing in heaviness. Desire affects our relations with everything. We no longer willingly look at things as the instruments of our free projects or at the world itself as the facticity of our future projections. Rather, we wish to be immersed in the world. Our attempt to strip our body of its future as beyondness is simultaneously an attempt to strip the world of any relation to a future.

Primarily, however, desire is a way of coping with the other's freedom through an objectivity. Normally, through the look, the other's subjectivity totally escapes us, and the body that one leaves before our eyes is but the silent origins of its unknown future projections. By desire, however, we attempt to have others freely limit themselves to their bodies and become the fleshly incarnation of freedom. In this way, the other's subjectivity will have become identified with its facticity and objectivity. Thus the true goal of desire is to possess the other's body precisely as this body is possessed by the other's freedom. But to choose the other as a body possessed by freedom is to choose ourselves in the same way. Thus our consciousness is disturbed because it is involved in a "magical language" in which our flesh attempts to beguile others to choose themselves as flesh.

Sexual desire, however, can never achieve its true goal. Our desire to possess the incarnated freedom before us leads us to take hold of the other's body and to attempt to appropriate it within our body. Now our body becomes the instrument of taking the other's body, our caresses turn into holds, and the delicate game of fascinating ourself and others within our body is upset. As we attempt to seize the other's body, our body becomes the mere tool of an intention of having each other. Our freedom thus escapes our prison and sexual desire degenerates into a frenzy of activity in which the original purpose has been forgotten.

The failure of desire can lead to sadism. The sadist experiences a troubled consciousness, but he is unwilling or embarrassed to admit that the meaning and value of his heaviness is the incarnation of the other's freedom through his own incarnated freedom. He persists in the partial goal of desire, the other's incarnation, while rejecting his own goal as incarnation. The sadist, Sartre notes, wants a nonreciprocal sexuality. He wishes the other to be incarnated before himself as pure freedom and is, therefore, led to use force rather than caresses to bring about the other's incarnation.

Strictly speaking, the sadist wishes the other to be incarnated differently than in sexual desire. He seeks the obscene, which is a certain kind of ungracefulness. In grace, the body constantly keeps its orientation to the future. Each movement appears as giving meaning to the previous movements, as being the natural and necessary consequent of the preceding movements, while still projecting toward a somewhat unpredictable future movement. Again, when this new movement occurs, it is seen as fitting into a natural synthetic totality that once more hints at a natural but unpredictable act about to come. The supreme test of grace is the nude body whose subtle movements invisibly cover its totally exposed flesh.

In the obscene act, however, a break appears in the body's relation to the future, a *nothing* slips into the totality of the bodily movements, and the flesh suddenly appears as simply *there,* moving with the natural laws of gravity—the legs or thighs moving no longer as part of the totality of a body in a situation, but as isolated folds of flesh.

The sadist aims at the obscene in order to strip the body of its grace, reducing it to a thing to capture within this thing the other's freedom. Unlike desire, in which freedom envelopes and incarnates the body as flesh, sadism aims at revealing flesh as capturing and containing freedom. The use of torture and pain to bring the other to renounce all that he cherishes reduces the body to a flesh that is this very enslaved freedom.

Sadism, as a project, must fail for two basic reasons. First, to the extent that the sadist succeeds in reducing the other's flesh to a mere thing, the flesh appears in the world as totally useless. The sadist either becomes disoriented by this useless spectacle or becomes "troubled" and desires it sexually. Second, and more basically, the sadist sees his failure in the very look of the other. Then he realizes that the other is still the alienated freedom and subjectivity that brings-to-be a "world" in which his own project of sadism has its very meaning.

The failure of desire, therefore, leads to either masochism or sadism, depending on whether we attempt to be absorbed in the other's freedom or have the other yield to our freedom. Furthermore, the failure of either masochism or sadism leads back to desire, and there is no way of breaking the circle of our relations with the other except by a pleasure that kills all passions without satisfying them.[2]

Thus all our efforts to cope with the other's freedom, whether

2. But, to repeat, Sartre still maintains a distinction between bad- and good-faith attitudes toward the other.

directly in its full subjectivity, as in love, or indirectly through its objectivity, as in desire, are doomed to failure. Each fundamental attitude can be the birth of the other and, in general, we continually slide from attempting to manage the other-as-object to confronting the other-as-subject. These basic attitudes are of course never found in their pure simplicity; they are modified by the individual's historicity and facticity, or to be more accurate, they are always chosen in a concrete form. But basically, we are always in a relation of conflict with the other, and as we will see, even our attempts to cooperate with the other never overcome these basic attitudes of conflict.

No matter how we attempt to handle the other's freedom, we are always led to use it and are thus always guilty before the other. Even if we try to help the other by providing him with comforts, by removing tyranny and injustice, we are still attempting to determine his freedom. He can no longer be the heroic resister or noble martyr. Thus, from the very moment of our existence, we put limits on the other's freedom and force him to become engaged in a world not of his choosing.

The conscious awareness of our unsuccessful attempts to relate to the other's freedom may lead us to freely seek the death of the other in the fundamental attitude of hate. The one who truly hates is disturbed, not by any particular trait in the other, but by the other's mere existence. *Although he may seek the death of only one person, he is really seeking to be a for-itself totally free from others.*

But hate, too, is doomed to failure and despair. For even if all others were to be successfully removed from existence, they still would have existed, and the being of the one who hates would be eternally a being-that-had-been-for-others.

III. "BEING-WITH" (*Mitsein*) AND THE "WE"

Sartre agrees with Heidegger that we do indeed collaborate with others and are conscious of ourselves as a "we." He denies, however, that Heidegger's description of "being-with" indicates a fundamental structure of the human reality. For Sartre, the "we" appears as either an object or a subject. The "we-object" or "us" is a true but secondary modification of our consciousness; it is a more complex form of our relation to the other through the look. The "we-subject," on the other hand, is a purely psychological apprehension of our cooperation with others. Following Sartre, we will first consider the "us."[3]

A. THE "US"

The experience of the "us" arises when the for-itself is aware that its original relation to the other is now modified by relations to the *"detotalized-totality"* humanity, that is, *a totality that can never be truly witnessed and formed into a synthetic whole by a consciousness divorced from the totality.* The detotalized-totality "humanity" is thus the background of the for-itself's relations to the other.

For Sartre, the background "humanity" can be examined more clearly if we limit our attention to the prototype, the for-itself's relation to the other in the presence of a "third." Although there are clearly many ways in which the presence of a third can modify our relation to the other, they eventually lead to the for-itself joining with the other either as a "we" or as an "us." The clearest example of the us-relation occurs when I am either in conflict or cooperating with another in some communal work and a third person appears as a witness to our conflict or cooperation. If, for example, I am defending myself against another's attack (the other) and a third appears, I am immediately aware of my conflict as objectivized before the look of the third. My "outside" is no longer the simple alienation of my objectification before the other's look. I now pre-reflectively and nonthematically (that is, not as an object) recognize my objectification as forming a totality with the other's behavior and I am aware that I am responsible for this totality.

In a similar way, class consciousness occurs when I assume my objectiveness as forming a synthetic totality with others before the look of "thirds"—for example, governmental officials. Indeed, it is in their look that I see my objectification with my fellowmen come into existence. It is before their freedom that I see my freedom transcended and made into the complex of dead possibilities that is the

3. As Hazel Barnes notes (BN, p. 444, n. 16), the French term *nous* can mean either "we" or "us." But in English, "we-subject" and "us-object" are redundant. Therefore, I will refer simply to the "us" and the "we."

relation of my freedom as objectified with other freedoms as objectified. I find my possibility not within my ability to transcend the in-itself, but as a possibility "out-there," limited and defined by innumerable other possibilities. I am humiliated and impotent before this world, for which I must nevertheless assume responsibility to the extent that I allow myself to come-to-be with others, before the thirds.

As with our being-before-the-other, the us-relation does not depend on the concrete existence of a particular *third*. By the mere fact that we are pre-reflectively aware of existing with many others, we are also aware that we *can* be united with them before a third. We are further aware of the possibility of considering ourselves as united with all men. But to the extent that we consider "humanity," or "all men," to be a completed totality, we are considering a mere abstract ideal that has no concrete meaning. For the totality mankind could exist only before some witness separated from humanity, such as God. "Humanity" will always have to be the detotalized-totality in which one group is united before another group as a third who witnesses and gives the group its unity as an "us."

B. THE "WE"

Our cooperation with others as subjects that use and control matter is revealed to us through the world of artifacts. A common subway map or railroad timetable reveals that we are using objects constructed by other men and that our future projections in some way involve the union with others as subjects. But for Sartre, there are two basic reasons why this we-relation is fundamentally different from the us-relation.

First, the we-relation does not presuppose any ontological modification of our relation to others. We have seen that the us-relation does indeed modify our very objectification before the other. It is true that this objectivity is finally reduced to the two basic attitudes of regarding the third as a subject or, in revolt, turning him into an object. But given our upsurge with the other before the third, we must recognize our objectivity as forming a new synthetic totality in which our free projections must now be involved.

The we-relation, on the other hand, does not affect our objectivity. We can use and transcend the complex of artifacts for our own purposes without our freedom becoming formally involved with the freedom of others. Thus I do not have to consider myself as a cooperating subject with the person who made the timetable. (Nor do I have to consider myself as part of a wished-for unity of humanity mastering nature.) In fact, I can use the timetable merely as a sheet of paper to wedge under a loose door. Furthermore, artifacts refer to me only in a very impersonal way: I am an anonymous person who should read the table as follows. . . . Indeed I can choose to become very personally involved with an enterprise indicated by an artifact, but this merely shows that the we-relation is a purely subjective modification and that it has no necessary ontological correlate.

Second, the we-relation, as a relation "with," presupposes the other as already given. If I am working with another, then this relation is already given on the more fundamental awareness that I am not the other. Also, I can recognize something as an artifact only if I already have the awareness that other consciousnesses exist. In a purely solipsistic world, an artifact would appear merely as one thing among many things. The we-relation is thus much weaker than the us-relation.

We can now conclude the discussion of the for-itself's concrete relations with others by noting that the for-itself is not simply the nihilation of the in-itself and a flight toward its own future. This flight, indeed, brings-to-be those nothings by which the in-itself comes-to-be as a thing, that is, as what-is-there. But through the other's look, the in-itself begins to recapture the for-itself's flight. The other externalizes the for-itself as that which exists and is seen among other things. The other makes the for-itself to be not only in a world but in-the-midst-of-the-world.

Nevertheless, Sartre notes that he is not at the end of his description of the for-itself's relation to the in-itself and cannot therefore give a general theory of being. He declares that he must begin to study something that Heidegger has overlooked in his description of being, namely, the being of action.

For Sartre, it is not incidental that the for-itself modifies the in-itself through action.[4] And he now investigates how and why man acts.

---

4. But, in the following chapters, Sartre himself does not examine, to any great extent, how the for-itself alters the in-itself. In fact, in the Conclusion (see p. 230), he suggests that it should be left to the metaphysician to examine the question of how action can alter being-in-itself.

HAVING, DOING, AND BEING

In the last part, Part Four, Sartre examines the relation of "doing" (*faire:* to do, or to make) and "having" (*avoir*) to the being (*l'être*) of the human reality. Knowledge is a form of having, and action is a mode of doing. The question is whether the modes of having and doing in some way flow from man's nature or, rather, from his fundamental choice of existence. Sartre's answer is clear. All of man's actions and possessions are modes of his being that reflect his fundamental choice of existence.

This fourth part complements Sartre's earlier description of bad faith as a choice of one's being.

1

Being and Doing: Freedom

In this chapter, Sartre brings together many of his earlier conclusions to focus on a concrete analysis of freedom. We have seen that the human reality is nihilation and that nihilation is freedom. Specifically, this nihilation and failure is the upsurge of nothing within a body, the birth of the for-itself, and the making-to-be of facticity. Finally, as nihilation and nothing, man is totally free and responsible for his being.

I. FREEDOM: THE FIRST CONDITION OF ACTION

Sartre begins the first—lengthy, but generally easily readable—section by reviewing his earlier conclusions about intentionality and negation. Then, after an examination of the traditional understanding of will, emotions, reasons, and motives of actions, he reaches an understanding of freedom as the original choice of the for-itself, the ekstatic nihilation in which will, emotion, reason, and motive arise and have their meaning.

Sartre reminds us that every truly human action is intentional. The difference between accidentally taking another's coat and stealing it is the difference between not intending and intending the end of appropriating the coat. But since the end or purpose of our intentional actions exists only in the future, intentionality presupposes a detachment and a separation from what is intended.

In general, one does not act until one sees something missing. The worker who lives as if his condition were his very being does not, Sartre notes, think of revolt. And if he considers a life better than his own, it is only in an abstract way as the life suited to the other. However, the moment he is awakened to the real possibility of new conditions for his life, he adopts a different attitude toward his being: he begins to view and live his present conditions as unbearable and is now ready for and capable of action. Clearly then, we act only when we nihilate and surpass the fullness of being toward the concrete nonbeing of our future.

But we must now begin a more concrete description of freedom. Freedom is often thought of as a struggle between the will and the emotions. The brave soldier uses his willpower to overcome his fear; the coward gives in to his fear. In this way, the emotions are viewed as latent forces that arise spontaneously in a given situation.

Sartre rejects this view of a battle between the will and the emotions. First, it leads to an inadmissible division within the for-itself. The for-itself would have to be viewed as having a pure mind and will that act on its body and passions. Second, this view fails to realize that passions themselves are intentional. Fear is always fear of *something* and has meaning only within a wider project of the for-itself. A soldier fears battle only if he wants to live; a worker fears losing his job only because of what this loss means in the future to himself and his family. Therefore, passions are themselves affected with *nothing* and arise by the for-itself's nihilation.

Consequently, we are led to take a new look at the for-itself as passion and as will. The very being of the for-itself, as nihilation, means that the ends of the for-itself must be of its own making. The for-itself arises as the temporal ekstasis in which the in-itself is negated as the immediate past, fled from as the present, and fulfilled as meaning in light of the projected future. The entire being of the for-itself is its projection from the in-itself. "Will" and "passion" are thus modes and manifestations of the for-itself's original being as nihilation and freedom. The for-itself "chooses" its being as passionate or deliberate; it projects itself as body or intellect, as immersed in the activity of the present or calmly attending to the future. Thus our free choice, which is our being, is not the result of a deliberation; it precedes and gives the context of all our deliberations.

In a similar way, the usual distinction between the reason and the motive of an action is rather the manifestation of a more fundamental freedom.[1] The "reason" for an act is generally understood to be the objective understanding of the situation: historians give "reasons" for the behavior of rulers and the outbreak of wars. In this way, Sartre notes, one can give as a reason for Clovis's conversion to Catholicism his desire to be favored by the hierarchy. Nevertheless, this desire to be favored emerges as a reason for Clovis's action only in the light of his purpose of conquering Gaul. If Clovis had had some other intention in mind, the episcopate's power could have been a reason for not converting. Thus, while the power of the hierarchy is indeed objective, this objectivity becomes a reason for action only in the light of a chosen end.

If, on the other hand, we are searching for the "motives" of Clovis's conversion, we are, according to the usual interpretation, after the deep subjective psychological forces that moved him to act this way: his ambition or, perhaps, simply his impulsiveness. The ideal of a perfectly free and deliberate act is thus viewed as one in which the subject has conquered his own motives and acts purely out of reasons.

According to Sartre, this usual explanation of the relation of reasons to motives fails to take into account that an objective situation is a reason only in the light of the more fundamental choice of the for-itself. Clovis's intention of conquering Gaul is not distinct from his ambition; and this ambition is not a subjective drive unconsciously moving him but a choice of his being, his way of nihilating the givens in the face of others. The true "motive" is nothing but Clovis's being as it reveals the world to him in a certain way.

In general, the "motive" is our pre-reflective and nonthetic project

1. Hazel Barnes translates *mobile* as "motive" and *motif* as "cause," noting that the latter is inadequate and possibly misleading. Since Sartre himself says here that *motif* means the reason for an act, we will distinguish reason from motive. In either translation, the context makes the meaning clear. It should be noted that the French *mobile* has the connotation of "mover" and that "motive" here signifies the inner subjective "movers" of a human action.

in the light of which the in-itself is revealed as reasons for our actions. We are, however, anticipating our analysis, since not every motive is the fundamental freedom of the for-itself. There are many secondary motives that, after they are lived, become objects of reflection, and it is these dead motives that the psychologist usually studies.

We are now in a position to return briefly to our earlier consideration of the will and the passions. Insofar as the will implies a deliberation or a "voluntary" act, it is reflective and consequent upon our more basic unreflective freedom, which is our motive. When we deliberate, the choice has already been made to act in accordance with reasons rather than to give ourselves to that spontaneity of action that is passion. Deliberation concerns only the means to an end, and since the end, to give ourselves to reflection, has already been chosen, Sartre notes, the "chips are down" when we begin to deliberate.

Consequently, the fundamental freedom of the for-itself is its very reality as a free project in relation to the in-itself and others. While this project, or choice of being, is not a deliberation, it is not thereby unconsciousness, but unreflective. It is the pre-reflective cogito seen as a project toward a goal and is the very ekstatic nature of the for-itself as a temporal spread in which reasons and secondary motives, will and passion, come-to-be. Since this fundamental freedom is the origin of all secondary motives and reasons, it is unmotivated but not capricious. It is the very being of the for-itself as it makes a world to-be-there and reveals the in-itself as reasons for action.

In the light of this fundamental freedom, Sartre gives a special meaning to the freedom of a particular act. He begins with a "theoretical" discussion.

Consider, he states, my decision to rest when on a hiking expedition with friends. The determinists are right when they see that this decision is always given in the context of reasons and motives. However, they erroneously conclude that my act could not have been otherwise than it was. It is true that my act had to fit into the complex of reasons and secondary motives that surrounded it; but it is also true that certain things were reasons and motives for me because of the fundamental way I choose my being. Indeed, assuming myself and my companions to be in the same physical condition, I may have chosen to exist my body in relation to the world and others differently from my companions. Consequently, before I am aware of my fatigue as an object of reflection, "I exist it" differently than do my companions. For example, my project may be to exist myself as body, to abandon myself to facticity, and to delight in the pleasures of the body. My companions, however, may exist their bodies as a means of attaining a union with nature. They are related differently to their fatigue, enjoying and throwing themselves into their surroundings, conquering and appropriating the hills and landscape that their fatigued eyes and bodies are approaching. It is therefore useless for them to tell me that I could go on. Of course I could—but only at the price of changing my fundamental project of being.

Sartre, consequently, agrees with Freud that each individual act has, as it were, layers of meaning. Our decision to rest, if properly analyzed, will reveal our fundamental project. He disagrees with Freud that this fundamental project is unconscious or determined by something that happened in the past. Rather, we arrive at the meaning of our actions not by going back to our childhood, but by revealing, to the reflective consciousness, the present, unreflective, free choice of our being. The way we behave, dress, or decorate our room reveals to us our choice of being. The past, indeed, gives us the facticity of our freedom, but the past is not our freedom. As we will see in the following section, although we must relate to our parents and our particular environment, we are absolutely free in how we relate to these givens.

The preceding analysis of freedom is very abstract. In the concrete, Sartre is aware that our individual acts are not so easily and necessarily connected with our fundamental project. Our acts are related to our fundamental project, not as a conclusion to a premise, but as a partial structure to a totality. Gestalt psychology has shown that totalities can absorb certain modifications without changing the basic form, as certain lines added to a sketch may not change its basic appearance as a face. In a similar way, certain varieties can occur within our primitive project. Furthermore, there is no a priori or objective way of judging what is secondary or primary, since I am the one who gives weight to my motives.

Our capability of performing actions contrary to our primitive project leads back to our earlier discussion of bad faith. It is clear that in bad faith we consciously commit actions that are against our original project while attempting consciously to deceive ourselves, often successfully, about our choice of being. Thus we can attempt to cure ourselves of stuttering, and we may succeed, while maintaining the very project of inferiority that brought the stuttering to be. The proof is that the inferiority complex will manifest itself in new symptoms.

Indeed, to choose to be inferior is simultaneously to choose to be in bad faith. Inferiority is not the modest contentment to be average and unnoticed. It is a restlessness, signifying a constant reflective appraisal of ourselves in shame and bitterness, for we desire to see ourselves unjustly penalized by our environment and heritage. We desire our own anger and seek to have it confirmed to us. If we go to an analyst, it is to confirm both that we have done all that we can do to help ourselves and that nature has cursed us. If, unwittingly, the analyst should bring us to face up to our self-deception, we will choose to be cured of our manifestations of inferiority rather than give up our fundamental project.[2]

The reason it is difficult to change our fundamental choice is not that there is any force or habit that inclines us to stay with it, but rather that there are never any reasons for changing it. All reasons and motives appear within our fundamental project, and even though we may view our choice as an object, we do so as an outsider. Nevertheless, change is always possible. Anguish is nothing but the awakening to the free, unmotivated choice of ourselves and the realization that what we now live as a project can be nihilated as our dead past. When this change occurs, there is a "conversion," and the whole world looks different to the for-itself; indeed, the world *is* different, since the for-itself, the in-itself, and others are a different complex of relations.

These conversions, according to Sartre, are the ontological justification of the instant. We have seen in the discussion of time that temporality is not composed of instants. But the instant does appear in a conversion, since in this profound change, the for-itself's funda-

2. I am somewhat interpreting Sartre's description.

mental project simultaneously becomes its past and the origin of its future.

Sartre concludes this section with the following summary:

1. The for-itself does not first have its being and then act; rather, to be is to act.

2. The for-itself's action and being is its free determination, the choice of its being.

3. This freedom is intentional. It is the choice of an end, or fundamental motive, in which reasons and secondary motives for action come-to-be.

4. The fundamental motive for *doing* is the pre-reflective being of my project; the reasons for my actions are the objective factors revealed by reflecting on my givens in the light of my motive.

5. The pure, or brute, given is an abstraction; in the concrete, the given already possesses its weight as a reason for action through the for-itself's fundamental choice.

6. The freedom of the for-itself is not the abstract freedom of a separated spirit; it is the freedom that is the nihilation of a given. The for-itself chooses its own direction from a given past, but it must always be a projection from some past.

7. The human reality must choose itself as free, and yet it cannot found its freedom. Its unconditioned freedom shares the universal contingency of all being; the for-itself is a failure of the in-itself to be its own foundation. Thus freedom, as a failure, is a perpetual attempt to escape contingency by interiorizing and justifying the very contingency that still remains the gratuity of choice.

8. The unity of the world is a reflection of the necessity of freely choosing myself as *one* way of being in the midst of the world. But this fundamental freedom is unstable, since each choice reveals to me the possibility of making other choices.

We thus see that freedom is always in relation to a given and that it shares the contingency of the given. Now we must describe the relation of freedom to this given, a relation that is freedom's facticity.

II. FREEDOM AND FACTICITY: THE SITUATION

Section II describes the way in which freedom is absolute and yet always arises in a context. We are already familiar with the outlines of Sartre's description of freedom; we must now examine more closely why conditions of birth and the resistance of nature are not true obstacles to freedom. We will see that only the freedom of the other can, in some respect, be a limitation on our freedom. After a brief general discussion, Sartre subdivides his description of freedom and facticity into a study of "My Place," "My Past," "My Environment," "My Fellowman," and "My Death."

Our previous considerations allow us to eliminate many of the determinist's more obvious objections and consider the relation of freedom and facticity in precise terms. First, it is clear that the so-called "coefficient of adversity in things," the resistance they offer to the fulfillment of our intentions, presupposes freedom, since things appear more or less difficult only in light of our freely chosen ends. The same mountain is a challenge to a climber, an object of beauty to a painter, and protection to a fugitive. Given these freely chosen ends, the mountain does indeed appear more or less scalable, beautiful, or protective. Nevertheless, the fact that a particular mountain is more difficult to climb than others reveals a brute resistance in things. Sartre will show in each of the following subdivisions that this brute resistance is a condition for freedom. Without resistance in things, the human reality could simply accomplish whatever it wished. Such a freedom and such a world would not be human. Yet, we must not equate freedom with the ability to accomplish successfully some intention. *The true philosophical notion of freedom distinguishes it both from a mere internal intention and from the ability to succeed in an enterprise.* It is sufficient that the captive does some action toward his escape in order to learn the value of his own intention and freedom.

Still, freedom is pure spontaneity and pure spontaneity cannot run into obstacles. Freedom, in the light of its freely choosen ends, makes the brute in-itself to be an obstacle; and the brute in-itself, as the origin of the for-itself's projections, makes an otherwise abstract freedom to be the for-itself's concrete freedom.

We can now understand the facticity of freedom. Both the in-itself and the for-itself are simple, unfounded happenings. Given these two happenings, or contingencies, a necessary relation arises: the for-itself must be the nihilation of the in-itself; the for-itself must be that freedom that is the constant attempt and failure to found the in-itself. Thus facticity, or freedom's situation, is a contingency-necessity-contingency relation. For example, this earth and stone simply *is*; it becomes meaningful as a mountain and as an obstacle to be climbed only in the light of man's consciousness of this earth and stone. However, we must not envision that the mountain has always been present but merely never previously named or known, for this understanding of the world would lead us back to realism.

To appreciate Sartre's view of the relation of the for-itself to the in-itself, it may help to picture what the world would be like if the for-itself had a different body. The very delineation of objects as "things" arises because of the way we are present to matter through our body. Suppose that we were gaseous beings responding only to temperature; then the spaces between various in-itselfs might be, for us, "things," and the in-itselfs might be distinguished by their temperatures rather than their functions. Thus two "stones" might be different "things," but a tree and a stone might be the same "thing." Consequently, the world and the for-itself reciprocally come-to-be, and this reciprocity is facticity.

Sartre will now consider the various ways this reciprocal relation, which is the for-itself's situation, occurs. He warns us to remember that these are merely the partial ways man expresses the choice of his being.

A. MY PLACE

My place is more than the mere geometric distances that surround me. Sartre notes that Heidegger has shown that a "lived" place is the accessibility or inaccessibility of things in relation to my ends. Paris can be far away if I wish to live there and have no money for the trip. There is, nevertheless, a certain brute given and absurdity to my place. Ultimately, my place is related to my birth, over which I had no choice. Consequently, the determinist claims that all our choices are limited by the place in which we were born, for it is from this place that all subsequent choices were made. There is admittedly a basic contingency in the place of our birth, which reflects the basic contingency of the for-itself and the in-itself, but this contingency must be understood correctly.

First, we must recognize that place comes into existence only through the for-itself as a nihilation and a temporality. The earth becomes a "place" only when man can truly project himself living on the moon or another planet. In relation to this free choice of the moon as a place for us, obstacles are raised. Conversely, the choice becomes a true choice because there are obstacles that are viewed as surmountable. It becomes impossible to distinguish the "brute" obstacle from the "pure" choice; both are abstractions. The temperature change upon leaving and reentering the atmosphere was an obstacle only in light of a relatively undeveloped skill of metallurgy, and conversely, the technique of metallurgy was relatively undeveloped only in relation to a project of landing on the moon.

The determinist's objection that freedom is limited, or choice restricted, by the place in which the for-itself chooses carries no weight. It originates from a conception of freedom as an in-itself that could be either here or there, the freedom of a would-be pure spirit that could survey the world better in this or that place. The human reality, as the nihilation of the in-itself, must be in a place by the very fact that its nihilations set up relations of lived distance in accord with its projected ends. It is indeed absurd that it be located in New York rather than Paris, but it encounters neither more nor fewer obstacles because of its "brute" location. There is no privileged place.

B. MY PAST

My past exhibits the same paradoxical relation between freedom and the in-itself as arises in every situation. I cannot exist except as a nihilation of a past and a projection toward the future, while the past arises as past because of my very projection to a future.

It is of course true that I cannot change the facts of my parents, my schools, or friends, nor the fact that I may have lost an arm or leg. But the meaning of these facts depends on my intentions. I may be a promising piano player who loses an arm. I could yield to self-pity and curse fate for depriving me of a greatness that I may have never achieved. Instead, I choose to become a one-arm piano player, and now I look upon my success as originating from that fortunate accident. My entire past, with all its growing obligations, thus weighs upon me only if I continue in my fundamental project. There is nothing preventing me from making this living past into an object and therefore into a dead past.

Nevertheless, because I am a being-for-others, once my past is chosen in the light of my future, it becomes part of the objective world and begins to exert an attracting force on me. Since my choice is not distinct from my doing, I begin to learn from the world the objective meaning of my choices. The moment I decide to become a one-arm piano player, I learn the meaning of my decision in my piano playing and in the reactions of others.

C. MY ENVIRONMENT

My environment is more than my place. It is the general instrumentality of things, the resistance or aid that things offer to fulfilling my intentions; it is also the unpredictable happenings that I meet with in my attempt to realize perfectly my intentions.

If I intend to visit a friend, my environment can be revealed as helping or hindering the fulfillment of my intention. The unreliable and uncomfortable subways, the traffic, the heat of the day, and the distance of the walk can all make for an unfavorable environment for the trip. Indeed, such catastrophes as flooding may even make the trip impossible. But again, the very unfavorableness or impossibility of the environment is revealed only in the light of my intended end. If, on the other hand, I really desire an excuse not to visit anyone and long for several days of solitude, this same environment is a blessing. It is clear, however, that certain unforeseeable happenings can occur to interfere with my intentions. The same inclement weather that encourages me to stay at home and write causes the lights to fail, the candle to fall, and my manuscript to be burned. Of course, depending on the intensity of my purpose, I can attempt to overcome these obstacles. But the fact remains that we do run into the unforeseeable.

According to Sartre, our intentions are always open because of this very unpredictability of nature. This openness is not learned, but an aspect of our original choice, which is itself a fundamental contingency. We have seen that the world comes-to-be with all its instrumentality and potentiality through this fundamental choice. This choice, however, is a failure; it fails to found being and leaves it purely contingent and factual. The unpredictability of a situation is the appearance of this brute contingency of the in-itself. In this way freedom arises only across the in-itself as contingent and unpredictable. Thus, Sartre states, we are never totally surprised by these unpredictables; we always expect the unforeseen. Thus, environment, as every situation, reveals the synthetic relation that is the in-itself as nihilated and as "world."

D. MY FELLOWMAN

The only possible limitation of my freedom arises from the factual existence of others. Sartre, however, makes it clear that this limitation is not an obstacle encountered by our freedom but a characteristic of the very in-itself as nihilated and presented as a given.

His point is that the in-itself that is nihilated is complex. Freedom is a nihilation of a brute given that is already laden with meanings and relations to others. We do not arise as a pure monad, contemplating the complex world, nor are we moved by this world as by some independent force challenging our independent freedom. Rather, the very meaning of freedom is to be situational, i.e., to arise as the nihilation of that which is already a complexity and to surpass this complexity toward one's own projects. True, there is no a priori reason why the human reality should arise as the nihilation of a "world" objectivized by the freedom of others. But given this absolute fact, the for-itself must be a nihilation and a surpassing, in the face of the alienating freedom of others, of a world not of its own choosing. We will follow Sartre's description of nationality and language to see in what way the freedom of others is a limit, but not an obstacle, to our freedom.

For Sartre, the "reality" of our belonging to the human race is the concrete reality of our nationality and, ultimately, of our precise city or district. Similarly, the reality of language is our particular dialect. On the other hand, the "truth" of belonging to a district or speaking a dialect is respectively the human race and language. Truth is the general and objectivized relations of the concrete; however, this must also be understood correctly.

The concrete, or the real, is not an instance of truth. Let us consider the relation between a dialect and language. At first, it may seem that the laws of grammar are a technique that man must learn in order to express his thoughts; we conceive that there is some imageless or verbless thought that precedes the actual use of sentences.[3] This conception of man's relation to techniques can be generalized: man is conceived as pure transcendence, or mind, that must use techniques to accomplish its purposes in the world. Besides the mind-body dualism that this conception implies, there is the more specific difficulty of regress of techniques; we would need a technique in order to learn how to use the techniques of grammer. We would then have to arrive at a technique of techniques, which might be related to some pure substance but not to the human reality. Rather, we must see how the techniques of language are a facticity of the human condition.

Clearly, words have meaning only within the context of a sentence, and we must also realize that the sentence itself has its meaning within that intentional act of the for-itself which is "to designate." The sentence "He is here" takes its meaning from the particular intention of the human reality: "(Thank heavens,) he is *here*," or "(Oh no,) *he* is here."

Nevertheless, one can still object that we are not free to construct words arbitrarily and that the for-itself is, indeed, limited by certain rules not of its own making. Man must arise as the nihilation of a particular fetus, born at a particular place, living in a particular environment, and communicating in a particular language. Man's dialect and vocabulary range are no more a limit on his freedom than is his place of birth. Rather, they are the very being of the for-itself as nihilated and surpassed. It would be meaningless to speculate what Shakespeare would have been like if he had been born in China. This is to conceive of a nature "Shakespeare" preexisting its embodiment.

---

3. Sartre is here concerned with our initial expression of our "thoughts," either to ourselves or others. Clearly, when we pre-reflectively attempt to express our thoughts, we do not first reflect on the laws of grammar.

Shakespeare is the very nihilation of a certain environment and language and a free projection from these as givens.

We need not conclude from this that there are no laws, or truths, of language. The laws of language are the for-itself's use of language as objectivized by the other. Similarities and regularities will, of necessity, appear because the for-itself does not arise in a vacuum creating its own language but as the nihilation of specific givens. In a living language, however, the laws are never fixed and clear, nor are they ever obstacles to freedom. Rather, they are the very means of making freedom realizable and not an abstract wish: James Joyce's freedom and experimentation with language, as in *Finnegans Wake*, would be meaningless without the given of English to be transcended.

What has been said about language applies to nationality. I am a member of the human race, not as an instance of some general nature, but as the nihilation of certain brute givens that are already the complex of a world made by others. As soon as I arise in existence, I arise as the nihilation of a civilization and culture already impregnated by the other, although I never face these givens as obstacles. Caesar had no more freedom than a Roman slave. To project Caesar's freedom onto the slave is again to conceive of the freedom of both as a nature. Only when the slave realistically projects himself toward some of Caesar's ends does the slave begin to choose with a freedom similar to Caesar's. The slave, of course, may not be able to fulfill his choice of what he understands Caesar's freedom to be, but then neither does Caesar always accomplish successfully the understanding of his own freedom.

The foregoing remarks, however, are not meant to overlook the fact that, in a sense, the freedom of our fellowman presents the only limits to our freedom. It is because of the other that we have an alienated outwardness: I am ruler, slave, teacher, or student, beautiful or ugly, because of the other. Tribes are not aware of themselves as black, tall, or short until they are aware of others recognizing them as such. From that moment, they must live these objectivized qualities as both alienated from them and as yet their own.

Still, we can freely yield to, or reappropriate, these "unrealizables." I am free to acknowledge the freedom of the other in his recognition of me as Christian or Jew, black or white; or I am free to turn the other into an object and transcend his objectification of me.

I freely assume my objectification by the other when I acknowledge his subjectivity. It is only by accepting the other as free to regard me as a Christian or Jew that I assume the responsibility of living as a Christian or Jew before him and thereby attempt to realize my "unrealizables." The Christian who sacrifices himself as a martyr and the Jew who chooses to live as a Jew before others freely choose their being before others as pride in Christianity or in Judaism. If they were totally unconcerned about realizing their externality before the other, they would not hesitate to change their names, mannerisms, and speech.

Thus, although we do not freely choose the brute givens of our freedom, we freely choose our reality in relation to them. Freedom is always in relation to certain givens, but these brute givens are never external obstacles to freedom. Rather, they are the very context and ground from which freedom arises as a nihilation.

E. MY DEATH

Death, for Sartre, is neither a gateway to another life nor the final meaning of human existence, as the last note of a melody is the final meaning of the melody. According to Sartre, Heidegger developed this latter view by considering death as the unique possibility of the human reality.

Death, like birth, is, for Sartre, simply an aspect of the fundamental facticity of the for-itself. It has no reasons to justify it; it is absurd; it is simply there. But before elaborating on the facticity of death, Sartre explains both why death is not that which gives meaning to life and why it is not the unique possibility of human reality.

We must first be aware of the qualitative difference between an unexpected death ending a short life and death from old age. Is it not clear that the very meaning of a man's work appears only in the light of his future work? What would James Joyce have been if he had written only that short volume of poems, *Chamber Music?* But even given a long life, we have no guarantee that death can be waited for as the natural completion of our life's work. We might outlive the meaning of our work, and our later works might prove to be "regressions." Thus Sartre states that the Christians are right when they insist we must live each moment as if we might die, although this does not mean that we must make of death an object to be contemplated, as if death reveals the meaning of our acts.

There are some, like Heidegger, who attempt to derive or equate death with the unique possibility of the human reality as a finite being. But finitude means the elimination of other choices by the fact of having made this choice. Consequently, if the for-itself were immortal, it would still be finite, and the choice of *A* over *B* could never be repeated: there would always be the history of having chosen *A*. Thus death is not a structure following the basic contingency of the for-itself in relation to the in-itself.

As with the brute givens of our place, our environment, and our fellowman, death represents another complexity of the brute given that the for-itself nihilates. It is thus pre-reflectively in all our acts, but it is never encountered as an obstacle. Of course, once reflected upon, death can be examined as a given already impregnated with the intentionality of our fundamental project.

Death is also an aspect of our being-for-others. If there were only one for-itself, there would be no consciousness of leaving the "world." Our death is one of those "unrealizables" that are thrown back to us by the existence of others. While we are alive, we are masters of our intentions; we can even appropriate the subjectivity of the other. But when we have died, we are perfectly exteriorized and in the hands of the other. Conversely, the other as alive is characterized by its attitude toward the dead. We arise in a world of the dead and even our indifference toward the dead characterizes the choice of our being.

Finally, death is the end of our possibilities, and as such, it cannot be truly conceived. For whatever our attitude is toward death, the fact remains that it puts an end to our attitudes. Even suicide, as the free termination of our life, does not make our life meaningful to us. For our suicide could take on meaning only in the light of our future; it could arise as meaningful only if it failed. We thus live our death, as our birth, as the facticity and gratuity of our condition.

We can now summarize some characteristics of our fundamental facticity, our situation:

1. De facto, I arise as the nihilation, or consciousness, of a brute complexity with its characteristics of instrumentality and adversity.

2. The situation is thus neither purely subjective nor purely

objective. It is the relation of the for-itself to the in-itself. It is the brute given as already illuminated and impregnated by the for-itself's surpassing. On the other hand, this surpassing is a surpassing only because it is the nihilation of a given.

3. The situation is the very being of the for-itself as a choice, a choice revealed as the in-itself illuminated by the for-itself's ends.

4. As the fundamental facticity of the human reality, the situation is always concrete and always illuminated by concrete ends.

5. The situation is thus not composed of laws and techniques that restrain man. All laws and connections between so-called brute givens arise from the temporality and intentionality of others, and human reality projects its own freedom across these connections.

6. Man's recognizable permanence, as in a condition fundamentally similar to others, does not arise from any substantive permanence but from his free engagement in his environment. While there is no external cause for our permanence, there are many things in our situation that support the continuation in our original project. We see ourselves in our very environment and we are attracted by the permanence of ourselves that we see. Nevertheless, our permanence is our choice. Sartre states that when a person claims that he is not easy to get along with, he is really taking a vow to remain true to his choice of himself.

Finally, we must keep in mind that the fundamental choice of our being is always an open choice: we are pre-reflectively aware of the brute contingency of the in-itself and of the unforeseeable. The unforeseeable can complicate our situation, although it can never be an external cause of changing our project.

III.   FREEDOM AND RESPONSIBILITY

In section III, Sartre points to the absolute responsibility that is man's freedom. Responsibility is the consciousness of being the sole author of an action or event. From all that has been said, it is clear that man stands without any excuse for his choice of being; it is through him that there is a world. Nor does the existence of others mitigate our freedom, since we are free to appropriate the others' freedom.

Our freedom is evident in our responsibility for war. We are all responsible, Sartre says, for the wars we have, and we get the wars we deserve. First, we choose our war by our attitude toward it. Of course, we can say that we did not declare a war and that we were born into it. But we are always born into a situation. Freedom is, not to be without a situation, but to be able to surpass and nihilate it according to our ends. Thus we are always responsible for our attitude toward our nation's war, whether one of indifference, cooperation, or active resistance. Furthermore, we could always leave this situation, by suicide or desertion or exile.

We thus bear the entire weight of the world on our shoulders. It is through us that meaning and purpose enter things. True, we did not choose to be born, but this is simply the facticity of our freedom. We do not found our freedom by our freedom. It remains an unjustifiable fact that, nevertheless, we freely support. The free man who is in good faith accepts his condemnation to be free and bears the total weight of this unfounded freedom in anguish. But as Sartre notes, most of the time we attempt, in bad faith, to reject and hide from our unfounded freedom.

2
Doing and Having

In the previous chapter, Sartre has made clear that the human reality exists as a choice of its being. This choice, which is man's behavior as a doing (making) and a having, takes its meaning from man's projected ends. Consequently, Sartre first considers the general psychoanalytic principles of the human reality's fundamental choice of being; then he describes some of the general ways consciousness appropriates its chosen being by *doing* and *having*; and he concludes by describing how the qualities of the in-itself and the being of the for-itself, as choices, mutually specify each other.

I. EXISTENTIAL PSYCHOANALYSIS

To understand the human reality in terms of freely chosen ends, we must neither view the desiring of these ends as things residing within consciousness nor regard the complex of desires and their interaction with environment as constitutive of personality. Sartre gives three basic objections to this type of psychology.

First, the individual is thereby considered in terms of some universal and abstract model; he becomes an instance of the universal that is considered as prior to and more true than the individual. Also, his individuality becomes nothing more than the intersection of several universal drives; the particular genius of Shakespeare would be explained as the unique intersection of drives common to all people, as well as the reaction of these drives to a specific environment.

Nevertheless, this view does touch upon a truth concerning human desires. For example, the propositions "gold is a body," "an elm is a body," "a man is a body," are all true. The error is to conclude that there is a common characteristic, namely, body (three-dimensionality) that preexists the individual mineral, tree, or man, and in which each individual somehow shares. Sartre, in his previous discussion on the truth of language and nationality, has already given us his answer to the relation between truth and reality. Truth is abstract; reality is concrete. Truth results from another person reflecting on our objectivized freedom; the similarities and categorizations characteristic of truth ontologically come after our "doing" and "being." To return to the example of the universality of "body": in the concrete, there are only the realities of flesh and blood, plant cells, and the crystalization of minerals (actually only *this* flesh and blood, and so on). There is, in reality, no common characteristic as pure and simple "three dimensions." That *by which* this man, this plant, and this mineral are extended in space are different concrete realities—flesh and blood, plant cells, and crystalization. Given the existence of these different realities, the mind compares them and considers the truth of their "bodiness," namely, their extension in three dimensions.[1]

Second, Sartre objects to understanding personality as the complex of one's drives because such an explanation both leaves crucial gaps in grasping the uniqueness of the person and further resorts either to unknowns or to mechanistic interpretations in bridging these gaps. For example, according to Sartre, to analyze Flaubert's writing as an outlet of a youthful intense desire for violent action is to leave unexplained both why this drive was diverted to writing and why the writing developed into a unique style. If we resort to unknown factors or environment as mechanical causes of Flaubert's writing, we abandon the free man who can be praised or blamed. Indeed, to insist on the reality of these causes in the face of our ignorance of their nature is merely to assume the truth of the mechanistic model.

1. Sartre is not clear on how comparisons of the concrete individual lead to the understanding of the universal structure. The above examples are not given in the text and involve some interpretation.

Furthermore, these psychologists arbitrarily stop their analysis at givens that either are not really ultimate or are implicitly viewed as received by a specific nature. Even Heidegger, according to Sartre, although he does not fall into the general class of the psychologists being considered, fails to see that the "authentic" and "inauthentic" ways of facing death cannot be ultimate, since they presuppose the choice to live. When these psychologists do arrive at something ultimate and irreducible, like Flaubert's ambition, they fail to recognize it as such and regard it as something received in "human nature."

Finally, most of these psychologists forget that many drives, such as sexual desires, are more than a specific urge satisfied by an object, such as an individual man or woman, but are concrete manifestations of the person's global way of relating himself to the world and others, a total way of appropriating, or "having," being. It is clear then that we cannot accept that the above views of man's desires provide the groundwork for an existential psychoanalysis.

In the previous chapter, we have already seen that the reality of man is a fundamental choice of being. Aside from certain "indifferents," man's every action indicates his fundamental choice of being; more properly, man *is* the fundamental choice as "expressed" here and now. Man's actions are not the result of separate drives, but are partial aspects of a totality, as, in the Introduction, the "profile" was seen to be a partial aspect of the apple through which the total apple was revealed. Consequently, an individual's actions are not like physical parts of some whole, as a piece of pie is part of the entire pie. Rather, the whole is contained in the part, as the whole pie is seen through its side view.

Thus, man's actions and ways of appropriating the in-itself and the *other* "express," in a particular historical situation, an already concrete choice of being. Each action is the entire human being existing in this particular way. If our choice of being is to exist our bodies as desire, every act we perform exists our body as desire: the way we walk, talk, gesture, play, and work. The ultimate that the existential psychoanalyst is seeking is the irreducible fact of the for-itself's contingent choice of its being. We must remember that every choice of being is unique and that reality is in no way abstract; existence precedes essence; and thus the ambition of Caesar is not the ambition of Alexander. Nevertheless, there is a truth to the general project of ambition or desire. Among the objectifications of each unique desire, there are resemblances that can be made by the other (or the subject regarding himself as other). Although these abstract structures come after the for-itself's pre-reflective choice of being, the for-itself can use these structures to reveal the meaning of its own being.

Man's necessity to exist freely as a choice of being thus leads to certain characteristics of existential psychoanalysis.

1. The principle of psychoanalysis is that man is a totality.

2. The goal is to reveal the meaning of each act and the behavior pattern of each person.

3. The origin is experience and the realization every person implicitly has of the meaning of his behavior.

4. The method is to compare the individual's actions in order to reveal to him his fundamental choice, which is often hidden by circumstances and his bad faith.

To the extent that the existential psychoanalyst is searching for the truth of human behavior, and insofar as he realizes that each action points to more than it immediately seems to indicate, he shares some things in common with the Freudian analyst. Both recognize that there is no definite given in the human reality, for even the libido is nothing but its concrete fixations. Both treat man as an adventurous being, growing in meaning and history. Both try to reconstruct, from all objective information available, man as a situational being. Both look for a fundamental attitude that characterizes the individual and that is often not known by the individual; for the Freudian, it is the unconscious psyche; for the existential psychoanalyst, it is the pre-reflective choice of our being that is not reflectively known by the subject. While the subject lives his project in full consciousness, he is without that delineation that enables him to fix and "know" it as a "this." He understands (*comprendre*), Sartre says, but does not know (*connaître*) his choice. Thus, for both psychoanalysts, the subject is not in a privileged position in respect to the meaning of his being. If the subject, as analyst, studies himself, he does it as the other. For the existential psychoanalyst, the subject's reflections will usually manifest the same characteristics as his fundamental choice and the same attempt to hide, perhaps, from this choice, for reflection is often another spontaneous attempt by the subject to found his being.

According to Sartre, there are several important differences between the two psychoanalytic theories. The empirical analysis has chosen a priori the libido or will to power as the ultimate of human behavior. We have seen, however, that the for-itself's choice of being is global; it is an attempt to reappropriate being in the face of the other. Thus both the libido and the will to power are themselves concrete aspects of a more fundamental choice of one's being.

But more important, all other analyses overlook the fact that the ultimate of the human being is a choice, a living choice that can be revoked. And because it is a living choice, the symbolic meaning of the for-itself's actions, such as stuttering, are not related to an unconscious but to the clear way the person has chosen his being. Sartre also notes that many times, in Freudian analysis, the subject is brought to face his choice, but the analyst fails to recognize this intention for what it is and continues to search for unconscious motivations. The subject under analysis should not have to *believe* that he is of such a character; rather, he should be led to see and acknowledge his own choice of being.

Finally, because the subject's actions are related to his freedom, to his being-in-the-world, the existential psychoanalyst will especially realize that he can never have clearly defined rules regulating the relation of symbols to reality. He will have to treat each case differently and allow the meaning of the subject's symbolic behavior to come from the subject. It would seem, therefore, that there is nothing wrong with approaching the subject with principles and conceptual schemata provided by ontology, as long as these are used artistically rather than mechanically.

II. "DOING" AND "HAVING": POSSESSION

All human behavior, according to Sartre, is an expression of a desire to do (or make), a desire to have, or a desire to be. Sartre shows that the desire to do and, to a lesser extent, the desire to have are "reduced" to the desire to be.[2] In general, desire, as the being of the

---

2. This "reduction" is clearly neither of a property to an essence nor of a phenomenon to being, but appears to mean that doing and having are secondary structures of the cogito as fundamental choice. Sartre does not elaborate how consciousness can have secondary structures or exactly what this would mean.

human reality, appears as the pure failure to be God. In the concrete, this desire expresses itself in such particular choices as walking, possessing a chair, or being casually dressed. Each of these choices—doing, having, and being—equally expresses the unity of the for-itself's choice of existence, although not equally in a direct way. First, "doing" (or "making") is clearly reducible to "having" or "being."

It is evident that whenever I make an artifact, I do so to *have* it and to claim that it is mine. I exercise, Sartre says, a creation over it; it is perpetually mine and yet perpetually independent of me. Here we see a symbol of the impossible ideal of God's creation, which is the very goal and value of the for-itself's desire.

"Knowing" is also a form of having. The ideal of knowledge is to possess the object within us and yet leave the object in its purity. My thoughts are intimately mine, and yet, to the extent that they are "true" and objective, they are independent of me and share a common existence. Again the ideal of possession occurs: to possess and to have as one's own that which is also independent and objective. Knowledge, as a form of discovery and revelation, has an added note of possession. Sartre speaks of the "Actaeon complex": the intimate revealing of the object to ourselves and our privileged grasping of it, as Actaeon cleared away the branches to see Diana. In the act of discovery, we wish both to assimilate the object and to have it retain its purity and nudity. Thus there are many similarities between knowing and eating, although in eating we destroy the object of our desire. The ideal of knowledge, however, is a totally digested and possessed object that retains its identity.

Sartre digresses to the activity of *play* to serve as an introduction to his careful study of having as a form of appropriation and posses-sion, and of possession as a way of being. Play is distinguished from seriousness, which Sartre conceives as characteristic of materialists and revolutionaries. The serious man attributes more reality to the world than to himself; he is in bad faith. Play, on the other hand, is an activity originating directly from man's subjectivity and freedom. In play, man sets his own rules and realizes himself, perhaps in anguish, as the complete source of his own activities.[3] Play often

---

3. Play, as an activity, is therefore reduced not to having but to being. The man of "play" (acting, sports, and so on) is the man who chooses himself in a world of undifferentiated simplicity, where the rules are all of his making.

exhibits a special aspect of appropriating and having that can lead us to the proper study of possession.

Sartre notes that in skiing, the expert skier possesses the snow by continually creating it as the delicate support of his activity. By his proper turns, his lightness and swiftness of movement, he creates snow to be the very support of these movements and appropriates the snow to himself. The skier's ideal is again the ideal of every desire: to perfectly possess its object by a continual creation and at the same time to leave it unmarred and independent as the pure in-itself. *Possession is the impossible union of the for-itself with the in-itself, which is the symbol of the desire to be God.*[4]

We are now in a position to examine the desire to have and its relation to the desire to be. First, we must realize that since having, or ownership, is an internal relation of the for-itself with the in-itself, it can in no way be explained as a social convention. At most, society makes the relation of appropriation legal, while not explaining it as a fact. If someone reappropriates property unjustly taken, he is affirming the basic relation of appropriation and possession. In a similar way, possession cannot be explained as an external relation existing between two independent substances. An external relation in no way affects the being of the realities related.

In Cartesian philosophy, possession is an external relation because the human reality, as a pure cogito, is not affected by possessing purely extended substances. In Cartesianism, "my chair" is simply an extrinsic denomination, which does not refer to any intrinsic aspect of the chair or my self. However, if I invite someone into my home and show him my living room and study, he clearly witnesses something of *me* in the arrangement and use of the objects before him. We must not conclude from this that possession is merely an external alteration of the object. Indeed, it is clear that in possession, the object—for example, a painting—is not physically changed by the act of ownership. Ownership, like knowledge, leaves the object physically unaffected, while totally metamorphosing it, revealing and appropriating it within that upsurge that is the for-itself's desire to be God. As with the "solitude" of the known, possession is the for-itself's

4. Sartre also notes the factor of "conquering" in sport is related to mastering the other.

attempt to be one with the in-itself and found the in-itself as a concrete manifestation of its desire to be God.

Possession is thus a certain relation of being to an object: to have the object totally for myself. "To possess" is to continually create the object as *mine*. The arrangement of my picture on the wall and its relation to all my other objects continually leaves the painting untouched and yet perpetually reveals it as mine. As the Creator is viewed as continually perserving the creature in existence, I must continually keep the object possessed in existence, as if it had a constant tendency to return to an indifferent in-itself. Since the objects in my room continually await me as mine, Sartre claims that in general, our possessions are also our attempt to protect ourselves from the other: we try to jump ahead of his attempt to objectivize us by trying to do and have this very objectification.[5]

The preceding discussion should not mislead us to think that we consciously seek to be God in every act of possession. The acts of our possessing are fundamentally nonthetic, and we live them rather than knowing them as symbols of our fundamental project to be God. Clearly then, the desire "to have" is basically a desire "to be"; it is a certain way of choosing our being in relation to the world. Further, we must always bear in mind that possession is a concrete act related to a concrete object. The man in love characteristically chooses *this* woman, although through this choice he assumes a unique attitude toward all women. In a similar way, the human reality chooses its total being in the face of individual being. Its choices are thus always specific and still always expressive of the total man. In seeking to be one with this particular object, I am, in my unique way, seeking to be one with being-in-itself. In seeking to found my facticity, I seek to found all of being (if there is a God, there is one God).

Our description of the for-itself's mode of possession is, nevertheless, still too abstract. Desire is intentional and thus differentiated by its object. In the concrete, the in-itself is not undifferentiated, but has

5. According to Sartre, the desire for possessions leads us to the desire to destroy the object possessed. For by destruction, we ultimately manifest our ownership in our attempt to reabsorb the object. "Giving" too is a form of destruction and enslavement of the other. When we are generous, we destroy the object for ourselves while simultaneously requiring the other to keep it in existence as something given to him by us.

specific qualities, albeit these qualities arise with the upsurge of the for-itself. Sartre now describes how qualities in things reciprocally give rise to the for-itself's unique choice of its being.

III. QUALITY AS A REVELATION OF BEING

One of the main theses of Sartre's work has been that the relation between consciousness and being is that portrayed neither by the idealist nor by the Cartesian realist. His constant theme is that consciousness is the pure revelation of something other than consciousness, the pure revelation of that which is transcendent to consciousness. Clearly then, the human reality's fundamental choice of being will be reciprocally characterized by these transcendent qualities. Thus the for-itself's choice is always an encountered choice within concrete qualities of things. Also, the for-itself attempts to found all being in its attempt to found particular qualities of things.

In section III, Sartre's point, seems to be twofold: (1) the for-itself freely chooses to found the in-itself through specific qualities, and these qualities are the symbol of the for-itself's attempt to found all being; and (2) the particular qualities in question, as well as the complex of all qualities related to others, reciprocally give rise to the for-itself as a nihilation in-the-midst-of-a-world of nihilations.

This internal bond between the in-itself and consciousness means that there must be objective characteristics in qualities that account for our admittedly subjective projections of psychic characteristics in qualities. Thus the existential psychoanalyst must accept from ontology the objective descriptions of transcendent qualities and relation between things before he can begin interpreting the symbolic meaning of qualities. These symbolic meanings, despite their subjective coloring, are ultimatedly based on objective characteristics of things. Unlike the empirical psychoanalyst, the existentialist, according to Sartre, accepts his general principles from ontology and, as much as possible, bases his analysis on the psychoanalysis of things.[6]

Sartre focuses most of his attention on a description and analysis

---

6. G. Bachelard, according to Sartre, has done great pioneering work in this field, although Sartre considers that his approach is not sufficiently ontological.

of the objective quality of the "slimy" or the "viscous" (*visqueux*). The usual explanation of why we label some things as slimy—"his handclasp is slimy"—is that we first have certain psychic repugnances, which we then project onto matter. But as Sartre notes, this explanation begs the question. We must still explain why we attribute and project these psychic feelings of repugnance onto this quality and not onto others. There must indeed already be an intimate bond between the psychic repugnance and the objective quality of sliminess.

The slimy is neither the clear fluidity of water nor the opaque density of rock. The clarity of water is rightly regarded as the symbol of consciousness; for clear water, like *nothing*, totally reveals things and, as in knowledge, leaves to things their identity. Water also freely flows from things, neither clinging nor attempting to absorb its object. The opaque stone, on the other hand, is the symbol of the pure in-itself, and the stone's density is opposed but not repugnant to consciousness. Also, the stone can be appropriated and possessed by the for-itself. The human reality can reveal a rock as an object of beauty, raise it to the level of a possession, and attempt thereby to found its being.

We are back then to the fundamental project of the for-itself as an appropriation and possession of the in-itself. The very repugnance of the slimy is to being appropriated. In Sartre's own example, if I put my finger in a jar of honey, the honey clings, preventing me from appropriating it according to my freedom; it stays on me, although I no longer wish its presence. This quality is not subjective, but is the very being of the viscous as a soft, moving thing.

Every quality of being arises from the original upsurge of the for-itself and in some way symbolically expresses the fundamental relation of the for-itself to being-in-itself. What then is the symbolic meaning of the slimy? First, we must recall that the usual relation of consciousness to "things" is to found "things" by choosing and raising them to the level of consciousness. Thus the for-itself attempts to found the synthesis "in-itself-for-itself," to absorb the in-itself in the for-itself. But the slimy, according to Sartre, is the revenge of the in-itself. The slimy attempts to absorb the for-itself, to bring consciousness down into its soft thickness. Consequently, the slimy, for Sartre, is the symbol of antivalue; it represents the triumph of the in-itself over the for-itself.

Although I may not choose the slimy as my project, I arise in a world in which the slimy is a quality. Therefore, whatever my project, I pre-reflectively grasp the slimy, as well as all other qualities of being, simultaneously surpassing it and illuminating my whole world with my obscure meanings of "slimy."

What has been said of the slimy can also be said for all sexual images. Such qualities as holes are, first, ontological characteristics in things that symbolically represent the for-itself's attempt to fill nothingness. Sexual intercourse is a symbolic instance of the for-itself's urge to fill and be filled by the in-itself.

The psychoanalyst can now use the ontological study of qualities to interpret the individual's free choice of being through particular qualities. What, for example, does it mean if someone loves the slimy?

Ontology, Sartre concludes, can give us only the principles and ultimate ends of the human reality. The psychoanalyst must do the detailed classification and interpretation. In general, each man is a unique attempt to found the world by freely assuming his being as the consciousness of certain transcendent qualities in the world. The human passion is to found the in-itself and to become the perfect synthesis that is God. But the ideal of God is an impossibility. "Man," Sartre concludes, "is a useless passion."

CONCLUSION

I. IN-ITSELF AND FOR-ITSELF:
METAPHYSICAL IMPLICATIONS

The analysis of being in the Introduction left us with two basic related tasks: (1) finding a solution to the problem of knowledge other than idealism and Cartesian realism, and (2) finding a solution to the problem of the apparent gap between the two realms of being, the for-itself and the in-itself.

The first task has already been fulfilled by a careful description of knowledge as intentional. Consciousness is totally the revelation of an object other than consciousness, and reciprocally, this other-than-consciousness is the in-itself as *realized* by consciousness. Also, consciousness, as a nihilation, "happens" to the in-itself, and reciprocally, this "happening" brings-to-be the in-itself as a *thing*, with qualities, instrumentalities, and potentialities. Thus Cartesian realism has been avoided—knowledge is a bond of being and not a relation of representations to things; and idealism has been avoided—there is a fundamental priority of brute contingent existence (the in-itself) over consciousness. In fact, it would seem that the ontological priority of brute "meaningless" existence over consciousness and reason is what fundamentally distinguishes Sartre's philosophy from all idealism.

But once granting the unmotivated happening of consciousness, we are indeed faced with a strange realism. Sartre insists that being-in-itself does not need consciousness, but it is not at all clear what this being-in-itself would be like without consciousness. In the chapter on transcendence, it seems clear that the *being* of consciousness not merely realizes things as "here" and "there," but brings-to-be the very distinction of things within a world. Sartre here uses the fictional image of the upheaval of the universe resulting from the *complete* annihilation of a single atom. In a similar way, he states, the upsurge of consciousness within the in-itself resulted in the happening of the world.[1]

The question of the for-itself's origin is, for Sartre, fundamentally one of metaphysics. Sartre conceives that metaphysics is related to ontology as history is related to sociology. Metaphysics concerns the concrete study of the history of things.[2] Ontology can both indicate to the metaphysician that certain questions are meaningless and provide the principles for the more meaningful investigations. First, it is meaningless to inquire into the origin of being, since all questions of "why" are consequent upon the existence of the for-itself. On the other hand, it is not meaningless to ask why there *is* being. But this question has already been answered by ontology, since the "there" of the in-itself comes to being only through the for-itself.

It is, however, a task for the metaphysician to inquire into the origin of the for-itself, because the for-itself is a reflective being. The study of the actual historical upsurges of the for-itselves, and the investigation of whether these were preceded by similar upheavals within being, do not, for Sartre, result in phenomenological descriptions of fundamental structures. Still, our preceding ontological study provides some fundamental information for this metaphysical investigation.

First, being appears as continually attempting to be the cause of its own reality. This attempt is revealed specifically as the passion of a self to be at one with its projected self. But this attempt results in a fundamental making-to-be of a concrete nothing within being that is consciousness' presence to being. The passion of being to be its own cause continually results in a split of being and nothingness, a split that does not progress toward any further synthesis, for neither reflection nor the "other" succeed in healing this failure of self-

1. Sartre notes that only through consciousness does true "otherness" come into being. For a tree to be "other" than a stone, either a third witness would be needed to recognize their "otherness," which would lead only to an extrinsic relation of "otherness"; or the tree must be conscious of itself as internally not the stone. Thus only through the for-itself arising as a consciousness can there be that which is "other" than the in-itself.

2. This analogy is not at all clear, nor is Sartre's brief allusion to the precise function of metaphysics.

identity. Second, the for-itself is being's perpetual desire and failure to be founded and become the in-itself-for-itself, or God.

The significant point is that being-in-itself does not present us with any reasons for this attempt at founding its own being. The for-itself is a happening to being that cannot be deduced from the nature of being. Thus metaphysics can assume, as a hypothesis, that being attempts to found itself, and the utility of this hypothesis will be judged by the degree it unifies the ontological descriptions of the in-itself.

It must, however, be emphasized that what is hypothetical is that being-in-itself truly attempts to found its existence; what is not hypothetical is the fact that the for-itself is de facto an attempt to found being. That is, there is no necessary connection between being-in-itself and the *appearance* of the for-itself as a passion to found being.

But we are now led to the second problem of the relation of the two realms of being, the for-itself and the in-itself. Do the for-itself and the in-itself both belong to the realm of being? If they do, then is there a fundamental synthesis between them?

In order for there to be a synthesis between a for-itself and an in-itself, they would have to be mutually and internally related, needing each other for their very existence. Now it is clear that a for-itself is internally related to an in-itself, since the for-itself is the concrete privation of a being. But the converse is not true of a being-in-itself. We have just seen that there is no intrinsic reason or internal relation of a being-in-itself to a consciousness. Being-in-itself simply is, and it does not need either its revelation or its project as its own cause. Thus, while a for-itself without an in-itself is an abstraction, this is not true of an in-itself without the for-itself.

The in-itself and the for-itself can be conceived as a completed totality, being, only as an ideal, an ideal that comes to being through the for-itself. The ideal and reality of the individual for-itself is to be God. And the ideal of being is to be the perfect cause and foundation of the in-itself—*at least, given the for-itself's own ideal, being can be conceived in this way.* Thus, being's totality is something that the metaphysician can consider as a hypothesis. He may realize that it is more profitable to consider the world as one phenomenon that has two dimensions of being, or he may return to a dualism of "consciousness-being." The latter, however, would seem to lead to the old errors of idealism and Cartesian realism. (We must remember that we are here considering the *explanation* of the appearance of the synthetic detotalized totality, consciousness-in-being, and not the phenomenological description of the phenomenon. The phenomenologist is not free to approach the phenomena of being and consciousness separately, since they do not manifest themselves as separate.)

Sartre concludes this section by expressing a hope that the metaphysician will consider how action modifies the reality of things. It makes no sense, he states, to claim that action merely affects the phenomenon of being, for this is to forget the intimate connection between phenomenon and being (phenomenon does not hide being as a noumenon; it reveals it). The metaphysician must thus explain how consciousness can affect the being of the in-itself.[3]

II. ETHICAL IMPLICATIONS

As with metaphysics, ontology can provide some of the fundamental principles of an ethics. We have already seen that the human reality is its own value insofar as the for-itself is a lack of identity with its projected goal. We have also seen that the goal of every human reality is the ever-escaping ideal to be God, an ideal that is a concrete choice of founding being through a certain quality in being. Further, this choice of being, as a project, is the meaning of the for-itself. There is thus a moral meaning in each of the for-itself's free choices of being, and it is the task of the existential psychoanalyst to describe and reveal these.

But for Sartre, the main goal of existential psychoanalysis is to eliminate seriousness. The spirit of seriousness is contrary to the spirit of freedom. To be serious is to attribute more meaning to things than to man; it is to put meaning in things as preceding man. It is to put essence before existence.

But if we repudiate seriousness and explicitly turn our consciousness on our freedom, will that freedom itself be changed? If existential psychoanalysis perfectly succeeds and we become totally aware of

3. It is difficult to understand why this is not an ontological problem.

ourselves as free, will we thereby make of our own freedom an object? Will our ideal then no longer be the identification of consciousness with being but the perpetual flight from being, the perpetual being-away from ourselves? Will this lead to a new form of bad faith as an attempt to escape our situation, or will it lead to a more accurate appraisal of our relation to facticity? Sartre claims he will investigate these questions in a work on ethics, a work we still await.[4]

4. It seems clear that we will not receive this work on ethics. First, Sartre's interest in Marx's philosophy has led him to the conviction that an ethics based on freedom must await social conditions in which individuals live truly free. This is not the place to consider the question of whether Sartre's unique Marxism is a "reversal" of the philosophy expressed in *Being and Nothingness*; it, however, is evident that the Marxism stated in the *Critique de la raison dialectique* (Paris: Gallimard, 1960)—only the introduction of which has thus far been translated by Hazel Barnes as *The Search For Method* (New York: Knopf, 1963)—is indeed significantly based on the existential philosophy of *Being and Nothingness*. Second, Sartre's distinctive biographies, such as his work on Genet, should, perhaps, be accepted as a substitute for the promised ethics. These works clearly investigate the concrete situation of an individual's good or bad faiths.

Index